Female Crime and Delinquency in Portugal

Sílvia Gomes • Vera Duarte
Editors

Female Crime and Delinquency in Portugal

In and Out of the Criminal
Justice System

palgrave
macmillan

Editors
Sílvia Gomes
CICS.NOVA Universidade do Minho
Braga, Portugal

Instituto Universitário da Maia
(ISMAI), Maia, Portugal

Vera Duarte
CICS.NOVA Universidade do Minho
Braga, Portugal

Instituto Universitário da Maia
(ISMAI), Maia, Portugal

ISBN 978-3-319-73533-7   ISBN 978-3-319-73534-4   (eBook)
https://doi.org/10.1007/978-3-319-73534-4

Library of Congress Control Number: 2018935259

© The Editor(s) (if applicable) and The Author(s) 2018
This work is subject to copyright. All rights are solely and exclusively licensed by the Publisher, whether the whole or part of the material is concerned, specifically the rights of translation, reprinting, reuse of illustrations, recitation, broadcasting, reproduction on microfilms or in any other physical way, and transmission or information storage and retrieval, electronic adaptation, computer software, or by similar or dissimilar methodology now known or hereafter developed.
The use of general descriptive names, registered names, trademarks, service marks, etc. in this publication does not imply, even in the absence of a specific statement, that such names are exempt from the relevant protective laws and regulations and therefore free for general use.
The publisher, the authors, and the editors are safe to assume that the advice and information in this book are believed to be true and accurate at the date of publication. Neither the publisher nor the authors or the editors give a warranty, express or implied, with respect to the material contained herein or for any errors or omissions that may have been made. The publisher remains neutral with regard to jurisdictional claims in published maps and institutional affiliations.

Cover credit: Samantha Johnson

Printed on acid-free paper

This Palgrave Macmillan imprint is published by the registered company Springer International Publishing AG part of Springer Nature.
The registered company address is: Gewerbestrasse 11, 6330 Cham, Switzerland

Acknowledgements

This book edition would not be possible without the strong support and complementary funding of the University Institute of Maia (ISMAI) and the Interdisciplinary Center for Social Sciences (CICS.NOVA).

We are both grateful to Fran Seftel, who helped with the proofreading of the manuscript. Sílvia Gomes would also like to thank the Foundation of Science and Technology (Portuguese Ministry of Science, Technology and Higher Education) for financing her research through a Post doctoral grant (ref. SFRH/BPD/102758/2014).

We want to thank the authors for having accepted our challenge to contribute to this book with their research, and for making other geographies more visible in scientific investigation on the topics of female crime and delinquency.

We want to thank Palgrave Macmillan for the support they have provided in making this book happen, particularly to Josie Taylor and Stephanie Carey for believing in this project since the beginning.

Contents

1 An Introduction to Female Crime and Delinquency: Portugal in the World   1
Sílvia Gomes and Vera Duarte

Part I Crime and Women: Gender Bias, Crime Trajectories and the Prison System   23

2 The Criminal Act at the Core of the Nexus Security–Insecurity: A Tentative Approach to Female Crime   25
Catarina Frois

3 Stalking by Women: Another Side of Gender Violence   41
Helena Grangeia and Margarida Santos

4 Onstage and Off: The Shifting Relevance of Gender in Women's Prisons   57
Manuela Ivone Cunha

vii

viii   Contents

5   How Do Foreign Women End Up in Prison?
    An Intersectional Approach of Criminal Pathways   75
    Sílvia Gomes

6   "To Kill or to Be Killed": Narratives of Female
    Victims of Intimate Partner Violence, Condemned
    for the Murder of Their Partners   105
    Mafalda Ferreira, Sofia Neves, and Sílvia Gomes

Part II   Female Juvenile Delinquency: Victimizations,
          Delinquencies and the Juvenile Justice System   123

7   Heterosexual Dating Violence and Social Gender
    Relations: Voices of Young Portuguese Girls   125
    Sofia Neves and Joana Torres

8   Constructing Meaning About the Delinquency
    of Young Girls in Public-Housing Neighbourhoods   143
    Maria João Leote de Carvalho

9   Gender and Crime in the Life Pathways of Young
    Women Offenders: Contrasting the Narratives
    of Girls and Professionals   163
    Raquel Matos

10 Girls and Transgressive Paths: A Case Study
    of Portuguese Girls in the Juvenile Justice System   183
    Vera Duarte and Ana Margarida Guerreiro

Index   205

Notes on Contributors

Manuela Ivone Cunha (CRIA, University of Minho) holds a Ph.D. in Anthropology and a degree in Sociology. Distinguished with a social sciences award for her ethnographic research on prisons and drug markets, she has also focused on intersections between criminal law, inequality and cultural difference. She was vice-president of EASA and is currently the editor-in-chief of Etnográfica. Besides several authored books, recent publications include "The ethnography of prisons and penal confinement", Annual Review of Anthropology, (2014); 'Addressing policy-oriented audiences. Relevance and persuasiveness', in D. Fassin (ed.) If Truth Be Told. The politics of public ethnography, Duke University Press (forthcoming).

Maria João Leote de Carvalho Ph.D. in Sociology, is a researcher at the Interdisciplinary Centre of Social Sciences (CICS.NOVA), Faculty of Social Sciences and Humanities (FCSH/NOVA), Portugal. Her interest in sociological research was based on her work as a teacher working with young offenders in a custodial institution for 16 years (1987–2003), and with at risk children and youth in state schools in social housing neighbourhoods in the last 13 years. The everyday experience of working with disadvantaged populations in such specific contexts is the basis for her choice to do sociological investigation exploring issues such as children and youth at risk, delinquency, urban violence, juvenile justice, rights of the child, and media studies. For 40 years she was member of the Commission for the Protection of Children and Youth in Oeiras. She has been a consultant for projects related to at risk children and youth and has been strongly active in international and national networking, including the Calouste Gulbenkian

x   Notes on Contributors

Foundation and the Child Poverty Working Group of the European Anti Poverty Network/Portugal. Since 2009, she has been a member of the Academic Section of the European Council for Juvenile Justice from the International Juvenile Justice Observatory. She was recently appointed to the National Council of the National Commission for the Promotion of Children's Rights and Protection of Children and Youth. With her Masters research she won the Teresa Ferreira Prize from the Dr. João dos Santos Centre of Studies in 2003.

Vera Duarte is a sociologist and holds a Ph.D. in Sociology (2011) from the University of Minho (Portugal), where she developed her thesis on "Discourses and Trajectories in Female Juvenile Delinquency". She has been a teacher in higher education since 2001. Nowadays she is Assistant Professor at the University Institute of Maia (ISMAI, Portugal); Executive Director of the Research Unit in Criminology and Behavioural Sciences (UICCC/ISMAI, Portugal); and researcher at the Interdisciplinary Centre of Social Science (CICS.NOVA.UMinho, Portugal). All her work of teaching, scientific production and research has been developed in the area of female juvenile delinquency, juvenile justice system and qualitative methodology.

Mafalda Ferreira (criminologist) holds a Master's degree in Forensic Medicine from the Abel Salazar Institute of Biomedical Sciences—University of Porto (ICBAS) and is currently a Ph.D. student in Forensic Sciences at the Faculty of Medicine of the University of Porto (FMUP). She performs technical and investigative functions at the UNi+, Prevention of Dating Violence Program, funded by the State Secretariat for Citizenship and Equality and at UNigualdade—Program for the Promotion of Equality and Social Diversity and Prevention of Domestic and Gender Violence, funded by the Commission for Citizenship and Equality. In the scope of volunteering carried out at the Portuguese Victim Support Association, she has been working with victims of intimate gender violence. She has a special interest in subjects such as women's rights, gender violence and femicide.

Catarina Frois is Senior Researcher at the Centre for Research in Anthropology, Portugal, and guest Assistant professor in the Department of Anthropology, Instituto Universitário de Lisboa (ISCTE- IUL) since 2010. Working extensively on the nexus between politics, security, surveillance, prison environments and confinement-related issues, her most recent publications include Female Imprisonment. An Ethnography of Everyday Life in Confinement (Palgrave) and Peripheral Vision. Politics, Technology and Surveillance (Berghahn).

Notes on Contributors   **xi**

Sílvia Gomes is currently a postdoctoral grantee in Sociology and Criminology (SFRH/BPD/102758/2014) at the Interdisciplinary Centre of Social Sciences (CICS.NOVA), University of Minho, and a guest assistant professor at the University Institute of Maia. She holds a Ph.D. in Sociology (2013). She is co-coordinating the Thematic Section on Sociology of Law and Justice of the Portuguese Sociological Association, and is a member of the Working Group on Immigration, Crime and Citizenship and on Gender, Crime and Justice, both part of the European Society of Criminology. Her main areas of research are focused on crime and media, prison studies, crime, ethnicity and social inequalities, intersectional approaches, re-entry, recidivism and criminal desistance.

Helena Grangeia Ph.D. in Psychology, is an Assistant Professor in the Department of Social and Behavioural Sciences of the University Institute of Maia (ISMAI), Portugal, and a Researcher at the Human Rights Centre for Interdisciplinary Research (DH-CII), University of Minho, Portugal. Her research interests are in the domain of Critical Victimology and Gender Violence and are particularly focused on intimate partner violence, harassment and stalking.

Ana Guerreiro (UMAR/ISMAI/FDUP, Portugal) works as a Criminologist in a Feminist Organization (UMAR), is a guest assistant professor at the University Institute of Maia, and is a Ph.D. student in Criminology at Faculty of Law of the University of Porto (FDUP). She is also a researcher at the Research Unit in Criminology and Behavioural Sciences (UICCC.ISMAI). She holds a degree in Criminology (2012) from the University Institute of Maia. Author of several book chapters and scientific papers, her main areas of research are focused on crime and gender, gender violence, organized crime and juvenile delinquency.

Raquel Matos is Associate Professor and Director of the Centre for Studies in Human Development at the Universidade Católica Portuguesa. She was awarded her Ph.D. in Psychology in 2008 from Universidade do Minho. In the last decades she has developed research projects on gender, crime and punishment, and has published articles and book chapters about women in prison as well as about gender and migration control. More recently, she has been coordinating several European projects in Portugal related to juvenile delinquency with a particular interest in exploring young offenders' life pathways and experiences in the justice system. Raquel Matos is currently coordinating the Portuguese team of the Project Promise—"Promoting Youth Involvement and Social Engagement—Opportunities and challenges for 'conflicted' young people across Europe", funded by Horizon 2020.

xii   Notes on Contributors

Sofia Neves is an Assistant Professor at University Institute of Maia (ISMAI, Portugal) and a member of Interdisciplinary Centre for Gender Studies (CIEG, ISCSP/ULisboa, Portugal). She holds a Ph.D. in Social Psychology (2005). Author of several books, book chapters and papers in scientific journals, her main area of research is Gender Violence. Currently she is the President of a non-governmental organization—Associação Plano i –, a member of the working group on Domestic and Gender Violence of the Commission for Citizenship and Gender Equality and a member of the working group on Psychologists' Intervention with LGBT people of the Association of Portuguese Psychologists.

Margarida Santos (Ph.D. degree in Juridical Sciences, specifically in the Public Juridical Science field, from the Law School of University of Minho) is an Assistant Professor at the Law School of University of Minho, Portugal, and at the Department of Social and Behavioural Sciences of the University Institute of Maia (ISMAI), Portugal. She is also a researcher at the Human Rights Centre for Interdisciplinary Research (DH-CII), University of Minho, Portugal. Her research interests are in the domain of Criminal Procedural Law, Criminal Law, Criminology, EU Criminal Law; Juvenile Justice.

Joana Torres holds a degree in Criminology from University Institute of Maia (ISMAI, Portugal), where she also completed a degree in Psychology and a Master's degree in Psychology of Justice. Her thesis focused on Dating Violence among young Cape Verdeans. Currently she is a Ph.D. student in Criminology at the University of Oporto. Her main area of research is gender violence.

List of Figures

Fig. 8.1	My neighbourhood	150
Fig. 8.2	My neighbourhood	153
Fig. 8.3	My neighbourhood	155

List of Tables

Table 9.1	Participants, with a description of: crime, prison sentence, criminal record, drug use and relatives involved in crime	170
Table 9.2	Number of participants, according to the type of institution where they work	174

1

An Introduction to Female Crime and Delinquency: Portugal in the World

Sílvia Gomes and Vera Duarte

1 Introduction

The idea of this book arose from informal discussions about our research subjects at different times during our academic careers. These conversations were informal because in the academic context in Portugal, it is common for one researcher to work within the crime and prison studies area while another works within the juvenile delinquency area. Recognizing the thriving body of recent gender-based research around female crime and delinquency in the country, we decided to create academic opportunities for sharing our studies and our views on the topic, while we tried to find a common basis for debate. In 2013 in Oporto, we organized a panel during the European Society of Criminology Meeting, with Portuguese submissions only. Despite our multidisciplinary fields of interest and diverse topics of analysis, we all felt we had some common ground and many new leads to consider.

S. Gomes (✉) • V. Duarte
CICS.NOVA Universidade do Minho, Braga, Portugal

Instituto Universitário da Maia (ISMAI), Maia, Portugal

© The Author(s) 2018
S. Gomes, V. Duarte (eds.), *Female Crime and Delinquency in Portugal*,
https://doi.org/10.1007/978-3-319-73534-4_1

Many questions arose during our discussion. Some of these were, What is the role that structural gender inequalities play in women's and girls' lives and in their relationship to the justice system? Are stories of victimization common to girls and women who end up in the justice system? Are there possible important connections between victimization and criminal behaviour? Is there a single story about the links between gender and delinquency or crime? Or, on the other hand, despite some similarities, are there differences among women when we focus on specific crimes or particular situations? What links are we able to establish between female crime and female delinquency?

So, we decided to expand what was a localised debate in a room at a conference into a wider net of possibilities by publishing it in book format. If on the one hand, multidisciplinary research on female crime and delinquency has increasingly focused on transgressive girls and women, on the other hand, discussions on the link between gender and crime or delinquency still have a long way to go. We have compiled this book in order to explore the interdisciplinary views on this link critically and reflectively, while supporting a gender-sensitive reading.

It is certain that there is room for much more discussion, and that this book does not intend to cover all recent trends in a wide range of phenomena, especially because many of these have not even been studied in Portugal yet. We hope, however, that this venture will be challenging enough to re-ignite discussions on female crime and delinquency internationally, leading lawmakers, politicians, academics and practitioners (in schools, neighbourhoods, the juvenile justice system, the criminal justice system, etc.) towards a better understanding of and more successful intervention in various contexts.

The goal is not only to give visibility to other contexts in which we may gain knowledge about female crime and delinquency, but also to find other ways of conceptualizing and reconfiguring how we think about society.

2 Why Do We Need To Talk About Portugal?

Many prospective readers may now be wondering why they should want to read about female crime and delinquency studies conducted in a small country in Europe. Or, at best, readers may be questioning whether the book will add something new to what is already known about girls and women in crime and the justice system.

As much of the gender and feminist criminological research on female crime and delinquency originates and is spread from the United States and United Kingdom, we aim to give visibility to the research being developed in more peripheral countries, thereby offering a valuable contribution to the existing literature on the subject. What many researchers may see as non-original is pioneering work in the Portuguese context in studies on female crime and delinquency and the justice system. Moreover, it is essential for understanding dynamics and content in a comparative cross-cultural way. If there is no space in the international context to understand cultural idiosyncrasies, knowledge is limited to what has been mainstream in these matters. These chapters do not ignore international studies and, therefore, major concepts and theoretical approaches from different contexts are used and support part of the work offered by the authors of this book. Even if these concepts converge with international studies, and even if theoretical approaches move national studies in certain common directions, together they also offer relevant and specific findings worthy of comparative exploration.

Although focused on female offenders and the criminal justice system in Portugal, all chapters consider international concepts and theoretical frameworks in order to understand both the differences and the similarities between Portuguese and international realities in the varied topics covered.

To examine the Portuguese context more searchingly, and to be able to understand its particular dynamics, it is important to clarify some legal aspects and to position it statistically in comparison with other societies. In Portugal, as in Italy and Spain, juvenile offenders are managed by authorities other than those within the Prison Administration. Legally, it is from the age of 16 onwards only that a person is considered to be responsible for his actions. Any offence committed up to this age limit, even if it could be qualified as a crime under criminal law, can be subject only to intervention that leads to the establishment of protective and educational measures. The child or young person is never subjected to criminal trial. Thus, nationally, it is not possible to talk about juvenile crime, except for acts committed by persons over 16 years old, when they are already considered criminally liable (see clarification by Duarte and Carvalho 2015, 2017). Therefore, we distinguish conceptually between delinquent practice and criminal practice, and we engage with two separate systems which focus on and deal with two different law-breaking populations: under 16, both girls and boys fall under a special measure called the Educational Guardianship Law (LTE); after turning 16, young adults and adults are under the Penal Code.

As opposed to what happens (more and more) internationally, with a very punitive approach to juvenile delinquents being practised in many countries, in Portugal the juvenile system maintains its educational and protective principles. Still, according to the latest data available in Council of Europe Penal Statistics—SPACE I (Aebi et al. 2016), Portugal has a total prison population rate of 138 prisoners per 100,000 inhabitants. This, in the European context, positions Portugal as a very punitive country. We thus see a country that has very distinct policies and actions depending on the age of its offending population.

The different chapters that make up this book will specify the national dynamics of and statistics on the diverse subjects under analysis. Nevertheless, it is important to mention that female prisoners continue to represent a minority in the entire prison system—the percentage of females is 6.1% in Portugal and 5.3% in the European Union. However, we have witnessed a marked increase in the female prison population in the last decade (Matos 2016), and we have an over-representation—well above the European average—of foreign women behind bars (see Gomes 2018, Chap. 5 in this volume).

3 Gender Differences in and Out of the Criminal Justice System

Gender is one of the most consistent differentiating dimensions in crime and delinquency studies (Belknap 1996; Carlen 1988; Faith 1993; Girschick 1997; Messerschmidt 1997; Naffine 1996): men commit more crimes; women are more often victims of crime. The statistical irrelevance of women's criminality and female delinquency, as well as their low rate of deviant or criminal recidivism contributed to the neglect of women's and girls' deviant and criminal practice for a long time (Duarte 2012; Machado 2008; Moore 2002). This lack of awareness of women and girls as offenders was also exacerbated by the fact that most crime studies were traditionally conducted by male sociologists, who studied street gangs and similar groups that reflected their male interests, and most female sociologists were prevented from studying women's crime (Heidensohn 1985; Moore 2002, pp. 261–262).

Even nowadays, the theoretical and empirical approach to crime is based primarily on the analysis of men's behaviour. From the perspective of many feminists, criminal sciences reveal an androcentric character, which may bias research, and traditional analytical tools may thus be unsuitable for the study of crime in the female world (Machado 2008, p. 102).

Only from the 1970s onwards, did more gender-sensitive literature appear with a feminist influence, first focusing on women (Adler 1975; Carlen 1983, 1988; Simon 1975), and then on girls in the 1990s (Chesney-Lind and Shelden 1992; Miller 2001; Steffensmeier and Allan 1996).

Freda Adler (1975) and Rita Simon (1975), while basing their research on different theories, have highlighted the progressive changes in women's behaviour and the growing rupture of traditional women's roles, also explaining that the low participation of women in criminal activity was due to their confinement to domestic roles and the discrimination that limited their aspirations and opportunities (Daly and Chesney-Lind 1988). Both works have come to be criticized by feminist authors, who pointed out that both theories overlook the material and structural forces that shape women's lives and experiences (Daly and Chesney-Lind 1988; Simpson 1989). As Vold et al. (2002, p. 270) suggest, the early work of feminist criminology sought only to fill the gaps of traditional criminology without breaking away from the analytical and conceptual tools of the past. These early studies were subsumed in so-called liberal feminism.

As a response to this feminist perspective, other critical feminist approaches have developed within the framework of crime studies, undertaking a deconstruction of the established and dominant systems of thought and knowledge, while considering that social structures mainly reproduce a masculine view of the world. In this context, we highlight the criminal approaches developed by Marxist feminism (see Machado 2008, pp. 103–104; Silva 2008, p. 71), socialist feminism (see Firestone 1970; Machado 2008, p. 104), and the third wave or postmodern feminism (see Machado 2008, p. 104; Smart 1989; Wonders 1998). The most recent feminist approaches emphasize multiculturalism, accentuating differences among women and girls in terms of class, race, ethnicity and experiences with crime, victimization and the justice system (Chesney-Lind 1997). Its origins are in black feminism, and have been recently adopted and developed into an intersectional approach (Crenshaw 1989, 1991) to the understanding of crime and delinquency (McCall 2005; Messerschmidt 1997) or intersectional criminology (Potter 2015).

In Portugal, research on female crime and delinquency appeared in the 1980s, but underwent a boom at the beginning of the millennium, with studies on women in law (Beleza 1993), women in prisons (Carmo and Fráguas 1982; Cunha 1994, 2002, 2010; Granja et al. 2013, 2015; Matos 2008), intervention, violence and imprisonment of women (Gomes and Granja 2015a), criminal trajectories of women in general (Leal 2007) and of foreign and Roma women in particular (Gomes 2014; Gomes and Granja 2015b; Matos 2014) and violence and female juvenile delinquency (Duarte-Fonseca 2000; Duarte 2012; Duarte and Carvalho 2013; Duarte and Cunha 2014).

Differences in behaviour between women and men in relation to crime, and girls and boys in relation to delinquency, are still explained today in terms of a system of patriarchy, which establishes a gendered division of social roles and hierarchies, through which behaviours are codified as masculine and feminine, functioning as such in the prevailing system of power relations between the sexes (Belknap 1996; Matos 2008). In this current social system, men are perceived as subjects more likely to develop violent behaviour (and, inherently, are "criminals"); and women are seen as more likely to be fragile and defenceless (hence, "victims") (Beleza 1993, 2002; Renzetti and Curran 1993). Differences in socialization in terms of gender tend to activate women and girls to greater compliance with social norms and to maintain more distance from risky behaviours (Chesney-Lind and Shelden 1992; Holsinger 2000). Likewise, women appear to be more subject to social control and surveillance processes, which seem to be more likely to avoid deviant behaviour (Vold et al. 2002, p. 276). In general, feminist theories or theories with a gender perspective reveal how socially, the offending girl and woman are doubly deviant, and point out the implications that the dominant social constructs of masculinity and femininity have within the justice system (Ballinger 2007; Machado 2007), especially in that they judge women and girls according to a masculine model identified as the norm, not taking into account their different life experiences as a counterpoint to the experiences of men and boys (Beleza 1993; Carlen 2002; Chesney-Lind 1997; Fonseca 2008; Piquero et al. 2005).

Women's crime and girls' delinquency are often underestimated (Silvestri and Crowther-Dowey 2008) and relegated to the hidden crime figures (Duarte 2012). Women and girls are more present in crime than statistics show (Matos 2008) and this may be related to a set of structural dimensions—social, political, economic—that relegate the categories of crime and gender to secondary status, in turn having repercussions for the way crime and delinquency are detected and treated. That is why Gelsthorpe (2010) states that studies similar to one that has been developed by Wacquant (2008), shifting the focus of analysis to women, would lead to understanding whether or not there is gender inequality in the criminal justice system that influences the relationship between women and crime.

The way the female figure has been seen in traditional theories has had a profound impact on how girls and women have been prosecuted in juvenile and criminal justice systems, respectively (Chesney-Lind 1997).

In this field, a single story has also been constructed about the relationship between femininity and offence, marked by biases of various natures (gender, race and ethnicity, age, social class, etc.), which have had an impact on the application of judicial procedures and on the maintenance of discriminatory situations (Holsinger 2000; Hoyt and Scherer 1998; Matos 2008).

As researchers focus on studies that link gender and prison studies, old dilemmas as well as new reasons for discussion are revealed. The invisibility of women, once again, is a highlighted matter (Belknap 1996), stressing the oblivion to which traditional criminology and criminal-legal sociology have relegated the specific problems of women in punishment (Cook and Davis 1999), while exposing and reinforcing a penitentiary policy designed to consider the masculine model as the universal model (Almeda 2003, 2005; Fonseca 2008). Following this idea, the importance of using gender analysis to understand and distinguish the phenomena of female and male seclusion (Girschick 1997) is accepted since there has been a rapid growth of women in prison (Carlen 1999; Cook and Davis 1999; Faith 1999; Gelsthorpe and Morris 2002; Owen 1999; Silvestri and Crowther-Dowey 2008). It is also necessary to observe certain segments of the female prison population with distinct life experiences, such as poor (Bloom 1996; Bloom and McDiarmid 2000; Diaz-Cotto 2002, Young and Reviere 2005) black, Hispanic and white prisoners (McQuaide and Ehrenreich 1998).

Pat Carlen (1983, 1990, 1994, 2002, 2007), one of the pioneers of feminist criminology, shows that while female imprisonment emphasizes the cultivation of domesticity and the reconstruction of family relationships, seclusion also interferes with the construction of such relations outside the prison (Carlen 1983). Later, even realizing that in some prisons there is an effort made for sentences to be served by women with the least possible harm, she advocates the development of a woman-wise penology based on feminist jurisprudence (Carlen 1990) because imprisonment is, above all, a punishment (1994). Several researchers have, meanwhile, looked at the characteristics, experiences and trajectories of women prisoners (e.g., Azaola 2005, 2007; Genders and Player 1995; Cunha 1994, 2002, 2008; Almeda 2005; Frois 2017; Gelsthorpe 2010; Gomes 2014; Granja 2015; Hawton et al. 2014; Matos 2008, 2016;

Moore and Scraton 2014, 2016). Others have focused on the inadequacy of programs and activities designed for the female prison context (Walklate 2004), since they do not consider the specific characteristics and needs inherent to the female prison population (Walklate 2004), as well as the socio-familial, cultural background and professional development of these women, with a view to a more effective intervention (Fonseca 2008; Pollock 1998).

The study of girls in the justice system became a focal point when, during the 1980s, the statistics from different Western countries showed that girls were more visible, both in the juvenile justice system (Burman et al. 2001; Chesney-Lind and Shelden 1992; Steffensmeier and Allan 1996; Zahn 2009), and in the representational field, produced mainly by media discourse (Chesney-Lind and Jones 2010; Duarte and Cunha 2014; Gelsthorpe and Sharp 2006). A first consequence resulting from this is that more gender-sensitive studies (Hubbard and Matthews 2008), mostly with a feminist influence, began to emerge. The studies developed in the scope of this research have indicated how girls end up having different paths in delinquency and in the juvenile justice system when compared to boys in the same situation (Belknap and Holsinger 2006; Burman et al. 2001; Duarte 2012; Holsinger et al. 2010; Darrell et al. 2005; Wong et al. 2010; Zahn 2009). If delinquent processes apparently seem to be similar, they vary qualitatively in the ways in which they are experienced in terms of gender. These studies have also discussed the paternalistic and sexist responses of the juvenile justice system (Belknap and Holsinger 2006; Chesney-Lind and Shelden 1992; Moore and Padavic 2010), demonstrating that intervention has generally been based on procedures founded on knowledge produced with male samples (Salisbury et al. 2009), without questioning how gender inequalities can shape participation and response to intervention (Foley 2008; Goodkind 2005). As Garcia and Lane (2013) stress, if the girls' detention patterns were changing, the responses of the system had changed very little; the system is poorly prepared to respond effectively to gender differences in delinquency (Bloom and Covington 2001; Chesney-Lind et al. 2008; Duarte and Carvalho 2017). A second consequence, which derives from the first, comes from the finding that girls and boys respond differently to the intervention and treatment programs to which they are subjected (OJJDP, Covington and Bloom 2006; Chesney-Lind et al. 2008; Holsinger et al.

1999; Zahn et al. 2009). This situation led practitioners, during the 1990s, especially in the United States, to seek effective responses and strategies based on gender.

In the juvenile justice system, poor girls belonging to ethnic minority groups are over-represented and tend to receive harsher punishments than rich white girls (Moore and Padavic 2010). As a result of the paternalistic and sexist response of the juvenile system, studies show that girls, compared to boys, tend to be punished more severely for less serious offences and are more likely to be institutionalized for protection in situations related to "immoral" and "deviant" behaviour, such as maladaptation within the family and at school, vagrancy, prostitution, debauchery and so on. (Belknap and Holsinger 2006; Duarte-Fonseca 2000). In their assessment of delinquent practice, Steffensmeier and Allan (1996) show that girls are less subject to the court procedures applied to boys; the courts tend to show some reluctance to detain girls, opting instead for supervisory measures or other alternatives to seclusion. In addition to this, legal practitioners continue to feel that it is more difficult to work with girls than boys, as they consider girls to be less controllable, less obedient and more problematic (Baines and Alder 1996).

In short, the single story of these women and girls seems to be linked to the effects of gender stratification and patriarchy on their life experiences and to a system that was designed to deal with men's and boys' problems and neglect women's and girls' needs.

The emergence of a more gender-sensitive literature has been fundamental in constructing a new understanding of criminal and delinquent behaviour, where the gender variable becomes an axis of analysis, allowing crime and delinquency to be conceptualized as a matter of gender and revealing important considerations about gender differences in transgression. Women and men, and girls and boys, have many common risk factors; however, some factors have shown gender idiosyncrasies (Zahn et al. 2010; Wong 2012).

Literature has pointed out that one of the major limitations of criminology research was, on the one hand, that little attention was directed to aetiology, prosecution and intervention with girl and women offenders (Worrall 1990; Chesney-Lind 1997; Burman et al. 2001); and, on the other hand, that the female figure in criminal and delinquency studies was neglected. This perpetuated stereotypical image related to the idea that women and girl offenders are victims of their past, their environment and their female condition and as such, are incompatible with the criminal world (Holsinger 2000) and ignored the ways in which the paths both to and in crime and within the justice system are themselves genderized (Belknap 1996; Belknap and Holsinger 2006; Cunha 2002; Duarte 2012; Duarte and Cunha 2014; Gomes and Granja 2015a, b; Matos 2008; Zahn 2009).

Another relevant fact is that the gendered-pathways perspective was developed and tested primarily in the United States; and, therefore, the applicability of the model in European contexts remains questionable (Nuytiens and Christiaens 2015). It is crucial to consider studies in other contexts to be able to understand these phenomena more comprehensively and consistently. US studies, as well as UK studies, should not be generalized and applied to (other) European females or to those in other geographical contexts without special attention to their environment. Cross-continental studies are still needed to gather evidence concerning the differences and similarities that girl and women offenders demonstrate.

4 Intersectional and Multidisciplinary Approaches: The Book

All this research aims to compare different theoretical positions for a broader understanding of these phenomena; so this book includes Portuguese researchers from different fields of study discussing their investigations into transgressive girls and women in and out of the criminal justice system. Part I is dedicated to crime and women, and part II is focused on female juvenile delinquency. Through the exploration of girls' and women's relationships with delinquency and crime, as well as with the justice system, our goal is to highlight the heterogeneity of girls' and women's experiences, while debating convergences and divergences between them. For this purpose, authors focus on different social groups, not only analysing age and gender, but also nationality, ethnicity and social class.

The first part of the book, focusing on women and crime in and out of the system, starts with Catarina Frois, an anthropologist who focuses around the security–criminality nexus, framed within the broader theoretical concept of human security with a specific focus on female crime. This exploratory reflection results from the analysis of a set of data collected at a female prison setting, through close observation of prison life, extensive interviews with inmates, as well as the study of court rulings that determined women resulting sentences.

Continuing the discussion of women as transgressors intersected with security issues, the following chapter focuses on a practice that has only been very recently included in the Portuguese Penal Code: stalking. Helena Grangeia, a psychologist, and Margarida Santos, from legal studies, analyse stalking perpetrated by women, from a gender perspective. Firstly, they examine the understanding of stalking as a form of gender violence that emerges from visible forms of gender inequalities and that affects women disproportionately. Then, they explore the way stalking could arise from gendered habits and practices, and, as a consequence, may polarize the interpretations of stalking by women as opposed to stalking by men. To promote the understanding of the need to consider specific explanatory gender frameworks, data from scientific studies is presented selecting women as stalkers.

Within the context of the Portuguese female prison, the anthropologist Manuela Ivone Cunha discusses the contextual shifts in the actual significance of gender as a category of identity and social life in women's prisons, spanning three decades. Considering that prison studies are not disconnected from broader theoretical debates on categories of identity and social life (e.g., gender, ethnicity/race, class), the author shows how a more "gendercentric" agenda is becoming further diversified, recognizing the multiplicity of women prisoners' experiences and identities, and considering a wider variety of aspects of prison life; however, she also states that the emphasis on gender should itself be treated as an empirical question, according to the relative relevance of gender as a category of identity, and depending on its variable potential to organize social relationships.

The following two chapters target specific female prison populations, showing how social and legal vulnerabilities and the processes of gender victimization may significantly influence the understanding of how and why imprisonment occurs. Sílvia Gomes, a sociologist, through an intersectional perspective, pays particular attention to the imprisonment of foreign women. Based on a theoretical framework that grants central importance to social inequalities in an attempt to understand both the causes of crime and the efficacy of the criminal and social control institutions, and on a qualitative empirical study, she exposes the idiosyncrasies in the links between crime and nationality (and class) when a gender perspective was introduced. The conclusions of her study underline the importance of prisoners' objective pre-prison living conditions and the intersections of gender, social class and nationality; they also clarify the understanding of criminal involvement, either by action or by the reaction of the criminal control agents.

The feminist criminologist Mafalda Ferreira and colleagues centre their analysis on female prisoners convicted for the murder of their partners or former partners. They examine the possible relationship between the practice of the crime and the exposure to a prior history of intimate gender violence, as well as arguing the role of the criminal justice system on criminalization. Data obtained allowed the authors to recognize the presence of gender violence experienced by the women, perpetrated by the person they eventually murder, and the existent gaps in the Portuguese criminal justice system regarding the conviction of these female offenders.

The second part of the book examines female juvenile delinquency, intersecting with victimization processes. Sofia Neves, a social psychologist, and Joana Torres, a criminologist, characterize dating violence and social gender relationships through the testimonies of young Portuguese girls. Data collected and analysed allowed the authors to confirm that dating violence is present in teens' lives, and is suffered and perpetrated by both girls and boys. However, gender specificities were discovered concerning practices, attitudes and motivation, with girls admitting to using violence towards boys as a right achieved by gender equality.

Maintaining the focus on the reasons given by female delinquents for their behaviour, Maria João Leote de Carvalho developed a sociological study to achieve a better understanding of children's socialization processes in multi-problematic spaces, particularly concerning their involvement in violence and delinquency. In the following chapter, she focuses on the development of girls' socialization in the field through their own accounts of their lives and examines their perspectives on offending behaviours. She argues that the transmission of delinquent values takes place most significantly within the female family circle or via female peers, rather than from the influence of male individuals (as many studies defend).

From within the prison system, Raquel Matos, a psychologist, focuses on gender and crime in the life pathways of young women offenders through the analysis of the narratives of both young women serving prison sentences and professionals who deal with young offenders. She stresses the advantages of assuming a gender perspective and contrasting different narratives on young women's delinquent behaviour.

The sociologist Vera Duarte and the criminologist Ana Margarida Guerreiro focus their analysis on the experiences and the meanings of the transgressions in the lives of girls under educational court orders (executed in a Juvenile Detention Centre or in the community) in Portugal. The aim is to understand the problems of female juvenile delinquency from the testimonies of the girls. The authors created profiles of the transgressive paths that show the heterogeneity of the phenomenon of female juvenile delinquency, and at the same time proposed a solution to the victimization vs. agency dichotomy.

As we may infer from the theoretical reflection, a multidisciplinary analysis of complex phenomena such as these is crucial. The chapters of this book investigate female crime and delinquency phenomena from different scientific and theoretical perspectives, and even if they are not always able to create a new theoretical and conceptual framework, they enrich our understanding.

Despite their theoretical and conceptual diversity, some features are integral to the chapters and, in certain way, translate what has been the main view of the study of female crime and delinquency in Portugal. Stitching them together and seeking to classify the various multidisciplinary contributions to this book, a common concern is present: how the processes of victimization and agency are rewritten in the practices of female violence, criminality and delinquency in and out of the criminal justice system. Therefore, the whole reflective process intersects and integrates victimization and criminal practice, agency and structure.

We present here an original, worthwhile and respectable collection of academic work. This book attempts to go beyond the same geographies of the production of knowledge. Of course, these cannot be ignored, and they are part of the discussion through which evidence concerning the differences and similarities that girl and women offenders demonstrate across the country is gathered. Furthermore, this book includes Portuguese researchers from different fields of study. This inclusion is essential to an understanding of the contexts within different but complementary views. Moreover, by placing together and exploring female delinquency and female crime, in and out of the criminal justice system, we are contributing to this field of study by tracing and exploring convergences and divergences between girls' and women's experiences.

Finally, understanding how women and girls explain, and justify, their offending behaviours and how they relate to the criminal justice system, is a crucial step toward reforming social and legal policies while aiming for greater efficiency in terms of preventing crime and delinquency.

References

Adler, F. (1975). *Sisters in crime: The raise of the new female criminal*. New York: McGraw Hill.

Aebi, M. F., Tiago, M. M., & Burkhardt, C. (2016). *SPACE I—Council of Europe annual penal statistics: Prison populations. Survey 2015*. Strasbourg: Council of Europe.

Almeda, E. (2003). *Mujeres encarceladas*. Barcelona: Editorial Ariel.

Almeda, E. (2005). Women's imprisonment In Spain. *Punishment and Society, 7*(2), 183–189.

Azaola, E. G. (2005). Las mujeres en el sistema de Justicia penal y la antropologia a la que adhiero. *Cuadernos de Antropologia Social, 22*, 11–26.

Azaola, E. G. (2007). Género y justicia penal en México. In E. Samaranch & E. González (Eds.), *Mujeres y castigo: Un enfoque sócio-jurídico y de género* (pp. 27–65). Madrid: Dykinson.

Baines, M., & Alder, C. (1996). Are girls more difficult to work with? Youth workers' perspectives in juvenile justice and related areas. *Crime & Delinquency, 42*(3), 467–485.

Ballinger, A. (2007). Masculinity in the dock: Legal responses to male violence and female retaliation in England and Wales, 1900–1965. *Social and Legal Studies, 16*(4), 459–481.

Beleza, T. P. (1993). *Mulheres, Direito, Crime ou a Perplexidade de Cassandra.* PhD thesis in Law, Lisbon, Faculdade de Direito de Lisboa.

Beleza, T. P. (2002). Antígona no reino de creonte: o impacte dos estudos feministas no direito. *Ex aequo, 6*, 77–89.

Belknap, J. (1996). *The invisible woman: Gender, crime, and justice.* Belmont: Wadsworth.

Belknap, J., & Holsinger, K. (2006). The gendered nature of risk factors for delinquency. *Feminist Criminology, 1*, 48–71.

Bloom, B. (1996). *Triple Jeopardy: Race, class, and gender as factors in women's imprisonment.* PhD thesis, Riverside, University of California.

Bloom, B., & Covington, S. (2001). *Effective gender responsive interventions in Juvenile justice: Addressing the lives of delinquent girls.* Retrieved from http://www.centerforgenderandjustice.org/pdf/7.pdf

Bloom, B., & McDiarmid, A. (2000). Gender-responsive supervision and programming for women offenders in the community. In *Topics in community corrections annual issue 2000: Responding to women in the community* (pp. 11–18). Washington, DC: U.S. Department of Justice.

Burman, M., Batchelor, S., & Brown, J. (2001). Researching girls and violence. *The British Journal of Criminology, 41*, 443–459.

Carlen, P. (1983). *Women's imprisonment – A study in social control.* Boston: Routledge.

Carlen, P. (1988). *Women, crime, and poverty.* Milton Keyes: Open University Press.

Carlen, P. (1990). *Alternatives to women's imprisonment.* Bristol: Open University Press.

Carlen, P. (1994). Why study women's imprisonment? Or anyone else's? In R. D. King & M. Maguire (Eds.), *Prisons in context* (pp. 131–140). Oxford: Clarendon Press.

Carlen, P. (1999). Women's imprisonment in England: Current issues. In S. Cook & S. Davies (Eds.), *Harsh punishment: International experiences of women's imprisonment* (pp. 123–141). Boston: Northeastern University Press.

Carlen, P. (Ed.). (2002). *Women and punishment: The struggle for justice.* Devon: Willan Publishing.

Carlen, P. (2007). A reclusão de mulheres e a indústria de reintegração. *Análise Social*, XLII, *185*, 1005–1019.

An Introduction to Female Crime and Delinquency: Portugal...   17

Carmo, I., & Fráguas, F. (1982). *Puta de prisão*. Lisboa: D. Quixote.

Chesney-Lind, M. (1997). *The female offender. Girls, women and crime*. Thousand Oaks: Sage.

Chesney-Lind, M., & Jones, N. (Eds.). (2010). *Fighting for girls. New perspectives on gender and violence*. New York: State University of New York Press.

Chesney-Lind, M., & Shelden, R. (1992). *Girls delinquency and juvenile justice*. Pacific Grove: Brooks/Cole Publishing Company.

Chesney-Lind, M., Morash, M., & Stevens, T. (2008). Girls' troubles, girls' delinquency and gender responsive programming: A review. *The Australian and New Zealand Journal of Criminology, 41*(1), 162–189.

Cook, S., & Davis, S. (Eds.). (1999). *Harsh punishment: International experiences of women's imprisonment*. Boston: Northeastern University Press.

Covington, S., & Bloom, B. (2006). Gender-responsive treatment and services in correctional settings. *Women and Therapy, 29*(3/4), 9–33.

Crenshaw, K. (1989). Demarginalizing the intersection of race and sex: A black feminist critique of antidiscrimination doctrine, feminist theory and antiracist politics. *University of Chicago Legal Forum, 8*(1), 139–167. Retrieved from http://chicagounbound.uchicago.edu/uclf/vol1989/iss1/8.

Crenshaw, K. (1991). Mapping the margins: Intersectionality, identity politics, and violence against women of color. *Stanford Law Review, 43*, 1241–1279.

Cunha, M. I. (1994). *Malhas que a reclusão tece: Questões de identidade numa prisão feminina*. Lisboa: Centro de Estudos Judiciários.

Cunha, M. I. (2002). *Entre o Bairro e a Prisão: tráfico e trajectos*. Lisboa: Fim do Século.

Cunha, M. I. (Ed.). (2008). *Aquém e Além da Prisão: Cruzamentos e Perspetivas*. Lisboa: 90 Graus Editora.

Cunha, M. I. (2010). Race, crime and criminal justice in Portugal. In A. Kalunta-Crumpton (Ed.), *Race, crime and criminal justice: International perspectives* (pp. 144–161). New York: Palgrave Macmillan.

Daly, K., & Chesney-Lind, M. (1988). Feminism and criminology. *Justice Quarterly, 5*(4), 497–538.

Diaz-Cotto, J. (2002). Race, ethnicity, and gender in studies of incarceration. In J. James (Ed.), *States of confinement: Policing, detention, and prisons*. New York: Palgrave.

Darrell, S., Schwartz, J., Zhong, H., & Ackerman, J. (2005). An assessment of recent trends in girls' violence using diverse longitudinal sources: Is the gender gap closing? *Criminology, 43*(2), 355–406.

Duarte, V. (2012). *Discursos e Percursos na Delinquência Juvenil Feminina*. Famalicão: Edições Húmus.

Duarte, V., & Carvalho, M. J. (2013). (Entre)Olhares sobre delinquência no feminino. *Ex-Aequo, 28*, 31–44.

Duarte, V., & Carvalho, M. J. (2015). Da delinquência juvenil: Contributos para a problematização de um conceito. In M. I. Cunha (Ed.), *Do Crime e do Castigo – Temas e Debates Contemporâneos* (pp. 99–112). Lisboa: Mundos Sociais.

Duarte, V., & Carvalho, M. J. L. (2017). Female delinquency in Portugal: What girls have to say about their offending behaviors. *Gender Issues, 34*, 258–274.

Duarte, V., & Cunha, M. I. (Eds.). (2014). *Violências e Delinquências Juvenis Femininas: Género e (in)visibilidades sociais.* Famalicão: Edições Húmus.

Duarte-Fonseca, A. (2000). *Condutas desviantes de raparigas nos anos 90.* Coimbra: Coimbra Editora.

Faith, K. (1993). *Unruly women: The politics of confinement and resistance.* Vancouver: Press Gang Publishers.

Faith, K. (1999). The politics of confinement and resistance: The confinement of women. In E. Roseblatt (Ed.), *Criminal injustice; confronting the prison crisis* (pp. 165–183). Boston: South End Press.

Firestone, S. (1970). *The dialectics of sex. The case for feminist revolution.* New York: William Morrow.

Foley, A. (2008). The current state of gender-specific delinquency programming. *Journal of Criminal Justice, 36*, 262–269.

Fonseca, A. C. (2008). *Mulheres em Cumprimento de Pena: Um Estudo Exploratório no Sistema Prisional Português.* Master dissertation, Porto, Universidade do Porto.

Frois, C. (2017). *Mulheres Condenadas – Histórias de Dentro da Prisão.* Lisboa: Tinta da China.

Garcia, C., & Lane, J. (2013). What a girl wants, what a girl needs: Findings from a gender-specific focus group study. *Crime & Delinquency, 59*(4), 536–561.

Gelsthorpe, L. (2010). Women, crime and control. *Criminology and Criminal Justice, 10*, 375–386.

Gelsthorpe, L., & Morris, A. (2002). Women's imprisonment in England and Wales: A penal paradox. *Criminology & Criminal Justice, 2*(3), 277–301.

Gelsthorpe, L., & Sharpe, G. (2006). Gender, youth crime and justice. In B. Goldson & J. Muncie (Eds.), *Youth crime and justice* (pp. 47–61). London: Sage.

Genders, E., & Player, E. (1995). *Grendon: A study of a therapeutic prison.* Oxford: Clarendon.

Girschick, L. (1997). The importance of using a gendered analysis to understand women in prison. *Journal of the Oklahoma Criminal Justice Research Consortium*, 4. Retrieved from http://www.doc.state.ok.us/offenders/ocjrc/97_98.htm

Gomes, S. (2014). *Caminhos para a Prisão – uma análise do fenómeno da criminalidade associada a grupos estrangeiros e étnicos em Portugal.* Famalicão: Editora Húmus.

Gomes, S. (2018). How do foreign women end up in prison? An intersectional approach of criminal pathways. In S. Gomes & V. Duarte (Eds.), *Female crime and delinquency: In and out of the criminal justice system* (pp. xx–xx). London: Palgrave Macmillan.

Gomes, S., & Granja, R. (Eds.). (2015a). *Mulheres e Crime – Perspectivas sobre intervenção, violência e reclusão.* Famalicão: Editora Húmus.

Gomes, S., & Granja, R. (2015b). Trajetórias de vida e experiências prisionais de mulheres ciganas recluídas. In S. Gomes & R. Granja (Eds.), *Mulheres e Crime – Perspectivas sobre intervenção, violência e reclusão* (pp. 47–66). Famalicão: Editora Húmus.

Goodkind, S. (2005). Gender-specific service in the justice system. A critical examination. *Affilia, 20*(52), 52–70.

Granja, R. (2015). *Para cá e para lá dos muros: Relações familiares na interface entre o interior e o exterior da prisão.* PhD thesis in sociology, Braga, Universidade do Minho.

Granja, R., Cunha, M. I., & Machado, H. (2013). Formas alternativas do exercício da parentalidade: Paternidade e maternidade em contexto prisional. *Ex Aequo, 28*, 73–86.

Granja, R., Cunha, M. I., & Machado, H. (2015). Mothering from prison and ideologies of intensive parenting: Enacting vulnerable resistance. *Journal of Family Issues, 36*(9), 1212–1232.

Hawton, K., Linsell, L., Adeniji, T., Sariaslan, A., & Fazel, S. (2014). Self-harm in prisons in England and Wales: An epidemiological study of prevalence, risk factors, clustering, and subsequent suicide. *The Lancet, 383*(9923), 1147–1154.

Heidensohn, F. (1985). *Women and crime.* New York: New York University Press.

Holsinger, K. (2000). Feminist perspectives on female offending: Examine real girls' lives. *Women & Criminal Justice, 12*(1), 23–51.

Holsinger, K., Belknap, J., & Sutherland, J. (1999). *Assessing the gender specific program and service needs for adolescent females in the juvenile justice system.* Report to the Office of Criminal Services, Columbus.

Holsinger, K., Like, T., & Hodge, J. (2010). Gender-specific programs: Where we are and where we need to go. *Women, Girls & Justice, 11*(1), 1–16.

Hoyt, S., & Scherer, D. (1998). Female juvenile delinquency: Misunderstood by the juvenile justice system, neglected by social sciences. *Law and Human Behavior, 22*(1), 81–107.

Hubbard, D., & Matthews, B. (2008). Reconciling the differences between the "gender responsive" and the "what-works" literatures to improve services for girls. *Crime & Delinquency, 54*(2), 225–258.

Leal, J. M. P. (2007). *Crime no Feminino: Trajectórias Delinquenciais de Mulheres.* Coimbra: Edições Almedina.

Machado, H. (2007). *Moralizar para Identificar. Cenários da Investigação Judicial de Paternidade.* Porto: Edições Afrontamento.

Machado, H. (2008). *Manual de Sociologia do Crime.* Porto: Edições Afrontamento.

Matos, R. (2008). *Vidas raras de mulheres comuns: Percursos de vida, significações do crime e construção da identidade em jovens reclusas.* Coimbra: Almedina.

Matos, R. (Ed.). (2014). *Género, Nacionalidade e reclusão – Olhares cruzados sobre migrações e reclusão feminina em Portugal.* Porto: Universidade Católica Editora.

Matos, R. (2016). Trajectories and identities of foreign national women: Rethinking prison through the lens of gender and citizenship. *Criminology & Criminal Justice, 16*(3), 350–365.

McCall, L. (2005). The complexity of intersectionality. *Signs, 30*(3), 1771–1800.

McQuaide, S., & Ehrenreich, J. (1998). Women in prison: Approaches to understanding the lives of a forgotten population. *Affilia, 13*, 233–246.

Messerschmidt, J. (1997). *Crime as structured action: Gender, race, class and crime in the making.* Thousand Oaks: Sage.

Miller, J. (2001). *One of the guys: Girls, gangs and gender.* New York: Oxford University Press.

Moore, S. (2002). *Sociologia.* Mem Martins: Publicações Europa-América.

Moore, L., & Padavic, I. (2010). Racial and ethnic disparities in girls' sentencing in the juvenile justice system. *Feminist Criminology, 5*, 263–285.

Moore, L., & Scraton, P. (2014). *The incarceration of women: Punishing bodies, breaking spirits.* Basingstoke: Palgrave Macmillan.

Moore, L., & Scraton, P. (2016). Doing gendered time: The harms of women's incarceration. In Y. Jewkes, J. Bennett, & B. Crewe (Eds.), *Handbook on prisons* (2nd ed., pp. 549–567). New York: Routledge.

Naffine, N. (1996). *Feminism and criminology*. Philadelphia: Temple University Press.

Nuytiens, A., & Christiaens, J. (2015). Female pathways to crime and prison: Challenging the (US) gendered pathways perspective. *European Journal of Criminology, 13*(2), 195–213.

Owen, B. (1999). Women and imprisonment in the United States: The gendered consequences of the U.S. imprisonment binge. In S. Cook & S. Davies (Eds.), *Harsh punishment: International experiences of women's imprisonment* (pp. 81–98). Boston: Northeastern University Press.

Piquero, N., Gover, A., MacDonald, J., & Piquero, A. (2005). The influence of delinquent peers on delinquency: Does gender matter? *Youth & Society, 36*(3), 251–275.

Pollock, J. M. (1998). *Counseling women in prison*. Thousand Oaks: Sage.

Potter, H. (2015). *Intersectionality and criminology: Disrupting and revolutionizing studies of crime*. New York: Routledge.

Renzetti, C., & Curran, D. (1993). *Women, men and society*. Boston: Allyn and Bacon.

Salisbury, E., Van Voorhis, P., & Spiripoulos, G. (2009). The predictive validity of a gender-responsive needs assessment: An exploratory study. *Crime & Delinquency, 55*(4), 550–585.

Silva, M. C. (2008). Desigualdades de género: esboço por um mapa pró-teórico. *Revista Configurações, 4*, 65–89.

Silvestri, M., & Crowther-Dowey, C. (2008). *Gender & Crime*. London: Sage Publications.

Simon, R. (1975). *Women and crime*. Lexington: Lexington Books.

Simpson, S. (1989). Feminist theory, crime and justice. *Criminology, 2*(4), 605–631.

Smart, C. (1989). *Feminism and the power of law*. London: Routledge.

Steffensmeier, D., & Allan, F. (1996). Gender and crime: Toward a gendered theory of female offending. *Annual Review of Sociology, 22*, 459–487.

Vold, G., Bernard, T., & Snipes, J. (2002). Gender and crime. In Vold et al. (Eds.), *Theoretical criminology* (pp. 267–282). New York: Oxford University Press.

Wacquant, L. (2008). Racial stigma in the making of the punitive America's punitive state. In G. Loury et al. (Eds.), *Race and mass incarceration in America: The Tanner lectures*. Cambridge: MIT Press.

Walklate, S. (2004). *Gender, crime and criminal justice*. Portland: Willan Publishing.

Wonders, N. (1998). Postmodern feminism and social justice. In B. Arrigo (Ed.), *Social justice/criminal justice*. Belmont: West/Wadsworth.

Wong, T. (2012). *Girls delinquency. A study on sex differences in (risk factors for) delinquency*. Oisterwijik: Uitgeverij Box Press.

Wong, T., Stotboom, A., & Bijleveld, C. (2010). Risk factors for delinquency in adolescent and young adult females: A European view. *European Journal of Criminology, 7*(4), 266–284.

Worrall, A. (1990). *Offending women. Female lawbreakers and the criminal justice system*. London: Routledge.

Young, V., & Reviere, R. (2005). *Women behind bars: Gender and race in U.S. prisons*. Boulder: Lynne Rienner.

Zahn, M. (2009). *Female Juvenile Delinquents*. EUA: Temple University Press.

Zahn, M., Day, J., Mihalic, S., & Tichavsky, L. (2009). Determining what works for girls in the juvenile justice system: A summary of evaluation evidence. *Crime & Delinquency, 55*, 266–293.

Zahn, M. et al. (2010). *Causes and correlates of girl's delinquency. OJJDP Girl Study Group: Understanding and responding to girl's delinquency*. Washington, DC: US Office of Justice Programs. Retrieved from https://www.ncjrs.gov/pdffiles1/ojjdp/226358.pdf

Part I

Crime and Women: Gender Bias, Crime Trajectories and the Prison System

2

The Criminal Act at the Core of the Nexus Security–Insecurity: A Tentative Approach to Female Crime

Catarina Frois

Three women of different origins, condition, age, personal and professional backgrounds were studied: Ana, 30 years old, serving a prison sentence of 5 years and 6 months for drug trafficking; Mariana, a woman of 60, convicted and sentenced to 12 years in prison for the murder of her husband; Camila, 46, arrested and charged on several counts of theft and robbery for which she was eventually convicted and sentenced to 7 years of imprisonment. What binds these women—besides their incarceration at Odemira prison facility, a small prison housing 50 women, in the interior south of Portugal—is that they share a personal history marked by abuse, physical and psychological violence, economic precariousness, and insufficient support from the welfare state's care institutions. Nevertheless, just as their individual trajectories are distinct, so too their rationalization and explanation of the motives underlying their criminal actions are also essentially subjective, idiosyncratic, and specific to their own case.

C. Frois (✉)
CRIA, Instituto Universitário de Lisboa (ISCTE), Lisbon, Portugal

© The Author(s) 2018
S. Gomes, V. Duarte (eds.), *Female Crime and Delinquency in Portugal*,
https://doi.org/10.1007/978-3-319-73534-4_2

This may be our interpretation as ethnographers who have followed everyday life inside prison and have gradually come to know the inmates' individual stories.[1] That is, as subjects who develop a relationship whose closeness grants us deeper insight into personal and familiar trajectories, beyond the abstract categories under which crimes are inscribed and the judicial rulings convicting these women to imprisonment—in these cases drug trafficking, homicide, theft, and criminal association. When moving beyond the personal and singular narratives of each one of these particular women, or in other words, when as social scientists we increase the level of complexity by contextualizing and problematizing the social, economic, circumstantial conditions underlying crime, we inevitably face a paradox: albeit unlawful, the criminal acts committed by these women—as with so many other incarcerated women—are simultaneously a manifestation of agency and autonomy, a reaction intended to guarantee or achieve security.

Exploring the possibility of reflecting upon crime (in this case female crime) as a strategy, a resource and even an inevitability found by individuals to deal with insecurity, is the theoretical and analytical proposal I develop in the following pages. It may seem like an exercise in tautology. After all, what value or meaning could we expect to reclaim by explaining a certain situation through its own proposition, namely, the same rhetorical devices? How can we validate or legitimate these women's offences by arguing that they were themselves victims—not necessarily of crime in the strict sense of the word, but of injustice, discrimination and prejudice?

It is on this point that the concept of human security becomes relevant as a theoretical tool, since by putting the individual at the core of the security nexus—as the subject at whom security policies and community practices should primarily be aimed—allows us to reflect upon the circumstances and contexts underlying these very same concerns. Broadly characterized, the human security concept—initially proposed in 1994 by the United Nations, but nowadays more complex and wide-ranging—has as its main purpose to broaden the focus of security concerns beyond state sovereignty or state intervention in war theatres, centering the attention on menaced individuals, communities and populations (see, amongst others, Burgess 2010; Eriksen et al. 2010; Kaldor 2014; Martin and

Owen 2013; Maguire et al. 2014). There are different types of threats to security: political, economic, environmental, personal, food, community, health. In this sense, the human security proposal assumes that problems of security extend beyond contexts of war to the suffering endured by individuals and populations from other types of danger, which sovereign states should also attend to and be aware of. As Mary Kaldor aptly explains, "just as human rights includes economic and social as well as civil and political rights, so human development is about more than a decent standard of living. It is also about feeling safe on the streets and being able to influence political decision-making" (2007: 279).

It is worth transcribing here the human security approach as stated by the United Nations Trust Fund for Human Security (n.d):

> Human security is a dynamic and practical policy framework for addressing widespread and cross-cutting threats facing Governments and people. Recognizing that threats to human security vary considerably across and within countries, and at different points in time, the application of human security calls for an assessment of human insecurities that is people-centered, comprehensive, context-specific, and preventive. Such an approach helps focus attention on current and emerging threats to the security and well-being of individuals and communities.

Furthermore, in a specific section specifying "the added value of human security as an operational tool", other important factors are emphasized: namely, "by contextualizing the causes and manifestations of threats and their impact on people, human security highlights the actual needs, vulnerabilities, and capacities of those impacted and strengthens the development of solutions that are targeted and prioritized".

My previous studies on surveillance devices and the use of video-surveillance in open areas (Frois 2008, 2011, 2013, 2014) already put the emphasis, like several other scholars studying related matters, on the ambivalent character of certain security policies and the resulting inefficiency of its mechanisms, which often failed to deal with problems that decision-makers and police force officials seemed to regard either as too elusive or too fastidious. Fear or insecurity is, to the common citizen much more than the fear of terrorism, or even of being the victim of a crime (and here I am alluding to the main political mottoes on the "war on crime" and "war on terror"). In contemporary society, as Robert Castel (2003) explained so adeptly, insecurity is mainly related to the absence of "protection"—understood in its broader scope—but also with the fear (as synonymous of worry and concern) about the present, the future, the unknown. Therefore, we may properly talk of insecurity in the economic sphere when people face economic deprivation or difficulties, unemployment, cuts in salaries, social benefits, or pension plans. Everyday insecurity may also arise when people fear for their children's or grandchildren's future in the face of adverse circumstances or bleak prospects; when the elderly fear for their health in light of the real possibility of not having money to buy medication, of not having anyone capable of looking after them in old age, considering state cuts in the public welfare system. This panorama, though specifically portrayed with the Portuguese context of the last decade in mind, could be extended to several other European countries afflicted by severe financial crisis.

More recently, other dimensions included in the human security sphere have gained prominence as a desirable goal—namely, "freedom from fear", "freedom from want", "freedom to live in dignity"—considering that people should be able to live in a peaceful environment, should have autonomy in their lives and choices, and must have the possibility to exercise their fundamental rights in democracy. If we take this framework, and apply its different propositions to reflect about female crime, and the Odemira inmates in particular, we confirm not only that they are valid, but also actually contribute to advance our theoretical efforts, even if originally they were not primarily conceived for this specific setting. On this point, I am closely following Ton Salman's argument that "risk-taking is just as much a 'natural' human action as are apparent efforts to increase security for oneself or one's beloved—and the concept of human security should be able to address both. People, for instance, often demonstrate a desire to avoid or escape forms of community and security that they experience as stiffing or oppressive. People may, moreover, want to engage in insecure and even dangerous actions if they no longer want to tolerate injustice or exclusion" (2010: 23–24).

Following this reasoning, what I propose in the following section is to analyze the conduct of three women—considering the motivations for the criminal offence committed—as a strategy conceived by themselves, as autonomous agents, to guarantee their own security and safety, albeit implying having to step outside the margins of the law.

1 Ana, Mariana, Camila: Three Different Persons, Three Different Crimes—The Same Insecurity?

The life histories of Ana, Mariana, and Camila, are explored in full detail elsewhere (Frois 2017). Here I must limit my incursion to a brief overview of their trajectories, specifically seeking to underline the common features of what, even if only superficially, are very diverse life histories.

As already mentioned, Ana is a 30-year-old woman incarcerated at Odemira for drug trafficking. As a single mother of a teenage daughter (who at the time of our conversations was also incarcerated in a youth detention center for petty theft), her marital experience was marked by recurrent abuse—physical aggression and verbal insults—at the hands of her companion. One day, in the middle of one of those violent outbursts, upon seeing her daughter reach for a kitchen knife with the intention of "killing the father", Ana decided it was time to leave the house, taking shelter at a halfway home for victims of domestic violence. A few months later, she decided to leave the home and share an apartment with a fellow victim she had met at the shelter. This situation did not last long, since her friend decided to go back to her ex-husband. With a job as house cleaner and the adolescent daughter to provide for, Ana sought help from social services in her area of residence. She was essentially seeking financial aid to cope with current expenses. The social worker responsible for assessing the case decided on a course of action that Ana considered unreasonably "radical", assigning the young girl to a children's home even without Ana's agreement. The alleged argument was that this would free Ana from the "burden" of providing for her daughter and thus dispense with any financial support for her. Finding herself on her own, she eventually moved in with a new boyfriend, a drug user and with whom she began using and trafficking drugs.

Less than two years after these events, both mother and daughter were incarcerated, a situation described by Ana in terms that can be interpreted as a paradox. On the one hand, when referring to the initial moment when she decided to abandon her daughter's father to start anew, she claimed, "I thought I was doing the best for us, that I was making things better, getting us out of a bad situation; but in the end, what I did was worse". By "In the end, what I did was worse", Ana was referring to the separation from her daughter, which she believed had precipitated the following events. Conversely, Ana claimed that her present confinement was a positive experience, and that even her daughter's confinement was the "best thing that could have happened to her". Ana reasoned that at least now there was someone to watch over her, and she was learning a trade. Ana made projections of a better future for both after their release from prison. Nevertheless, she was very critical of the social worker and municipal services assigned to her case, in what she described as a "bad job". What she had expected at the time she sought out their help was to be awarded some kind of income support allowance that would allow her to live with her daughter—to pay the rent, to find a workplace—but the result was exactly its opposite. In other words, she questioned the kind of help that found it preferable to break apart a family than to secure its subsistence.

This perplexity is not entirely different from what Camila conveyed to me as she described the background in which she had committed the crimes leading to her conviction. In this instance, being a woman of gipsy ethnic origin, it would be among a group of her own ethnic community that she would finally seek shelter when the outcome of her efforts to obtain help from social services to take care of her four underage children resulted in an ultimatum presented by the social worker assigned to her case: she had six months to find a "suitable" house to accommodate her children, or the children would be put into care. Camila's case is highly relevant to our discussion, since it clearly reveals the kind of ineffectiveness that can introduce itself in the management of public mechanisms devised to support persons in situations of urgent need or acute deprivation.

Her story is intricate, but may be summed up thus: during her adolescence, Camila rejected what she called "the gypsy lifestyle" (referring to the communal and nomadic custom of her family and community) and married a man who would ultimately abandon her after 14 years of life together, leaving her without the means to support her children, so she filed an appeal with the family court to demand alimony from her husband. Camila also asked help from municipal services to find her a proper residence to live with her children (at the time they were living in a run-down shanty with no plumbing or electricity) and she signed-up at the local employment center as well as applying for the Minimum Wage Income from Social Security services. When all these possibilities had been exhausted, she was faced with the social worker's six-month ultimatum.

That was when she made up her mind to try what she characterized as the "last available resource": crime. When she joined the group of gypsies mentioned at the beginning of this story, Camila was aware that they made money from robberies and theft. Initially her idea was to raise enough money to "show the social worker", as she put it, that she was capable of supporting the children within a proper environment. However, her new-found associates were a large group already under police investigation, and shortly after she had joined, more than a dozen of them (men and women) were arrested, including Camila. Even though the minors were in fact put into care, it was now her family of origin that supported her and sought ways to be granted custody of her children while she was incarcerated.

Mariana's trajectory diverges from these two narratives in several aspects. In her case, she had only once needed to seek the help of state institutions to cope with the daily insecurity she faced. Nevertheless, even in that single instance the response obtained had been quite different from what she had expected. Throughout 40 years of marriage—from which she had two children who were now already adults—she was a constant victim of assaults and maltreatment by her husband. She concealed these episodes from the family, friends, and working colleagues. In all cases, as she told me, she did this either out of fear or out of shame.

Family gatherings and socializing were reduced to a minimum; she had no relationships with friends, discouraged by her husband's bouts of jealousy and suspicion. At work she never allowed herself to confide in anyone about her domestic problems. Mariana described her husband as a "bad person, a mean man", but she never sought an alternative, that is, she never found the courage to leave her house. Mariana's reasoning was that since she was the victim, why should she have to be forced out of her home, and not him? Having suffered death threats at gun point on several occasions, and realizing no one was ever "coming to help her", one day, only hours after she had been once again threatened by her husband, she decided to take her husband's gun to the police station. The police officers filed the complaint, kept the gun, and then followed what seemed to be the usual practice in that particular precinct: they called her husband up and returned the gun to him, letting him go with no further consequences. A few years after this isolated attempt to find help through the proper channels, one day she ended up taking another gun her husband kept and used to threaten her with, and shot him to death.

Viewed within the Portuguese context, Mariana's case is exemplary of a notorious incongruity between the existing data regarding domestic violence and/or conjugal homicide, and the action of judges and magistrates. In a phenomenon that is so deeply rooted in conjugal custom, where inequalities between men and women are so generalized—the latter generally in a position of dependency and vulnerability—the majority of condemnations still favor suspended sentences even when the facts are proved in court—something which despite no longer depending on the victims' accusation, still depends largely upon their testimony—we find that judges (and the common citizen for that matter) still have difficulty in identifying the aggressor with the figure of the criminal who deserves an effective prison sentence, and thus the high rate of condemned offenders on probation, often serving consecutive suspended sentences for the same crimes.[2] As a result, the number of women killed (or suffering attempted murder) by those same partners while on probation—regardless of any additional measures, such as restraining orders or electronic bracelets—continues to rise.

2 Pre-Penitentiary Institutions, or the Paradoxes of the Welfare State

In societies like the Portuguese, the role of the state in securing social welfare is of vital importance to its citizens—in areas such as health, education, security, and all manner of benefits—the most disadvantaged sectors of the population are especially vulnerable to relations of dependence, a dependence which, we might say, is twofold: there is the dependence upon public institutions' ability to respond to dire and urgent necessities—of their ability to provide effective care, monitoring, intervention, and protection. In this domain, an individual's financial situation is of extreme importance, insofar as it defines the possibility of choice or autonomy—for instance, to afford a health insurance or pension plan, to access a wider range of schools for his/her children, and so on. On the other hand, said dependence upon public institutions—even when it proves sufficiently effective—engages its subjects in another form of relationship that demands a certain *quid pro quo* which many would find intrusive or humiliating: to "demonstrate" one's own failure to cope, to offer proof of one's own destitution, and then accept the assessment and probing (albeit helpful or well-intended) of third parties, such as social workers, sanitary technicians, youth protection committees, among others.

I believe these situations are an instance of what Michel Foucault (1977) characterized as extensions of the penitentiary system, although in the case of the imprisoned female population I worked with, I find that we could venture to describe them as institutions which appear to comprise a *pre-penitentiary* system. Although the state's legitimacy, as an apparatus of power, to intervene more radically in the life of the citizens is more evident after incarceration—most significantly through deprivation of freedom—this intervention actually starts well before the practice of criminal actions, as if in anticipation of them. Without necessarily signaling a woman as an offender or delinquent, her situation of poverty or instability marks her under the category of "risk"—as someone whose need for early intervention (with financial or family problems, namely, where children are involved) targets her as a "candidate" for a more vigorous, and ultimately more extreme, kind of intervention in the near future. Didier Fassin sums up this process accurately when he states, "Because these populations [i.e. immigrants, prisoners, youth offenders, refugees] are socially, economically and often legally precarious, their government involves three rationalities: the welfare state, which protects the subjects from the hazards of life; the penal state, which decides which crime to punish and how, and the liberal state, which mobilizes simultaneously individual rights and individual obligations" (Fassin et al. 2015: xi).

The typical profile of the incarcerated women at Odemira prison facility shows that in general terms imprisoned women lived in a situation of extreme precariousness—born into families of low socioeconomic status (usually accompanied by situations involving violence and maltreatment)—and presented a high rate of illiteracy or education levels far below the national average (Gomes and Granja 2015). At the time of their conviction, the majority were unemployed or working in unskilled and temporary jobs, relying on state welfare services or charity organizations. A large percentage are single mothers or lived with partners who were not the father of their children, with teenage or young motherhood being the norm. In turn, this also corresponded to a large number of children in the care of relatives other than their progenitors, or situations of repeated institutionalization—whether they were voluntarily handed over by their mothers or retrieved by state agencies such as social security services or the Child and Youth Protection Services (Frois 2017).

For female offenders, these different aspects merge with trajectories that while being perceived by them as unique and absolutely specific to their own case, usually present a number of recurrent features—upbringings marked by lack of opportunities, lack of family support networks, economic instability within unstructured environments or communities. These factors are not alien to the gender roles that characterize the still largely patriarchal frame of Portuguese society, which is more acutely felt among women of lower education and professional skills, and therefore also more dependent on relations (family, husband, boyfriend, neighbors) that establish certain roles and duties for them to comply with (Pina Cabral 2003; Wall and Amâncio 2007). Vunerability, the exposure to situations of insecurity, and the resulting impotence manifested in different spheres of their existence, becomes intrinsic amongst these sectors in Portuguese society, and that is precisely the portrait presented by the population at Odemira prison facility, our case study.

The dialectic relation between practices and representations found here is not reproduced totally detached from the normative society. It is actually framed by the state apparatus in multiple ways, the most important and visible of which are the mechanisms of the welfare system: child benefits or the so-called national family allowance, guaranteed minimum income for disadvantaged persons and families, social housing and rents, unemployment benefits, solidarity supplements for the elderly, and so on (e.g., Carmo and Costa 2015; Lima 2016). Social solidarity institutions—child daycare centers, old people's homes, charity institutions (such as *Santa Casa da Misericordia*[3] or other NGOs), churches, food and clothing banks, among others—have a more direct or indirect effect within a broader network built to fulfill the needs of men and women of all ages. Invariably, it falls upon women to secure this kind of minimum subsistence. We might say that socially, in Portugal it is part of the female role to seek and deal with social institutions (formally or informally), whether because it is considered part of the domestic sphere for which they are responsible (since they are usually the element in the household who doesn't have a "proper job"), or simply because men find it embarrassing or beneath them to "beg" for help from others.

Many of the women currently at Odemira fit into this profile. Throughout my work at this prison facility, in this respect the discourse of imprisoned women fell into a pattern—clearly distinct from what I have observed in male prisons (Frois 2016)—regarding their motivations (for lack of a more suitable term) for their initiation in criminal activities. It was extremely rare to find justifications based on the desire to earn the "respect" of their peers (Bourgois 2002; Crewe 2009; Ugelvik 2014)—which is a common rationalization in male prison environments—or to fulfill an ideal of ostentation and wealth (even if only apparent or transient), in sum, as a measure of success within a given value system. Individual trajectories and life experiences are, in most cases, narrated by the inmates as justification for their crimes, in what is undoubtedly a most extreme reflection of subjectivity: arguments such as "I had to kill him or else I would die, but I still love him", in the case of conjugal homicide in a marriage characterized by domestic violence. "How else would I feed my children if not drug trafficking?" in the case of women unemployed living on the minimum income benefit. "I robbed to support my drug habit", in the case of drug addicts. This list of examples could go on endlessly.

How, and why, may crime be considered (whether alternatively, successively, or simultaneously): primarily as a choice, an opportunity, or even a last resort? What legitimacy or relevance does such a claim still carry after we have in our possession all the information surrounding these women's socio-economic background and context, and we have identified all the situations of vulnerability, inequity, stigma, and often social exclusion, by which they were bound?

In light of the arguments I have been presenting, I believe that at least it may provide a viable, and indeed fruitful, instrument of analysis considering (1) that it avoids pathologizing or profiling stereotypes that tend to accommodate and account for categories such as that of "bad mother/ bad wife" (e.g., Carlen 1985); (2) it resists a rationale of presumptive victimization, as if poverty or structural (and sometimes endemic) violence predetermined the course of their lives (as still seems to be the view taken by many magistrates and social workers); (3) it acknowledges the identity and status of women as individual persons endowed with autonomy and agency, even if sometimes against their own self-perception. To be sure, when a woman states that she sought help from several institutions to guarantee hers and her children's subsistence and welfare, and that either due to their rejection or insufficiency she had to get involved in robberies or drug-trafficking—explaining that the crime was her ultimate resort—she is in fact revealing that the illegal activity was a conscious, thought-out, and purposeful decision.

We might speculate on whether such a choice would pose itself had she succeeded in finding a job or had financial resources, for instance, but that is hardly the point in question. For our argument, what matters is that faced with adversity, this woman found a solution that was unsafe and risky, but one which became a form securing the stability that had escaped her reach when she pursued certain legal mechanisms at her disposal. Even if we are willing to take a more objective and hard analysis of such a case as an "exception", an example of the inevitable fallibility of such a system, it remains equally significant that the welfare state failed this woman as well as the community it serves. In a certain way, the crime could almost be viewed as an "alternative" plan for these women, beyond any legal, moral, or even ethical distinctions (Comaroff and Comaroff 2016).

Admittedly, the present hypothesis may initially confuse the reader, given that the human-security approach aims precisely to move beyond crime-fighting policies. However, the reason is rather straightforward: the female authors of criminal actions, such as Ana, Mariana, or Camila, are first and foremost people for whom this broader intervention should have been triggered, with its preventive positive impacts on their lives. That is, these were women living with economic frailties and precariousness and facing numerous types of threats to their safety and physical and psychological well-being, as well as that of their own families and especially their offspring (Merry 2008). As such, notwithstanding the moral or normative standards in a given community, the crimes they have committed—the unlawful element of their actions—could plausibly be subsumed under their broader struggle to achieve those same above-mentioned purposes: to live without fear (namely, of abuse and domestic violence); to have the possibility of being autonomous and able to decide and make choices in situations of financial deprivation and to preserve their dignity as individuals, faced with decisions by state institutions that the average person would consider intrusive—such as those measures conditioning the most basic decisions of family life.

On many levels, we are thus confronted with the issue of security—or lack thereof—which we are interested in. Security as an ideal; as part of a lived-in experience; security identified with physical, psychological, and material well-being. Its absence implies a necessarily alternate set of decisions and choices, since an individual's agency will not yield to a condition of absolute passivity, and will exhaust all the resources at his/her disposal—resources which, if anything, largely depend upon their known and surrounding networks of support and solidarity, whether formal or informal.

Notes

1. The use of the ethnographic method in prison studies is the subject of a comprehensive handbook edited by Drake et al. (2015).
2. In 2015 was created the *Equipa de Análise Retrospectiva de Homicidio em Violência Doméstica* (the Portuguese counterpart of, for example the North-American National Domestic Violence Fatality Review Initiative) composed by members of different ministries with the aim of studying and examining judicial cases of conjugal homicide in context of domestic violence. This team evaluates the efficiency of the adopted proceedings in similar situations (for example, security forces, social workers, magistrates, etc.) https://earhvd.sg.mai.gov.pt/Pages/default.aspx. According with the Observatory of Assassinated Women of UMAR (Women's Union, Alternative and Response) between 2004 and 2016, 454 women were killed by men with whom they maintained or had in the past a romantic or conjugal relationship http://www.umarfeminismos.org/index.php/observatorio-de-mulheres-assassinadas. Domestic violence annual statistic are available at https://apav.pt/apav_v3/index.php/pt/
3. A Portuguese charity founded in Lisbon in 1498. It is currently the oldest working NGO in the world, if not the first. It isn't supervised by the church or the state.

References

Bourgois, P. (2002). *Search of respect. Selling crack in El Barrio*. New York: Cambridge University Press.

Burgess, P. (Ed.). (2010). *Handbook of new security studies*. New York: Routledge.

Carlen, P. (Ed.). (1985). *Criminal women. Autobiographical accounts*. Cambridge: Polity Press.

Carmo, R., & da Costa, A. F. (2015). *Desigualdades em Questão. Análise e Problemáticas*. Lisbon: Mundos Sociais.

Castel, R. (2003). *L'Insécurité sociale. Qu'est-ce qu'être protégé?* Paris: Seuil.

Comaroff, J., & Comaroff, J. (2016). *The truth about crime. Sovereignty, knowledge, social order*. Chicago: Chicago University Press.

Crewe, B. (2009). *The prisoner society: Power, adaptation, and social life in an English prison*. Oxford: Oxford University Press.

Drake, D., Earle, R., & Sloan, J. (Eds.). (2015). *Palgrave handbook of prison ethnography*. London/New York: Palgrave Macmillan.

Eriksen, T. H., Bal, E., & Salemink, O. (Eds.). (2010). *A world of insecurity. Anthropological perspectives on human security*. London: Pluto Press.

Fassin, D., et al. (2015). *At the heart of the state. The moral world of institutions*. London: Pluto Press.

Foucault, M. (1977). *Discipline and punish. The birth of the prison* (trans: Sheridan, A.). London: Penguin.

Frois, C. (Ed.). (2008). *A Sociedade Vigilante. Ensaios sobre Identificação, Vigilância e Privacidade*. Lisbon: Imprensa de Ciências Sociais.

Frois, C. (2011). Video-surveillance in Portugal: Analysis of a transitional process. *Social Analysis, 55*(3), 35–53.

Frois, C. (2013). *Peripheral vision. Politics, technology and surveillance*. Oxford/New York: Berghahn.

Frois, C. (2014). Video-surveillance and the political use of discretionary power in the name of security and defence. In M. Maguire, C. Frois, & N. Zurawski (Eds.), *The anthropology of security. Perspectives from the frontline of policing, counter-terrorism and border control* (pp. 45–61). London: Pluto Press.

Frois, C. (2016). Close insecurity: Inmates' perceptions and discourses in Portugal. *Social Anthropology, 24*(3), 309–323.

Frois, C. (2017). *Female imprisonment. An ethnography of everyday life in confinement*. London/New York: Palgrave.

Gomes, S., & Granja, R. (Eds.). (2015). *Mulheres e Crime. Perspectivas sobre Intervenção, Violência e Reclusão*. Vila Nova de Famalicão: Húmus.

Kaldor, M. (2014). Human security. In M. Kaldor & I. Rangelov (Eds.), *The handbook of global security policy* (pp. 85–102). Oxford: Wiley-Blackwell.

Kaldor, M., Martin, M., & Selchow, S. (2007). Human security: A new strategic narrative for Europe. *International Affairs, 83*(2), 273–288.

Lima, A. P. (2016). Care as a factor for sustainability in situations of crisis: Portugal between the welfare state and interpersonal relationships. *Cadernos Pagu, 46*, 79–105.

Maguire, M., Frois, C., & Zurawski, N. (Eds.). (2014). *The anthropology of security. Perspectives from the frontline of policing, counter-terrorism and border control*. London: Pluto Press.

Martin, M., & Owen, T. (Eds.). (2013). *Routledge handbook of human security*. New York: Routledge.

Merry, S. E. (2008). *Gender violence: A cultural perspective*. Oxford: Wiley-Blackwell.

Pina Cabral, J. (2003). *O Homem na Família. Cinco Ensaios de Antropologia*. Lisbon: Imprensa de Ciências Sociais.

Salman, T. (2010). Taking risks for security's sale: Bolivians resisting their state and its economic policies. In T. H. Eriksen, E. Bal, & O. Salemink (Eds.), *A world of insecurity. Anthropological perspectives on human security* (pp. 22–44). London: Pluto Press.

Ugelvik, T. (2014). *Power and resistance in prison: Doing time, doing freedom*. London/New York: Palgrave.

United Nations Trust Fund for Human Security. http://www.un.org/humansecurity/

Wall, K., & Amâncio, L. (Eds.). (2007). *Família e Género em Portugal e na Europa*. Lisbon: Imprensa de Ciências Sociais.

3

Stalking by Women: Another Side of Gender Violence

Helena Grangeia and Margarida Santos

1 Stalking as Gender Violence

Initially, stalking was conceptualized as predatory violence, restricted to celebrities, particularly in the Anglo-Saxon world. Since the 1990s, stalking has become one of the multiple, complex facets of violence against women (cf. Grangeia and Matos 2011). This view is founded primarily on the traditional association between stalking and domestic violence, encompassing behaviours of control, harassment and interfering after the breakup of the relationship (e.g., Burgess et al. 1997; Coleman 1997; Douglas and Dutton 2001; Kurt 1995; Logan et al 2002). Secondly, the larger focus on women victims is based on the marked discrepancy between men and women, with a greater percentage of men as offenders and women as victims. (cf. meta-analyses of Spitzberg et al. 2010).

H. Grangeia (✉) • M. Santos
Instituto Universitário da Maia (ISMAI), Maia, Portugal

JusGov Universidade do Minho, Braga, Portugal

© The Author(s) 2018
S. Gomes, V. Duarte (eds.), *Female Crime and Delinquency in Portugal*,
https://doi.org/10.1007/978-3-319-73534-4_3

This difference corresponds to a greater focus on and more research devoted to the dynamics and impact of the victimization of women through stalking (e.g., Buhi et al. 2009; Fisher et al. 2002), particularly stalking which occurs in relationship contexts (e.g., Ferreira and Matos 2013).

The analysis of the disproportionate victimization of women versus men has gradually taken into consideration the historical and cultural aspects that assign to female victimization a different meaning from the violence against men. These aspects also explain the epidemic nature of female victimization and clarify why it is easily perceived as natural (Sottomayor 2015). In this way, stalking is currently understood as a form of gender violence as it disproportionately affects women because they are women. (Article 3° of the Istanbul Convention, Council of Europe, 2011). Thus, it makes sense that stalking should not be viewed as an experience of victimization that could occur during the life of a woman, disconnected from other forms of violence. One should rather consider gender violence as a global problem that results from and in diverse forms of violence—many of which are present in the daily lives of women—which overlap, interconnect and combine. This argument strengthens the view of stalking as harassment, defended by Grangeia (2017), and as based on the concept of the continuum of sexual violence proposed by Liz Kelly (1988).

This perspective informs the European Union's initiatives that seek to support and develop an integrated approach to gender violence, like the study led by the European Union's Fundamental Rights Agency on Violence Against Women (FRA 2014). This study gathered data for comparison among the 28 countries of the European Union about the dimension, nature and consequences of various forms of gender violence. Further, a wider definition of violence against women was adopted, which allows for the collecting of data concerning forms of violence that are traditionally not subjects of attention, like stalking and sexual harassment, in line with the recommendations of the Istanbul Convention.

Regarding stalking, the results of this study indicate that in the 28 countries of the European Union, one in five women (18%) has been a victim of stalking since the age of 15; and in this group, one in 10 women (9%) has been stalked by a former partner.

Despite the existence of various legal instruments, the Istanbul Convention on preventing and combating violence against women and domestic violence plays an important role in the prevention of violence against women, and is noteworthy for its wide scope of prevention, including the prevention of violence, the protection of victims, penal procedures and integrated policies. In effect, this convention is an innovative text, representing the first legal European instrument that provides a regulatory framework for preventing and combating gender violence. The Preamble to the Istanbul Convention acknowledges that "violence against women is a manifestation of historically unequal power relations between women and men, which have led to domination over, and discrimination against, women by men and to the prevention of the full advancement of women" (p. 5) and recognizes "the structural nature of violence against women as gender-based violence, and that violence against women is one of the crucial social mechanisms by which women are forced into a subordinate position compared with men" (p. 6).

It is important to highlight that within this convention, stalking is recognized as a form of violence against women. Article 34 (Stalking) maintains, "Parties shall take the necessary legislative or other measures to ensure that the intentional conduct of repeatedly engaging in threatening conduct directed at another person, causing her or him to fear for her or his safety, is criminalised" (p. 17). Despite the growing social awareness of the phenomenon in Europe, and the pressure of academia and some judicial professionals to criminalize the phenomenon (Grangeia 2012), only after the ratification of the Istanbul Convention[1] did stalking become a crime. In Portugal, Law 83/2015 (5th of August), which complied with the convention, brought a series of alterations to the penal code, one of which was the creation of the crime of stalking. This has resulted in a strengthening of criminal legal protection where "doctrine undoubtedly follows the spirit of the Istanbul Convention, in the sense that new convictions are imbued with a significance and symbolism that are clearly based on the protection of the victim, particularly the woman... as an equal subject, on the one hand, but requiring a different perspective on the other, deserving greater positive discrimination to guarantee effective criminal legal protection" (Monte 2016, pp. 283, 284).

Nevertheless, the gender perspective is not evident within the Portuguese criminal legal arsenal, as in other legal frameworks, offering the same protection to men as women. Thus, in spite of the growing importance of the expression "gender violence" (cf. Álvarez Garcia 2013) on international (cf. Torrado Tarríno 2013) and national fronts (e.g., II

National Action Plan for the Implementation of the United Nations Security Council Resolution 1325(2000) on Women, Peace and Security 2014–2018, Resolution of the Council of Ministers No. 50/2014), there are no direct penal repercussions.

2 Implications of a Gender Perspective on Stalking

Considering stalking as a form of gender violence implies recognition that it violates human rights, openly revealing gender inequalities, and disproportionately affects women. One can also assume the gendered nature of stalking based on subtle forms of power that regulate subjects, reinforcing hegemonic patterns of masculinity and femininity through submission to socially entrenched practices and habits (Grangeia 2015). An example is the common romanticizing of stalking behaviours founded upon heteronormative ideas and resulting in traditional relationship dynamics. This reinforces the role differences between men and women as polarized, complementary and standardized. Or rather, the romantic discourse that legitimizes the masculine initiative and encourages feminine passivity in relational contexts of seduction and romance frames the culturally acceptable practices that lead to stalking (Grangeia and Matos 2013). Lee (1998) refers to a stalking-supportive culture that normalizes and absolves male stalking, taking for granted the woman's acceptance.

In this sense, gender becomes central to the historical, social and cultural genesis of stalking, whether perpetrated by a man or a woman (cf. Kamir 2001). In other words, the categorization of stalking as a normative or deviant practice depends on gender codes and not so much on the behaviour itself. For example, the same behaviour could be considered more threatening if perpetrated by a man rather than a woman (Davis and Frieze 2000; Langhrinshsen-Rohling 2012; Lyndon et al. 2012; Spitzberg et al. 2010). However, male targets of stalking could have more difficulty understanding the female behaviour as a form of abuse or violence, as it challenges hegemonic constructs of the "adequate" or "idealized" victim and the typical offender (Eckstein 2007; Wigman 2009).

The gender perspective on the perceived seriousness of stalking could, however, seem paradoxical because of its dynamic nature. When the stalker is male and in the initial phase—referred to by Emerson, Ferris and Gardner (1998) as pre- stalking, or the phase that precedes the victim's recognition of the intrusive, threatening nature of the harassment—the behaviours of approach and even control and following are easily interpreted by the female target as innocuous and flattering. In these cases, the significance of the stalking behaviour is coloured by the romantic discourse, leading to normalization and banalization.

Nevertheless, the romanticizing/normalizing of male stalking is easily replaced by the notion of danger associated with the increasingly persistent and intrusive behaviours (Grangeia and Matos 2017), with the reinterpretation of initial behaviours as threatening (Dunn 2002). In the case of women stalkers, the violence of women against men is construed as less serious than that of men against women (Thompson et al. 2012; Wigman 2009). These stereotypical constructs that minimize female violence seem to occur mainly in the initial phase of stalking (Grangeia and Matos 2017; Thompson et al. 2012). However, if romanticizing/normalizing male stalking could lead to the perception of danger, the minimizing of female stalking could be seen as associated with psychopathology based on its exceptional nature (Grangeia 2015). Or rather, the stalking by a woman of a man is not backed by dominant social discourse (e.g., romanticizing), thus breaking away from the gender norms, and so viewed as an inadequate social behaviour, quite unexpected in the face of traditional social roles assigned to women (e.g., Grangeia and Matos 2013).

To conclude, it is important to remember that the perception of stalking as gender violence is necessary and relevant as it acknowledges the insidious, invasive character of this phenomenon. This allows for the uncovering of a common root of violence against women, and validates ways of responding to this violence that place stalking in the wider context of oppression and victimization of women.

However, professing the importance of a gender perspective on stalking does not exclude other perspectives. In fact, the gender focus allows the decoding of different interpretations that could be applied to particular cases of stalking, whether perpetrated by men or women.

3   Stalking Perpetrated by Women

If we consider the scientific publications that analyse data on stalking, we can conclude that stalking is mainly perpetrated by men. Studies of meta-analyses (Spitzberg et al. 2010) confirm this fact, indicating a greater prevalence of men stalkers (23.9%) than women stalkers (11.92%). Notwithstanding the apparent clarity of the data, a critical examination is necessary.

Firstly, much of the data available about stalkers is obtained from reports by the victims. For example, in a study by the European Union Agency for Fundamental Rights (FRA 2014), the participants (in this case only women) were asked to report a "situation where the same person has been repeatedly offensive or threatening towards you" (p. 8) in order to identify a possible scenario involving stalking. Knowing that stalking perpetrated by men is considered more serious and causes more security concerns than stalking by women (Cass and Rosay 2012; Phillips et al. 2004; Sheridan et al. 2003), it is possible that women victims define experiences of victimization perpetrated by men more easily. In spite of this limitation and the fact that the majority of perpetrators are men, the following data should not be ignored: 7% of cases of victimization by stalking were perpetrated by women, 8% of the victims indicated perpetrators of the male or female gender and in 22% of cases, the victim could not indicate the sex of the perpetrator (FRA 2014). The results of the Portuguese study on stalking (Matos et al. 2011) could be considered as another example of the need to analyse data on the sex of stalkers with caution. In this case, after approximately one-fifth of participants identified themselves as victims of stalking based on the definition provided, 40.3% indicated that they had been targets of victimization perpetrated by more than one stalker. Following this, the victims were invited to respond to the rest of the survey based on more significant experience. It is based on this experience perceived as more significant—that could eventually mean the most disturbing—that once again, male stalkers predominated (68%), with 28.1% of women stalkers and 3.9% of cases where the victim could not indicate the sex of the offender.

In contrast, the few studies that approach stalking from the perspective of the perpetrator (e.g., Davis et al. 2000; Fremouw et al. 1997; Grangeia and Matos 2017; Langhinrichsen-Rohling et al. 2000; Thompson and Dennison 2008) face other limitations. Unlike the surveys on victimization by stalking, perpetration is normally evaluated independently of the impact on and perception of the victim. Yet the results should reflect the capacity of participants to refrain from giving socially desirable responses. (Grangeia and Matos 2017). Also, these studies often use behaviour inventories with a university population and the results are described based on the levels of perpetration rather than on the dichotomy stalker/non-stalker (cf. Lyndon et al. 2012), typically more symmetrical between men and women stalkers, in line with findings in studies on violence in intimate relationships between young people (e.g., Archer 2000; Langhinrichsen-Rohling 2005).

Another question to consider in the critical interpretation of rates of perpetration, and one which demands caution regarding the banalization of stalking perpetrated by women, is the overlap of the roles of victim and stalker, rarely identified in studies of victimization or perpetration. One Portuguese study with a sample of 3367 university students aged between 18 and 30 produced a self-reported perpetration rate of 16.9% among male respondents and 6.7% among women (Grangeia and Matos 2017). Nevertheless, 185 participants admitted a dual position, or rather, recognized experiences as both victim and stalker. This overlap of victim–stalker represents a majority in reports of perpetration (62.1% perpetration rate), mainly concerning women, for whom the dual position represents 68.4% of women stalkers (Grangeia and Matos 2017). In this study, positioning as victim (rate of self-reported victimization) is almost exclusively among women, while when men report victimization, they indicate cumulative experiences of the perpetration of stalking. Nevertheless, when women assume having perpetrated stalking, they typically also report experiences of victimization. This result that indicates that women stalkers have cumulative experiences of victimization could be explained from a gender perspective. Women could report more easily or become involved in the perpetration of stalking if they had previously been victims of the same situation, minimizing in this way the perception that they are adopting a subversive gender behaviour, or rather, one that is not expected for women and socially "reserved" for men.

4 An Important Minority of Women Stalkers

In view of the findings in the previous section, it is now important to investigate whether stalking perpetrated by women is exceptional or not, so that we can adopt or dismiss specific explanatory frameworks that are differentiated for stalking perpetrated by men.

There are a few studies that focus specifically on women as stalkers, which recommend a specific approach to these offenders. The first study of Purcell, Pathé and Mullen (2001) sought to understand whether women and men stalkers differ regarding psychopathology, motivation, behaviour types and risks of violence. Based on a forensic clinical sample of 40 women and 150 men stalkers, the authors concluded that the two groups differed mainly regarding motivation (more restricted to searching for delusional intimacy in the case of women) and to the types of victims chosen (who tend to be professional contacts in the case of women stalkers). Curiously, men and women stalkers do not differ with regard to propensity toward threats and violence, leading the authors to conclude that "there is no reason to presume that the impact of being stalked by a female would be any less devastating than that of a man (…)" (Purcell et al. 2001, p. 2059).

In 2003, Meloy and Boyd present conclusions of a study in which women stalkers are characterized based on data collected by mental health and law enforcement professionals in United States, Canada and Australia. The sociodemographic features of women stalkers do not differ from those of men stalkers, in spite of the fact that there was no direct comparison between groups. The authors highlighted that these women were typically single, heterosexual, aged around 30 and with higher educational qualifications than women offenders in general. The data included in the study suggest the presence of major mental disturbances, in particular borderline personality disorder—which is more commonly diagnosed in women than in men—and stresses the absence of antisocial personality disorder, similar to what is normally found in male stalkers. Women stalkers included in this study stalked people with whom they had not had a previous intimate relationship. They used threats in more than half the cases, which increased the risk of violence in the same way as was identified in stalking perpetrated by men.

A study by Meloy, Mohandie and Green (2011) resulted in a forensic sample of 1005 cases of stalking in the USA and attempted to update and typify the characteristics of the woman stalker (n = 143). The woman stalker is characterized as single, separated or divorced, aged 30, with a psychiatric disorder, usually a mood disorder. The authors suggest that "as in virtually all stalking studies that have gathered clinical and forensic data, female stalkers are multi-problem individuals who display criminal, psychiatric, and drug abuse difficulties and also engage in the crime of stalking" (p. 250). Apart from this, the results of this study corroborate previous studies on the differentiation between male and female stalkers concerning the type of victim–stalker relationship, given that it is more probable that women stalkers follow someone with whom they have not had any previous intimate relationship. Considering the whole sample and although women stalkers present with lower rates of threat and violence than men stalkers, the data justify a risk of moderate violence. This risk intensifies when we consider the cases where a woman stalker had a previous intimate relationship with the victim, which represents the most dangerous group.

A superficial interpretation of the studies seems to reveal more common characteristics than specific ones in the case of women stalkers. In general terms, it is the relationship scenario that seems to differentiate women stalkers from men stalkers as well as the motivation for stalking. Considering that these studies analyse the most severe cases of stalking—those identified by the justice/health system—male stalking seems to have a different nature from female stalking. Stalking perpetrated by men seems to be mostly a form of gender violence, as women are stalked in relationship contexts in an attempt to maintain an intimate relationship and to enable power, control and other abusive dynamics within in a relationship maintained unilaterally. In the case of stalking perpetrated by women, the cases in this study generally reflect a desire for intimacy and the search for a relationship, and perhaps for this reason, these are the cases traditionally more associated with psychopathological motivations.

However, it is important to remember that the differences among these relational and motivational scenarios are based on cases that were flagged, or rather, those that for reasons of severity and/or exceptionality broke with social, legal or clinical norms. It is therefore necessary to consider a sociocultural framework in which these cases would be deviant and in this sense, once again, gender becomes relevant as it allows to clarify results that seem paradoxical.

For example, an explanation for the differences in the flagged cases among men and women, whether based on number or relational and motivational characteristics, could be related to the banalization of violence in cases of women stalking men, portraying it as more acceptable and less serious than the violence of men towards women (Thompson et al. 2012). In this way, in contrast with what is commonly acceptable, the risk of threats and violence could be a distinguishing factor among the cases of stalking by men and by women, particularly if we consider the stalking of partners and ex-partners (Meloy et al. 2011; Stran and McEwan 2012). Meloy and his collaborators (2011) conclude "gender plays a role in shaping the behaviour of the female stalker, although the relationship between the stalker and the victim appears paramount. Female gender mitigates aggression, but attachment aggravates it" (p. 252).

Another aspect that stands out in the studies on women stalkers is the association of their behaviour with psychopathological characteristics. This seems to reinforce the divide between men and women stalkers; for example, in spite of considering an approach to risk assessment common to both groups, routine psychiatric evaluations are still recommended for women stalkers (Strand and McEwan 2012).

To this end, Grangeia (2015) proposes examining what could be an uncritical reproduction of the pathologization of women stalkers in scientific studies, and suggests the adoption of an analytical framework based on sociocultural factors that contribute to the appearance of certain psychopathological conditions and gender biases, and that go beyond intra-individual explanations. Firstly, the author cautions against generalizing the results of exclusively forensic and clinical studies, reflecting the most serious cases, to all types of stalking situations. Secondly, stalking by women is more easily associated with deviant behaviour on an individual level (not expected in terms of gender roles), and easily understood as a clinical disorder rather than a social disorder, as in the case of men stalkers (e.g., crime, Grangeia and Matos 2013).

To conclude, with the analysis of the relational and motivational contexts of stalking, its association with threats and violence, and the psychopathological characteristics of stalkers, one finds arguments for both the adoption of a common framework for female and male stalking as well as for a differentiating approach.

This paper proposes an interpretation that goes beyond superficial numbers that point to a minority of women stalkers. We stress that this is an important minority, and despite the fact that female stalkers share many features with male stalkers, the social definition of who is a stalker and of what stalking means (banalizing, romanticizing, danger, crime, psychopathology) depends on gender. Thus, for all these reasons, we defend a differentiated approach for women stalkers based on a critical perspective that considers the gender of the offender.

Note

1. On the 11th of May 2011 the Convention of Istanbul was approved; it was ratified by Portugal with a decree of the President of the Republic no. 13/2013, on the 21st of January, taking effect on the 1st of August 2014.

References

Álvarez Garcia, F. J. (2013). Indicadores de violência de género. In R. Castillejo Manzanares (Ed.), *Violencia de género y Justicia* (p. 90). Santiago de Compostela: Universidade de Santiago de Compostela.

Archer, J. (2000). Sex differences in aggression between heterosexual partners: A metaanalytic review. *Psychological Bulletin, 26*(5), 651–680.

Buhi, E. R., Clayton, H., & Surrency, H. H. (2009). Stalking victimization among college women and subsequent help-seeking behaviors. *Journal of American College Health, 57*, 419–426.

Burgess, A. W., Baker, T., Greening, D., Hartman, C. R., Burgess, A. G., Douglas, J. E., & Halloran, R. (1997). Stalking behaviors within domestic violence. *Journal of Family Violence, 12*, 389–403.

Cass, A. I., & Rosay, A. B. (2012). College student perceptions of criminal justice system responses to stalking. *Sex Roles, 66*, 392–404.

Coleman, F. L. (1997). Stalking behavior and the cycle of domestic violence. *Journal of Interpersonal Violence, 57*, 110–119.

Davis, K., & Frieze, I. (2000). Research on stalking: What do we know and where do we go? *Violence and Victims, 15*, 473–487.

Davis, K. E., Ace, A., & Andra, M. (2000). Stalking perpetrators and psychological maltreatment of partners: Anger-jealousy, attachment insecurity, need for control, and breakup context. *Violence and Victims, 15*, 407–425.

Douglas, K. S., & Dutton, D. G. (2001). Assessing the link between stalking and domestic violence. *Aggression and Violent Behavior, 6*, 519–546.

Dunn, J. L. (2002). *Courting disaster: Intimate stalking, culture, and criminal justice.* New York: Aldine de Gruyter.

Eckstein, J. J. (2007). *Constructing gendered victimization: Examining the narratives of men experiencing violence from female partners.* Paper presented at the annual meeting of the NCA 93rd annual convention, TBA, Chicago. Available online at http://www.allacademic.com/meta/p191171_index.html

Emerson, R. M., Ferris, K. O., & Gardner, C. B. (1998). On being stalked. *Social Problems, 45*, 289–314.

European Union Agency for Fundamental Rights (FRA). (2014). *Violence against women: An EU-wide survey. Main results report.* Luxemburgo: Publications Office of the European Union. Available online at http://fra.europa.eu/en/publication/2014/violence-against-women-eu-wide-survey-main-results-report

Ferreira, C., & Matos, M. (2013). Post-relationship stalking: The experience of victims with and without history of partner abuse. *Journal of Family Violence, 4*, 393–402.

Fisher, B. S., Cullen, F. T., & Turner, M. G. (2002). Being pursued: Stalking victimization in a national study of college women. *Criminology & Public Policy, 1*, 257–308.

Fremouw, W. J., Westrup, D., & Pennypacker, J. (1997). Stalking on campus: The prevalence and strategies for coping. *Journal of Forensic Sciences, 42*, 666–669.

Grangeia, H. (2012). *Stalking entre jovens: da sedução ao assédio persistente.* PhD thesis in Psychology, Braga: Escola de Psicologia, Universidade do Minho.

Grangeia, H. (2015). Genderização do stalking: mulheres que perseguem, mulheres perseguidas'. In S. Gomes & R. Granja (Eds.), *Mulheres e Crime: perspetivas sobre intervenção, violência e reclusão* (pp. 31–46). Famalicão: Editora Húmus.

Grangeia, H. (2017). Assédio persistente, perseguição, stalking. In A. S. Neves & D. Costa (Eds.), *Violência de Género* (pp. 127–151). Lisboa: ISCSP.

Grangeia, H., & Matos, M. (2011). Da invisibilidade ao reconhecimento do stalking. In A. I. Sani (Ed.), *Temas em vitimologia: realidades emergentes na vitimação e respostas sociais* (pp. 61–84). Coimbra: Almedina.

Grangeia, H., & Matos, M. (2013). Stalking—The Portuguese case: Discursive constructions of stalking and their implications. In S. Petrie (Ed.), *Controversies in policy research: Critical analysis for a new era of austerity and privation* (pp. 53–81). Hampshire: Palgrave.

Grangeia, H., & Matos, M. (2017). Persistent harassment: Targets and perpetrators among young adults. *Victims & Offenders: An International Journal of Evidence-based Research, Policy, and Practice.* Available online at http://www.tandfonline.com/doi/abs/10.1080/15564886.2016.1268987?journalCode=uvao20

Kamir, O. (2001). *Every breath you take: Stalking narratives and the law.* The Ann Arbor: University of Michigan Press.

Kelly, L. (1988). *Surviving sexual violence.* Cambridge: Polity Press.

Kurt, J. (1995). Stalking as a variant of domestic violence. *Bulletin of the American Academy of Psychiatry and Law, 23,* 219–230.

Langhinrichsen-Rohling, J. (2005). Top 10 greatest "hits": Important findings and future directions for intimate partner violence research. *Journal of Interpersonal Violence, 20,* 108–118.

Langhinrichsen-Rohling, J., Palarea, R. F., Cohen, J., & Rohling, M. L. (2000). Breaking up is hard to do: Unwanted pursuit behaviors following the dissolution of a romantic relationship. *Violence and Victims, 15,* 73–90.

Langhrinshsen-Rohling, J. (2012). Gender and stalking: Current intersections and future directions. *Sex Roles, 66,* 418–426.

Lee, R. K. (1998). Romantic and electronic stalking in a college context. *William & Mary Journal of Women and the Law, 4,* 373–409.

Logan, T. K., Leukefeld, C., & Walker, B. (2002). Stalking as a variant of intimate violence: Implications from a young adult sample. In K. E. Davis, I. H. Frieze, & R. D. Maiuro (Eds.), *Stalking: Perspectives on victims and perpetrators* (pp. 265–291). New York: Springer.

Lyndon, A. E., Sinclair, H. C., MacArthur, J. R., Fay, B. A., Ratajack, E., & Collier, K. E. (2012). An introduction to issues of gender in stalking research. *Sex Roles, 66*, 299–310.

Matos, M., Grangeia, H., Ferreira, C., & Azevedo, V. (2011). *Inquérito de vitimação por stalking: Relatório de investigação.* Braga: Grupo de Investigação sobre Stalking em Portugal.

Meloy, J. R., & Boyd, C. (2003). Female stalkers and their victims. *Journal of the American Academy of Psychiatry and the Law, 31*, 211–219.

Meloy, J. R., Mohandie, K., & Green, M. (2011). The female stalker. *Behavioral Sciences and the Law, 29*, 240–254.

Monte, M. F. (2016). O resgate político-penal da vítima (mulher) em matéria de direitos humanos—considerações em torno da Convenção do Conselho da Europa para a prevenção e o combate à violência contra as mulheres e a violência doméstica, adotada em Istambul, a 11 de maio de 2011, e da Lei n.º 83/2015, de 5 de agosto. In P. Jerónimo (Ed.), *Temas de investigação em direitos humanos para o século XXI—edição comemorativa do 10.º Aniversário do Mestrado em Direitos Humanos da Universidade do Minho.* Braga: Direitos Humanos—Centro de Investigação Interdisciplinar/Escola de Direito da Universidade do Minho.

Phillips, L., Quirk, R., Rosenfeld, B., & O'Connor, M. (2004). Is it stalking? Perceptions of stalking among college undergraduates. *Criminal Justice and Behavior, 31*, 73–96.

Purcell, P., Pathe, M., & Mullen, P. E. (2001). A study of women who stalk. *American Journal of Psychiatry, 158*, 2056–2060.

Sheridan, L., Gillett, R., Davies, G. M., Blaauw, E., & Patel, D. (2003). There's no smoke without fire': Are male ex–partners perceived as more 'entitled' to stalk than acquaintance or stranger stalkers? *British Journal of Psychology, 94*, 87–98.

Sottomayor, M. C. (2015). A Convenção de Istambul e o Novo Paradigma da Violência de Género. *Ex Æquo, 31*(2015), 105–121.

Spitzberg, B. H., Cupach, W. R., & Ciceraro, L. D. L. (2010). Sex differences in stalking and obsessive relational intrusion: Two meta-analyses. *Partner Abuse, 1*, 259–285.

Strand, S., & McEwan, T. E. (2012). Violence among female stalkers. *Psychological Medicine, 42*(3), 545–555.

Thompson, C. M., & Dennison, S. M. (2008). Defining relational stalking in research: Understanding sample composition in relation to repetition and duration of harassment. *Psychiatry, Psychology and Law, 15*, 482–499.

Thompson, C. M., Dennison, S. M., & Stewart, A. (2012). Are female stalkers more violent than male stalkers? Understanding gender differences in stalking violence using contemporary sociocultural beliefs. *Sex Roles, 66*(5–6), 351–365.

Torrado Tarríno, C. (2013). Violência doméstica versus violência de género. Transitando por el universo psico-jurídico. In R. Castillejo Manzanares (Ed.), *Violencia de género y Justicia* (pp. 68–69). Santiago de Compostela: Universidade de Santiago de Compostela.

Wigman, S. A. (2009). Male victims of former-intimate stalking: A selected review. *International Journal of Men's Health, 8*(2), 101–115.

4

Onstage and Off: The Shifting Relevance of Gender in Women's Prisons

Manuela Ivone Cunha

1 Introduction

Prison studies are not unconnected with broader theoretical debates on categories of identity and social life such as gender, ethnicity/race, class and the intersections between these categories. Gender, however, has informed prison research in a peculiar way. The very descriptive reference to gender, to begin with, or the lack of it, is not itself gender-neutral and appears to depend on the gender of those imprisoned. A random glance through publications in prison studies will likely show that an explicit mention of gender finds its way to the title only if a penal institution or carceral research site imprisons women. This institution will appear designated as a 'women's prison'. Single-word 'prisons', without gender specifications, are male by default, unless they are the objects of a specific comparison with their female counterpart.

(UID/Ant/04038/2013)

M. I. Cunha (✉)
CRIA, Universidade do Minho, Braga, Portugal

© The Author(s) 2018
S. Gomes, V. Duarte (eds.), *Female Crime and Delinquency in Portugal*,
https://doi.org/10.1007/978-3-319-73534-4_4

This dual pattern of identification of prisons for men and prisons for women is far from being a simple effect of disproportion in numbers of men and women prisoners, or of relative carceral demography, in which women are invariably in the minority. Rather, it is a discrepancy that matches the asymmetry characterizing the history of prison research itself, which in turn is not altogether immune to long-standing gender issues of symbolic domination and inequality. Research on men's imprisonment has framed the debate in a universal mode, oblivious to gender. It is true that this research has more recently come to acknowledge the gender dimension, especially by focusing on the ideologies of masculinity that shape prison culture (Newton 1994; Sabo et al. 2001). Research on women's prisons, however, was built on the very basis of gender and has tended to be more gender-bound as a whole.

Besides having informed a reflexive agenda addressing issues of representation, such as the conundrums of representing women as victims and/or agents (Fili 2013), the angle of gender has presided over most research issues. Among the most pervasive is the gendered nature of prison regimes, whether they are portrayed as based on normative femininity and domesticity, or as more gender-neutral (Bosworth 1999; Carlen 1983; Kruttschnitt and Gartner 2005; Miller and Carbone-Lopez 2013; McCorkell 2003). Another prominent topic is the gendered character of prison cultures, socialities and 'pains of imprisonment', presented as predicated on gender roles and identities, and contrasted with their male equivalents (Giallombardo 1966; Heffernan 1972; Walker and Worrall 2000; Ward and Kassebaum 1965; Zaitzow and Thomas 2003). Overall, the characterization of the former has been endowed with a distinctly comparative tone, perhaps owing to the fact that configurations found within men's prisons were taken as the compass and reference model for analysing women's.

One example can be found in the depiction of prison cultures—a pervading topic in the study of prisoners' social world. Where women prisoners were concerned, either this sub-culture was deemed non-existent or considered an inverted version of the male one. In the first case, descriptions were in the negative mode: the *absence* of cohesion and solidarity among women prisoners (that is, by reference to the forms it took in men's institutions), the *absence* of groups, the *absence* of an 'inmate code' and the *absence* of a local repertoire of social roles, which in turn was also *absent* from a less complex prison slang (e.g. Ward 1982; Tittle 1969; Kruttschnitt 1981; Williams and Fish 1974). In the second case, characterizations were made by contrast. Women's prison culture was supposedly based on pseudo-families and/or homoaffective dyads (e.g., Selling 1931; Heffernan 1972; Foster 1975; Giallombardo 1966; Ward and Kassebaum 1965; Statler 1986). Both phenomena have been described mostly as an emotional response to the deprivation of affection, ignoring other kinds of social and identity dimensions. This emphasized the contrast between the nature of women aggregates and the structure of male prisoners' sociality, which was viewed mostly from a socio-economic angle.

As I have shown elsewhere (Cunha 1994), this long-standing tendency to establish symmetrical contrasts between female and male experiences of punitive confinement may have contributed to over-simplifying and distorting far more complex realities. However, favouring different descriptive models to account for men and women's carceral configurations—one more 'psychological', the other more 'sociological'—was not entirely new. To a certain extent, it recreated within prison studies the trajectory of perspectives on male and female criminality, respectively. While in mid-twentieth century the social, economic and cultural dimensions of crime were increasingly highlighted, this did not occur evenly in theoretical perspectives on both genders. Approaches to female criminality would still remain excluded from this inflection for a long time (Smart 1977; Heidensohn 1985; Dobash et al. 1986).

Nowadays, this more 'gendercentric' agenda is nevertheless increasingly diversified for theoretical and empirical reasons alike. These involve recognition of the diversity of women prisoners' experiences and identities and attention to a wider variety of aspects of carceral life, but also changes inside and outside prison walls (e.g. Boutron and Constant 2013; Greer 2000; Mandaraka-Sheppard 1986; Owen 1998; Rowe 2011). Drawing on fieldwork in a Portuguese carceral setting in different decades, I propose to contribute an additional aspect to this debate by focusing on contextual shifts in the actual (current?) saliency of gender as a category of identity and social life in women's prisons. These shifts have occurred without major changes in prison regimes, even if these have become formally less gendered.[1]

2 A Changing Prison Landscape

Portugal is no exception to the worldwide imbalance between men's and women's incarceration rates. Women have consistently been the minority among the population behind bars. Currently (and also until the 1990s) they represent less than 6% of the prison population. However, after the democratic revolution in 1974, which decriminalized one of the main causes of women's imprisonment during the dictatorship (prostitution), this proportion rose steeply during the second half of the 1990s up to nearly 10% by the end of the century—one of the highest percentages in the European Union.

In fact, during the 1990s the percentage of Portugal's population behind bars (men and women) registered an unprecedented increase, and Portugal attained one the highest imprisonment rates per 100,000 inhabitants (145) in the European Union.[2] One of the aspects of this substantial change in the prison population was its massive provenance from the same low-income-stigmatized urban areas. As a result, co-prisoners were often neighbours, relatives or previous acquaintances, an aspect that altered the social world of prisons (cf. Cunha 2008, 2014). This was both a consequence of selective drug control (intensive law enforcement targeting specific areas) and of the workings of the Portuguese retail drug economy (Cunha 2005).

Although this change took place in both male and female prisons, it has been more concentrated—and therefore more conspicuous—in the latter. Its prominence in women's institutions stems partly from the relative homogeneity of their population. In the 1990s, the variety of offenses leading to women's imprisonment was sharply reduced. Although the population of male prisoners was also fairly homogeneous (property offenses and drug-related crimes accounted together for the majority of convictions), its internal distribution was more balanced than that of its female counterpart, which was concentrated overwhelmingly on drug trafficking.[3] Drug-related offenses already stood out as an important cause of women's imprisonment in the 1980s, along with property offenses (Cunha 1994). But it has mainly been since the 1990s that they became a top cause of women's incarceration (Cunha 2002; Cunha and Granja 2014; Matos 2008; Matos et al. 2017).

Imprisoned women were involved mostly in small-scale drug trafficking, whether as international drug couriers, or in domestic retail drug dealing (see below). Two scenarios have been reported in the relevant literature in Portugal: (i) young women whose participation in drug trafficking is associated with drug use and/or abusive male partners (Matos 2008); (ii) primarily adult but also young women from economically depressed milieus for whom drug trafficking is an income-generating strategy often engaged in to support their households. These women operate autonomously as free-lancers or in non-hierarchical partnerships with neighbours or family members. This is mostly the case in domestic drug trafficking, which reveals some particular aspects in Portugal (cf. Cunha 2005).

Be that as it may, women are proportionally more convicted to prison sentences for drug-related offenses than men. The centrality of drug offenses in women's convictions is also what has best explained the faster rise of female incarceration rates: these are the crimes with the highest conviction rates and are among the most harshly sentenced. This means that the rise in women's incarceration rates owed little to possible changes in the way courts deal with this gender.

I conducted field research in the main Portuguese women's prison (*Estabelecimento Prisional de Tires*, *Tires* hereafter) in two periods that, in retrospect, emerge as defining moments in a changing carceral sociology (the late eighties and the late nineties, cf. Cunha 1994, 2002, 2008).[4] These two decades revealed in their most pronounced form different patterns that can now be found combined or reproduced in other prison settings, albeit more mitigated in some respects. This is the case, for example, with the prison of Santa Cruz do Bispo *(Estabelecimento Prisional de Santa Cruz do Bispo)*, which was the object of a recent controlled comparison with Tires (Cunha and Granja 2014).[5] I will, therefore, focus on these different configurations as they emerged in a clearly defined fashion in these two periods in *Tires*.[6]

3 Gendered Regimes

The 'therapeutic' approach that shaped the history of women's penitentiary regimes during the first half of the twentieth century (Carlen and Tombs 2006; Heidensohn 1985)[7] never fully occurred in Portugal. Instead of a strong medical and psychiatric influence in the definition and implementation of these regimes, in Portugal the main concern at that time was to carry out a systematic programme for the 'moral regeneration' of delinquents (Cunha 1994). Against the backdrop of religious exhortation, discipline and ascetic austerity, the adopted treatment model was based on two ingredients, both drawing heavily on dominant gender ideologies: domesticity and motherhood. In Portugal as elsewhere, delinquent women were considered 'double deviants', that is, both as members of society and as members of their gender. Rehabilitation therefore meant putting them back on track for the female roles and spheres from which they had supposedly strayed.

This perspective was in perfect harmony with the state ideology of the *Estado Novo* dictatorial regime in Portugal (1933–1974) (Cunha 1994). Its symbolic conflation of 'home' and 'nation' presented women as the nation's ultimate moral base and emphasized the need for their dedicated performance as wives and mothers as the only route for women's social existence and participation in the collective destiny (see Beleza dos Santos 1947; Salazar 1977). This state ideology was at odds with social realities, in that it could only be fulfilled—or afforded—by the elites. With the exception of these groups, women in Portugal—and more so among the poor—have always resorted to work and wage labour as a survival strategy, without this being considered a transgression of a gender cultural script within their social milieus (Cole 1991; Pujadas 1994).

The above ingredients would nevertheless linger, albeit more tenuously, in prison institutions long after the democratic revolution of 1974 and still permeate prison life today. The first ingredient in this foundational treatment model was the inculcation of domestic habits (Cunha 1994, 2013). *Tires* was a clear illustration of this model. The penitentiary treatment program was built around domestic skills. This was expressed both in the spatial configuration of the institutional wards itself, as in the range of activities offered to prisoners. If laundry, cleaning and kitchen services were oversized, it was only because they were meant to respond not just to *Tires* prison's internal needs, but also to supply male prison facilities nearby. The whole rationale and organization of the domestic sphere was thus transferred to the carceral institution on a large scale. Most activities, whether for maintenance or production, were an extension of the domestic order.

The predominance of so-called feminine activities would last for decades. Gradually, however, it would cease to be presented as a method or a program for regeneration, designed and pursued with that explicit purpose. It became a mere effect of the status quo and disengagement from the outside world, which is not uncommon in these institutions (Goffman 1999 [1961]). It also reflected the occupational skills of inmates themselves, which were scant and for the most part limited to domestic training. Even in today's most 'modern' prison, *Santa Cruz*, the range of activities available is, with a few exceptions, mostly centred on the domestic sphere (Cunha and Granja 2014). In any case, the geography of gender would continue to sharply determine the prison regime.

A second ingredient in the moral regeneration which was shaped by social notions of gender consisted of the attempt to instill feelings of maternal responsibility in inmates and cultivate mothering skills. Although permission to keep infant children in prison took the children's interests into account, it was primarily justified by the program's aim to educate the mothers. Aiming at the 'social promotion of the delinquent woman', it was determined that 'offspring, in the case of infants, should remain with the mothers so as to maintain and promote their sense of natural responsibilities' (Pinto 1969, p. 56). Prison regulations also explicitly stipulated that prisoners should be taught to attend to their infant children inside the institution and that children should spend time with their mothers on a daily basis (Correia 1981, p. 279).

Official regulations and institutional rules have remained stable over time in their general principles: namely, the age limit for children allowed to live in the institution with their mothers (up to three years old, exceptionally five)[8]; the provision of a day nursery within the prison compound, but physically separated from prison blocks, where children remain during mothers' working hours, and where they are cared for by trained personnel; a prison wing that houses prisoners with children together. These conditions are common to most major women's prisons in the country. Although stable in these aspects, explicitly gendered moral considerations have since long been expunged from official decrees, and their focus has shifted from the moral regeneration of prisoners (via leading them into proper motherhood) to accommodating the interest of the child.

Considerations involving the mother role did not disappear from prison daily life however. They remained infused in informal institutional practices and interactions (cf. Cunha 1994; Cunha and Granja 2014). Prisoners continued to be aware that their inmate and mother conditions were somehow merged, and some went as far as to suspect that their performance as mothers was assessed in the same way as their behaviour as prisoners—that is, with the potential to influence parole board deliberations. In any case, they sense all too well that the in-prison relationship with their offspring, and the language of *care* itself, are inescapably encompassed in the coercive management of the 'total institution' (Cunha 1994; Goffman 1999 [1961]).

4   Doing and Undoing Gender

In the previous section it was suggested that women's penitentiary treatment in Portugal was dictated mainly by gender ideologies, insofar as it was aimed at returning delinquents to the 'feminine' roles they had supposedly deviated from. Thus, the institution insisted on motherhood as part of the penitentiary's program of moral regeneration. Yet, contrary to this gendered image of the stranded woman, inmates have for the most part tended to express *conformity*—not 'deviance'—to conventional definitions of their gender. In *Tires* during the 1980s, this conformity was even clearly inscribed in prisoners' sociality itself, which was centred on in-prison mother–child relationships or marital-like couples, and was otherwise highly atomized: inmates generally did not act nor see themselves as a group, and actually developed a refined rhetoric of mutual denigration.[9]

Although the importance of these dyadic relationships was expressed by inmates in the language of affection and emotions, the support they provided had an identitarian aspect that confirmed them first of all as relational beings, more specifically in the relational roles which were normative markers of their gender ('mother', 'wife'/'romantic partner'). Gender identity occupied the front stage of the prison scene, both by the way it was performed through this sociality and how it was repeatedly asserted in 'prison talk', which focused mainly on children and partners, namely, on how the separation from them was paramount among the 'pains of imprisonment'. In the case of women with children in prison, mothers' narratives express a highly idealized maternal self-image and focus on a recurrent theme: the way their children's presence fulfills them, helps them cope and softens their prison experience (Cunha 1994, p. 156; Cunha and Granja 2014; Serra and Pires 2004, p. 420).

Indeed, the gendered regime of the prison was amplified both by women's discursive construction of gender and by prisoners' management of their stigmatized social identities (Cunha 1994). Motherhood was an important aspect in this respect. As also noted by Palomar (2007, p. 372), the prison environment does allow for experiencing motherhood in new ways, creating new subjectivities through which mothers in turn re-signify previous experiences of maternity: sheltered from the pressures of everyday survival, poverty and violence, with time available to dedicate to their children (who now also receive specialized medical and psychological attention); constantly near their children and exposed to expert educational and pedagogical input and programs, they may experience a bond with their children with unprecedented intensity and endow it with a meaning that takes centre stage in their lives thereon. It is hardly surprising that in such a context motherhood becomes hyperbolized in narratives of personal identity, including the way it is perceived in retrospect or projected in the future.

Women's prisons like *Tires* invite and promote an exaltation of motherhood not only because they have persistently emphasized reproduction and domesticity or because the idea of 'inmate fathers' is still as alien to prison organizations as the one of "inmate mothers" (and their 'special needs') is central to women's.[10] They also do so because their environment focuses on motherhood and the mother–child bond in a way that is highly idealized and disconnected from the actual experiences and harsh realities of these women's lives. Prisons thereby participate in the essentializing of motherhood, both as a naturalized aspect of gender and as an ideal hardly within the reach of the populations it incarcerates. It is behind bars that mothers find the time, the structure or the resources necessary to measure up to such an ideal.

Not surprisingly, however, it is also behind bars that this ideal contributes to deepening feelings of self-blame, inadequacy and dysfunctionality in performing the mother role.[11] Although motherhood is repeatedly invoked as a motive and justification for their offence (*I did it for my children; I had to feed my kids*)—thus as a gendered 'technique of neutralization' (to extend a term coined by Sykes and Matza [1957])—prisoners blame themselves, and are blamed by prison personnel, not only for having offended, but also for failing to live up to motherly responsibilities (Cunha 1994, p. 71).

Besides being a source of meaning that reshapes, recreates or reinvents a personal identity, motherhood in prison has conveyed, however, another identity effect as an anchor of a 'non-deviant' social identity. As I have detailed elsewhere (1994), in the eighties, the adherence to conventional gender roles also emerged as a way to shelter social identity from the stigma attached to imprisonment, that is, as a viable route to negotiate and exorcize stigma. In other words, the narrative importance of the 'good mother' was also instrumental in rejecting a "deviant" identity and invoked as a synonym of a 'good citizen'.

Ten years later, mothering and motherhood were less emphasized in identity management and in the prison social scene. Firstly, categories of identity and social forms were made more complex by hyper-incarceration and by the co-imprisonment of relatives. Since the nineties, in-prison family forms have become more varied. The sociography of relatedness, as well as the 'ethics of care' once identified with women *qua* mothers, have no longer been limited to mother–child dyads anymore, but have involved wider circles of relationships (Cunha 2002, 2013). Co-imprisoned family members and other prisoners participate collectively in the in-prison care of children, for example, sharing food, affection and assistance.

Furthermore, since co-imprisoned mothers and daughters were often both adults, and the ethics of care involved more than two generations simultaneously (see Cunha 2002, 2013), care is now enmeshed in a wider and more (even if not altogether) gender-neutral ethics of respect, reciprocity and moral obligation between family members.[12] Daughters, as well as sons, are supposed to respect and support their parents within and from beyond prison walls. It is disrespectful not to be loyal, deferential, or not to reciprocate the care they received from their parents when they were children.

In addition, prison stigma ceased to be a crucial issue. Prison merely compounds the structural and symbolic marginalization that now affects imprisoned populations collectively and much more profoundly than before. Stigma is no longer negotiable—either through gender conformity or otherwise (Cunha 2008).

Finally, the prominence of gender identity in the prison scene would give way to a new sense of collective identity, based on the prisoners' sharing of a common provenance from the same destitute urban areas, on kin, friendship and neighbourhood ties, and on a shared position at the lowest level of the class structure. Class-based collective solidarities gained strength in the prison scenario and became an important facet of prisoners' social identity. There was now an unprecedented rhetoric of 'community', constantly reasserted in prison talk, reiterating the perception that *we're all in the same boat*, and sustaining wider forms of solidarity and resistance. The notion of a shared destiny was now emphasized over other identities—gender and race/ethnicity alike (Cunha 2010). In the face of these collective categories of agency and identity, within which prisoners came to react to their common marginalization, other levels of identity such as gender became more discreet in prison life.

5 Final Remarks

Although prisons for men and for women are both gendered institutions, perspectives on these two kinds of settings have been unevenly gendered, and research on women's prisons has tended to be more gender-bound in general. This gendercentrism has partly been justified by the historical centrality of gender systems prioritizing reproduction and domesticity over other aspects of life in the definition of prison regimes for women. These aspects can be amplified by women prisoners' own discursive construction of gender and strategically emphasized in the management of stigmatized identities in the prison social scene. However, the very saliency of gender as a category of identity and social life can be highly contextual, even in confinement situations where there is more continuity than change in gendered prison regimes over time. Firstly, as we have seen, prisons reflect broader structural shifts that have a variable impact on forms of marginality and are not without influence on shaping different forms of stigmatization. Secondly, social identities are situational. For all the intersections—rightly indicated by intersectionalist perspectives—of gender, ethnicity/race, class and other facets of an altogether plural identity, these facets can nevertheless be more or less relevant in different social situations. Even taking into account the power structures that shape multiple aspects of identity, in some circumstances one facet can appear overshadowed or subdued in favour of other contextual variants of that identity.

The two ethnographic inquiries conducted in a women's Portuguese prison in different decades showed that while in the eighties gender identity occupied the front stage of the prison scene, ten years later the prominence of gender would give way to a new sense of collective identity and forms of relatedness, associated with hyper-incarceration and the co-imprisonment of relatives, friends and neighbours. In the face of this powerful collective identity with which prisoners came to react to their common deeper social marginalization, other levels of identity such as gender were played down and became less visible in the prison social scene. Gender still matters, evidently, and gender inequality has not become less relevant in shaping these women's lives. Nevertheless, these two inquiries led me to be cautious about treating gender as a fixed dimension of the prisoners' moral and social world, and showed the importance of historicizing gender in prison studies in more than one way.

In my own research, the focus on gender has followed the movement of my imprisoned interlocutors, and receded from the foreground to the background of the analysis. As an analytical angle it remained important to situate women's participation in the drug economy, the repression of which triggered a rise in imprisonment rates, and to investigate the reasons these rates rose faster for women than for men. Otherwise, I considered a women's prison like *Tires* mainly as a vantage point to better capture important processes linking prisons to a range of economically depressed urban neighbourhoods, as well as the resulting sociological mutations that emerged in prison life by the end of the century. These mutations affected both male and female prison settings, but were more clearly visible in women's (cf. Cunha 2002, 2008).

Taken together, the two inquiries informing this chapter can contribute to a reflection on how a more or less important focus on gender should be decided less on the basis of general agendas (theoretical or political), than on the basis of gender's contextual importance, specifically assessed. In other words, the emphasis on gender should itself be treated as an empirical question, that is, according to the relative relevance of gender as a category of identity, and depending on its variable potential to organize social relations.

Notes

1. The tensions between what is formally defined in the legal requirements (which promote gender equality) and everyday social practices are particularly visible in parenting in prison, for example. Prison regulations have also incorporated the principles of neutrality and formal equality between women and men. Currently, the law regulating children's stay in prison is gender neutral; that is, both imprisoned mothers and fathers are allowed to keep their offspring with them inside prison facilities (Law 115/2009). However, the implementation of this principle is unequal. Logistics and practical dispositions render most men's prisons hardly suitable for children to reside with their imprisoned fathers. For example, there are no day-care centres in male institutions, nor adequate cells that are physically separated from other prison blocks (cf. Law 51/2011). Furthermore, although the need to meet female prisoners' 'special needs' regarding motherhood is mentioned in state guidelines about parenting in prison, there is no equivalent reference regarding fathering (Law 115/2009).

2. Estatísticas da Justiça, Ministério da Justiça (1987–2000).
3. As an example analysed in Cunha's study (2002) documenting these shifts during the 1990s, in 1997 46% of incarcerated men were imprisoned for property offenses and 34% for drug-related crimes, against 16% and 69%, respectively, in the female case (*Estatísticas da Justiça, Ministério da Justiça, 1997*).
4. Fieldwork was conducted in two- and one-year periods (1987–1989 and 1997, respectively). It benefitted from unrestricted access to all prison facilities. Besides 70 in-depth interviews, this allowed for the observation and participation in most prison activities and daily life, as well as for engaging in informal individual and group conversations with prisoners on a regular basis and under varied circumstances. In both periods a trusting relationship with prisoners was established, although not at the same pace or by the same processes (see Cunha 2002). In both periods women were selected by combining a snowball progression that followed 'natural' networks and a systematic sampling that diversified inmates along lines of penal and social profile, as well as length and experience of confinement (Cunha 1994, 2002).
5. *Tires* was created in 1954 on the outskirts of Lisbon and continues to be the main female penal institution in the country; *Santa Cruz* opened in 2005 near the northern city of Oporto, and was intended for a similar kind of penal population.
6. The prison population of *Tires*, which in 1997 reached 823 inmates, had developed a striking social and penal homogeneity in the span of only a decade. In 1997, a total of 76% of the women there were imprisoned for drug trafficking, compared to the 37% registered 10 years earlier, and property offenders represented no more than 13%. The majority of those convicted (69%) were serving sentences of more than five years. Prisoners increasingly came from the segments of the working class most deprived of economic and educational capital: from 1987 to 1997 the proportion of women who held jobs in the bottom tier of the service economy rose from 4% to 33%, and the proportion of those who had never attended school or gone beyond the fourth grade rose from 47% to 59%. A significant proportion of prisoners had relatives imprisoned in the same institution or in other prison facilities. According to a conservative estimate based on data registered in social-educational files, between one-half and two-thirds of the inmates in *Tires* had family members inside the same institution (sisters, cousins, aunts, nieces, mothers, grandmothers). This estimate does not include male partners and kin serving their own sentences in other facilities.

7. Based on neo-Lombrosian perspectives addressing female criminality, during the first half of the 20th century prison policies in some European countries and in the United States adopted a therapeutic treatment based on medical and psychiatric intervention. Although this trend has lessened over the years, according to Carlen and Tombs (2006) there is a revival of these approaches in policies that address women's socio-economic problems by repositioning them as 'cognitive' problems.
8. For recent general regulations see the General Regulation for Portuguese Prisons, Law 51/2011.
9. Among other examples of mutual disqualification, one prisoner could justify her offence as a fortuitous result of unique circumstances, while essentializing those of her companions as matters of a criminal nature (cf. Cunha 1994, 2008, for development of this point).
10. For the way prisons and the judicial system fail to include fathers in sharing the burdens of parenthood see Palomar (2007) and Machado and Granja (2013).
11. This ideal further excludes fathers and exonerates them from their own emotional, socio-economic and moral responsibilities.
12. Mothers, grandmothers, mothers-in-law, aunts, cousins, sisters and sisters-in-law now find themselves doing time together, in a circle of kin that often amounts to more than a dozen people, sometimes encompassing four generations (when a great-grandson is born in prison to a prisoner whose daughter and granddaughter are also imprisoned).

References

Beleza dos Santos, J. (1947). *Nova organização prisional Portuguesa*. Coimbra: Coimbra Editora.

Bosworth, M. (1999). *Engendering resistance: Agency and power in women's prisons*. Dartmouth: Ashgate.

Boutron, C., & Constant, C. (2013). Gendering transnational criminality. The case of women's imprisonment in Peru. *Signs, 39*(1), 177–195.

Carlen, P. (1983). *Women's imprisonment: A study in social control*. London: Routledge & Kegan Paul.

Carlen, P., & Tombs, J. (2006). Reconfigurations of penality. The ongoing case of the women's imprisonment and reintegration industries. *Theoretical Criminology, 10*(13), 337–360.

Cole, S. (1991). *Women of the praia. Work and lives in a Portuguese coastal community*. Princeton: Princeton University Press.

Correia, A. M. (1981). *Tratamento penitenciário*. Lisbon: Centro do Livro Brasileiro.

Cunha, M. I. (1994). *Malhas que a reclusão tece. Questões de identidade numa prisão feminina*. Lisbon: CEJ.

Cunha, M. I. (2002). *Entre o Bairro e a Prisão: Tráfico e Trajectos*. Lisbon: Fim de Século.

Cunha, M. I. (2005). From neighborhood to prison: Women and the war on drugs in Portugal. In J. Sudbury (Ed.), *Global lockdown: Imprisoning women* (pp. 155–165). New York/London: Routledge.

Cunha, M. I. (2008). Closed circuits: Kinship, neighborhood and imprisonment in urban Portugal. *Ethnography, 9*(3), 325–350.

Cunha, M. I. (2010). Race, crime and criminal justice in Portugal. In A. Kalunta-Crumpton (Ed.), *Race, crime and criminal justice: International perspectives* (pp. 144–161). New York: Palgrave Macmillan.

Cunha, M. I. (2013). The changing scale of imprisonment and the transformation of care: The erosion of the 'welfare society' by the 'penal state' in contemporary Portugal. In M. Schlecker & F. Fleischer (Eds.), *Ethnographies of social support* (pp. 81–101). New York: Palgrave Macmillan.

Cunha, M. I. (2014). The ethnography of prisons and penal confinement. *Annual Review of Anthropology, 43*(1), 217–233.

Cunha, M., & Granja, R. (2014). Gender asymmetries, parenthood and confinement in two Portuguese prisons. *Champ Pénal/Penal Field*, XI. https://doi.org/10.4000/champpenal.8809.

Dobash, R., Dobash, E., & Gutteridge, S. (1986). *The imprisonment of women*. Oxford: Basil Blackwell.

Fili, A. (2013). Women in prison: Victims or resisters. Representations of agency in women's prisons in Greece. *Signs, 39*(1), 1–26.

Foster, T. (1975). Make-believe families: A response of women and girls to the deprivations of imprisonment. *International Journal of Criminology and Penology, 3*, 71–78.

Giallombardo, R. (1966). *Society of women. A study of a Women's prison*. New York: Wiley.

Goffman, E. (1999 [1961]). *Asylums. Essays on the social situation of mental and other inmates*. New York: Garden Books.

Greer, K. (2000). The changing nature of interpersonal relationships in a women's prison. *Prison Journal, 80*(4), 442–468.

Onstage and Off: The Shifting Relevance of Gender... 73

Heffernan, E. (1972). *Making it in prison. The square, the cool and the life.* New York: Wiley.

Heidensohn, F. (1985). *Women and crime.* London: Macmillan.

Kruttschnitt, C. (1981). Prison codes, inmate solidarity and women: A reexamination. In M. Warren (Ed.), *Comparing Male and Female Offenders* (pp. 143–141). London: Sage.

Kruttschnitt, C., & Gartner, R. (2005). *Marking time in the golden state: Women's imprisonment in California.* Cambridge: Cambridge University Press.

Law 115. (2009, October 12). Código da Execução das Penas e Medidas Privativas da Liberdade, *Diário da República, 1*(197).

Law 51. (2011, April 11). Regulamento Geral dos Estabelecimentos Prisionais, *Diário da República, 1*(71).

Machado, H., & Granja, R. (2013). Paternidades fragmentadas. Género, emoções e (des)conexões biogenéticas e prisionais. *Análise Social, 208,* xlviii(3), 550–571.

Mandaraka-Sheppard, A. (1986). *The dynamics of agression in women's prisons in England.* London: Gower.

Matos, R. (2008). *Vidas raras de mulheres comuns: Percursos de vida, significações do crime e construção da identidade em jovens reclusas.* Coimbra: Almedina.

Matos, R., Cunha, M., Carvalho, P., Tavares, R., & Miranda Pereira, L. (2017). Women in prison. Portugal. In P. Hein van Kempen & M. Krabbe (Eds.), *Women in prison. The Bangkok rules and beyond, International Penal and Penitentiary Foundation* (Vol. 46, pp. 613–644). Portland: Intersentia Uitgevers N.V.

McCorkell, J. A. (2003). Embodied surveillance and the gendering of punishment. *Journal of Contemporary Ethnography, 32*(1), 41–76.

Miller, J., & Carbone-Lopez, K. (2013). Gendered carceral regimes in Sri-Lanka: Colonial laws, post-colonial practices and the social control of sex workers. *Signs, 39*(1), 79–103.

Newton, C. (1994). Gender theory and prison sociology: Using theories of masculinities to interpret the sociology of prisons for men. *The Howard Journal of Criminal Justice, 33,* 193–202.

Owen, B. (1998). *In the mix: Struggle and survival in a women's prison.* Albany: State University of New York Press.

Palomar Verea, C. (2007). *Maternidad en prisión.* Guadalajara: Universidad de Guadalajara.

Pinto, J. R. (1969). O tratamento penitenciário de mulheres. *Boletim da administração penitenciária e dos institutos de criminologia, 25*: 21–91.

Pujadas, J. (1994). Processos sociais e construção de identidades nas periferias urbanas: os casos de Lisboa e Catalunha. *Mediterrâneo, 4*, 11–19.

Rowe, A. (2011). Narratives of self and identity in women's prisons: Stigma and the struggle for self-definition in penal regimes. *Punishment and Society, 13*, 571–591.

Sabo, D., Kupers, T. A., & London, W. (Eds.). (2001). *Prison masculinities.* Philadelphia: Temple University Press.

Salazar, A. O. (1977). *Como se levanta um Estado.* Lisbon: Golden Books.

Selling, L. (1931). The pseudo-family. *American Journal of Sociology, 37*, 247–253.

Serra, D., & Pires, A. (2004). Maternidade atrás das grades: Comportamento parental em contexto prisional. *Análise Psicológica, 2*(XXII), 413–425.

Smart, C. (1977). *Women, crime and criminology.* London: Routledge & Kegan Paul.

Statler, J. (1986). *Mitchellville: A study of the adaptation responses of women in prison.* PhD dissertation, Iowa State University.

Sykes, G., & Matza, D. (1957). Techniques of neutralization: A theory of delinquency. *American Sociological Review, 22*(6), 664–670.

Tittle, C. (1969). Inmate organization: Sex differentiation and the influence of criminal sub-cultures. *American Sociological Review, 34*, 492–505.

Walker, S., & Worrall, A. (2000). Life as a woman. The gendered pains of indeterminate imprisonment. *Prison Service Journal, 132*, 27–37.

Ward, J. (1982). Telling tales in prison. In R. Frankenberger (Ed.), *Custom and conflict in British society* (pp. 234–257). Manchester: Manchester University Press.

Ward, D., & Kassebaum, G. (1965). *Women's prison: Sex and social structure.* Chicago: Aldine.

Williams, V., & Fish, M. (1974). *Convicts, codes and contraband: The prison life of men and women.* Cambridge: Ballinger.

Zaitzow, B., & Thomas, T. (Eds.). (2003). *Women in prison: Gender and social control.* Boulder: Lynn Rienner Publishers.

5

How Do Foreign Women End Up in Prison? An Intersectional Approach of Criminal Pathways

Sílvia Gomes

1 Introduction

Foreigners, non-Western immigrants, immigrant children and people of colour, who make up the most vulnerable social categories because of their lower-class status and the multiple discriminations inflicted on them (Wacquant 1999, 2005), are over-represented among the prison population across Europe (Marshall 1997; Tournier 1996; Kalunta-Crumpton 2006; Albrecht 1991; Junger-Tas 1997; Wacquant 2005; Alonso et al. 2008)—in many cases, to a degree comparable to the "disproportionality" that affects blacks in the United States (Wacquant 2000, p. 110).

According to the *Council of Europe Annual Penal Statistics* for 2015 (Aebi et al. 2016), the average percentage of foreign prisoners in European prisons was 22.1%. When looking at the data on Portuguese prisons, we confirm that foreign men and women are over -represented in prison: male foreigners represent 17.0% of the male prisoners (European average

---

S. Gomes (✉)
CICS.NOVA Universidade do Minho, Braga, Portugal

Instituto Universitário da Maia (ISMAI), Maia, Portugal

© The Author(s) 2018
S. Gomes, V. Duarte (eds.), *Female Crime and Delinquency in Portugal*,
https://doi.org/10.1007/978-3-319-73534-4_5

20.4%), and female foreigners represent 26.6% of the female prisoners (European average 20.4%). Although the percentage of female prisoners is significantly lower than that of male prisoners (6.1% vs. 93.9%), following the European trend (5.3% vs. 94.4%), the prevalence of foreign women is so large that, even in such a low proportion, it manages to increase the percentage of foreigners in the context of imprisonment: 17.5%. While this percentage is lower than figures already gathered by Portugal a few years ago, which documented a visible tendency towards an increasing foreign population behind bars and their over-representation in some nationalities (see Esteves and Malheiros 2001; Seabra and Santos 2005; Guia 2008; Gomes 2014), it is still an extensive number when compared to national prisoners.

Between 1994 and 2011, there were two periods of significant increase in the foreign prison population in Portugal: from 1994 to 1996 and from 2001 to 2006, the latter distinctly marked by the entry of Eastern European prisoners from countries such as Ukraine, Moldova and Russia (Seabra and Santos 2005). This new wave of foreigners contrasted with the traditional influx from the African Portuguese-Speaking countries (PALOP), which comprised a large number of Cape Verdean nationals. The largest proportion of foreign prisoners is still from Cape Verde, although the volume of these immigrants has decreased substantially (Guia 2008, p. 185; Rocha 2001, p. 33; Esteves and Malheiros 2001, p. 103; Seabra and Santos 2005, p. 211).

This article focuses on a fragment of a major research study developed during these years, when there was an upsurge in the foreign population in Portugal. This research[1] sought to analyse the mechanisms that allow us to understand the (over)representation of ethnic and foreign groups inside prisons. The objective was twofold: (i) apprehend the factors and potential causes of crime in men and women from foreign and ethnic minority groups as well as (ii) understand the possible implications of the attribution of the criminal label by moral entrepreneurs. The life trajectories of foreign women prisoners, namely, nationals from PALOP and Eastern European countries, will be examined, studying their objective living conditions[2] up to the time of their incarceration. Through an analysis of these objective living conditions, based on an intersectional approach, we aim to verify to what extent certain crimes and imprisonment are a result of combined effects, melding processes of social inequality, exclusion, prejudice, daily and institutional racism; and, when comparing this finding with national and international studies, we aim to expose the idiosyncrasies in the links between crime and nationality (and class) when we introduce a gender perspective.

Therefore, this article starts with a brief theoretical analysis of the relationship between crime and nationality, moving onto a discussion on the importance of developing an intersectional approach to the understanding of crime and the realities of the criminal justice system. Following this, analytical and methodological options of the study are presented, in order to clarify the perspectives through which data analysis is developed and then presented. Results are divided into two main groups, starting with the pre-prison contexts, where objective living conditions are explored through the analysis of female prisoners' narratives, and moving to the reasons shown for their crime and imprisonment. These women's diverse backgrounds, corresponding to multiple social vulnerabilities such as being poor, female and foreign, end up explaining their life trajectories and their entry into in the prison system.

2 Articulations Between Crime and Nationality

European studies focusing on explaining the link between crime and nationality show how police, judicial and penal practices are applied with particular severity to people with a non-European phenotype (Tournier 1996; Hood 1992; Heaven and Hudson 2005; FitzGerald 1997). These individuals are easily identified and tracked by police and are targeted by the judicial system (Bowling and Phillips 2002; Bonelli 2005; Gomes 2017) or racism (Albrecht 1991). As a result, we can state that we are facing a process of criminalization of foreigners and immigrants. In addition, since foreigners or immigrants have been continuously segregated in the suburbs of large cities, living in degrading conditions and under socioeconomic inequalities (Albrecht 1997; Bonelli 2005), socioeconomic reasons also explain the disparity between foreign and nationals in the criminal justice system (Albrecht 1997; Bowling and Phillips

2002; FitzGerald 1997; Rocha 2001; Esteves and Malheiros 2001; Seabra and Santos 2005). These reasons are reinforced by the sense of frustration about social mobility experienced by young people from immigrant families when they become aware of relative deprivation and socio-economic inequalities (Bonelli 2005). In the United States, immigrants generally had a low level of crime involvement, which then grew with their children owing to high expectations that were frustrated by the existence of discrimination (Marshall 1997).

Although these studies are consensual, we cannot assume a *single story* about the relationship between crime and certain social groups (Duarte and Gomes 2015), because there is significant diversity among them and within the foreigner and immigrant groups as well. Webster (2007, pp. 62–63) acknowledges some of the nuances and diversities when analysing the phenomenon of crime and its links to foreign/immigrant groups.

Firstly, Tonry (1997, pp. 22–25) discovered that economic immigrants from many countries of Asian culture in England and in the United States have lower crime rates than the resident population in the first and subsequent generations. Secondly, he also found that cultural differences between structurally similar immigrants, regardless of age or class composition, could result in markedly different patterns of crime, just as cultural differences can predict more crime. Thirdly, the policies adopted by some countries to assist immigrant insertion and absorption can reduce crime rates, including those among second and third generations of descendants. Fourthly, the reasons that groups migrate, such as low self-esteem and alienation, which are expressed in reduced self-control and social isolation, can be powerful factors that shape crime. In the same way, these reasons can also encourage successful adaptation. Finally, some categories of immigrants have social and economic characteristics, such as belonging to the middle class and having relatively good academic and vocational qualifications, which discourage criminality. Or, as other authors would say, there is less routine surveillance, because of their social class, leading to less contact with the criminal justice system and, therefore, a reduced presence in crime statistics. It is important not to forget that official statistics reflect more the action of the criminal justice system in its different stages, based on penal policies, than crime itself.

Then, there is a category that has been persistently missing from these studies, namely, gender. When a society is organized along nationality/ethnicity and sex/gender lines, amongst others, we cannot assume that the explanation for crime involvement, responses to crime or the application of criminal justice are neutral in their effects and consequences (Peterson 2012; Potter 2015). The link between several identities and statuses (Potter 2015) is mandatory in crime studies, since in some situations all of the diverse identities or statuses we possess, or the intersection amongst several of them, in many combinations, can be central to understanding crime and the criminal justice system (Agozino 1997).

3 Gender and Intersectional Approaches in Crime and Justice Studies

Gender studies have been theoretically, analytically and conceptually valuable to explain crime and the deviant pathways of particular social groups. However, for a long time they were not able to explain existing inequalities among women themselves. Researchers from around the world began to realize that it was important to have gender intersected with variables such as age, race, ethnicity, nationality and class in gender studies in general, but also in crime studies in particular (Agozino 1997; Barak et al. 2006; Reasons et al. 2002; Diaz-Cotto 2002; Schwartz and Milovanovic 1996; Sudbury 2005), to overcome this barrier.

The intersectionality perspective is perceived as the most significant contribution that women's studies have made so far (McCall 2005, p. 177). Black feminist legal scholar Kimberley Crenshaw (1989, 1991, 2001) is acknowledged as the creator of the term intersectionality. It is today a whole area of research that studies the meanings and consequences of multiple interconnected identities (Oliveira 2010), but it was traditionally a way of addressing the experiences and struggles of black women who were wedged between feminist discourses and anti-racist discourses (Davis 2008, p. 68). It was though Crenshaw's retooling and special application of black feminist thought and critical race theory

(Potter 2015) that this perspective was born. Thus, for Crenshaw (1989), intersectionality was used to signify ways in which black people relate to and intersect with gender; the focus was then on the variables of race and gender. However, as the studies focused on members of the black population who were poor and marginalized, the social class dimension was often involved in the theoretical analyses and reflections (Crenshaw 1991).

In the realm of the sociology of crime and deviance studies, gender, race, social class and age have been simultaneously marginalized and at the centre (Heitzeg 1994). If sometimes such variables are "veiled", remaining in the subtext of the criminal behaviour, other times they are dominant. Nevertheless, it is undeniable that the relationships among race, gender, class and age;—and further variables—are complex; and academics today have defended the relevance of these variables for the understanding and explanation of crime, as it is insufficient to choose only one or two of these variables, since they are all intertwined with social structure and identity (Heitzeg 1994; Burgess-Proctor 2006). Additionally, the relationship among different variables cannot be isolated from its role in the systems of oppression. This means that the experience of racism, sexism, classism and any other kind of prejudice can contribute to the rejection of dominant social norms and, subsequently, be correlated with deviant behaviour, in the same way that it can contribute to stigmatization and social control and a subsequent sense of impotence (Heitzeg 1994, pp. 2–9). In this sense, Potter (2015) has very recently launched a pioneering book that advances a literature review on intersectionality and criminology. Placing *intersectional criminology* on the podium of the discussion, Potter advocates the requirement and use of intersectionality in the study of crime, criminality and the criminal justice system.

Although the intersectional approach is still in developing and is subject of debate, feminists and other scholars have begun to analyse crime and criminal justice, if not adopting entirely an intersectional approach, at least interconnecting gender with other relevant social forces. Illustrating this in studies of female incarceration,[3] Girschick (1997) proves that incarcerated women face different obstacles, one of which is belonging to a certain "race" and a certain social class, as well as to victimization paths; women in prison are disproportionately "women of colour", predominantly poor and were mistreated and abused in their life trajectory. Also, Bloom (1996) and Bloom and McDiarmid (2000) mention that the characteristics of women involved in the criminal justice system reflect a population that is threefold marginalized by race, class and gender. Young and Reviere (2005) verify that today's prisons are full of poor, *dark-skinned* and single-mother prisoners, imprisoned for minor drug offences. By using differentiated lenses—gender, race and class—the authors argue that women prisoners are punished twice: first, by criminal sentences and then because the policies which were developed to govern the time spent behind bars were not designed for women's responsibilities and problems. Brown (2010, p. 18) shows how Afro-American women, as a result of their ethnic affiliation, gender, poverty and incarceration, find it difficult to reintegrate into their communities after incarceration. Ruiz-Gargía and Castillo Algarra (2015) state, on the one hand, that the Spanish prison system has not yet adjusted to the circumstances and demands of its growing number of foreign-national female prisoners, and, on the other hand, that these women (i) accentuate their gender role as mothers because of their position as head of the family, and (ii) do not consider themselves to be criminals, since the illegal act that led them to prison was something out of the ordinary, a behaviour caused by on-going deprivation and social exclusion. In Portugal, two studies focus on the intersections between gender and ethnicity/nationality for the understanding of the trajectories and identities of female prisoners. Cunha (2001), studying intra-prison sociabilities, realizes the importance of ethnic categories in the relationship between prisoners, as well as the blurring of the ethnic category when coupled with class and neighbourhood experiences (Cunha 2005). Matos (2016) also shows that nationality and ethnicity play an important role as organizers of female prisoners' social relations inside prison, as well as attributing meaning to their trajectory to prison. For instance, a conformity was verified in the expected gender roles in foreign women's narratives regarding their families and intimate (violent) relationships; but some adjustments in this conformity were also verified: for example, when these women chose to migrate or to engage in criminal activity to overcome social vulnerabilities and exclusion or how they faced incarceration as non-national citizens.

From this brief description, as in the studies that articulate crime and nationality, we realize how social exclusion and social inequalities are transversal as we attempt to understand both the causes of crime and the performance of the criminal- and social-control institutions. Not surprisingly, we are considering social forces that are undervalued in the dominant system, with several systems of oppression. That is why, though race, ethnicity or nationality, gender and social class are ubiquitous, the meaning of the relationship among them changes according to the context in which they operate (Messerschmitt 1997). Thus, in the study of crime, if in some cases gender and nationality may be more important in certain contexts, in other circumstances linking social class and gender may be more appropriate. All social categories are not equally important in every social environment in which crime is committed; throughout life trajectories, we have multiple possible combinations. For this reason, it is essential to consider all variables, as a way to gauge how they are applied or not.

4 Understanding Life Trajectories: Analytical and Methodological Options

Analysing life trajectories of women prisoners requires the construction of an analytical framework that is capable of accounting for the intricacy of how they construct and report their objective living conditions and how they convert them afterwards into subjective initiatives, on the one hand, and give visibility to variables that are considered central to the research on the other hand, because they are relevant in shaping these objective living conditions.

Following these assumptions, we approach crime as a phenomenon with different layers of analysis. Social inequalities and vulnerabilities are produced and reproduced by the social action of the various types of social actors and this, in turn, is structured by the pre-existing conditions of inequalities and vulnerabilities (Silva 2009b, p. 37). In order to avoid any kind of circular reasoning, it is necessary not only to articulate the different types of prospective inequalities—class, gender, nationality—in women's objective living conditions, but also to establish a hierarchy of levels of analysis. Although each level has its relative autonomy, logic and specific fields, the following hierarchy of understanding/explaining levels must be maintained: (i) the socio-structural level, though it does not totally determine, structure and integrate, (ii) the organizational, and (iii) the interactional (see Silva 2009a,b).

Life trajectories are understood based on connecting two main theoretical approaches, combining macro and micro features. Firstly, we adopt theories of structured action, focusing on Bourdieu's (1979, 1998) concept of habitus, because women make their own history, but do not do it through categories of their own choosing, as they are inserted into a set of long-lasting dispositions that act systematically in all practices, determining the possible spectrum of choices and probabilities (Bourdieu 1998, p. 89). Secondly, we look at intersectionality perspectives in general (Crenshaw 2001; Brown 2010; Coster and Heimer 2006), and intersectional criminology in particular (Potter 2015), owing to the impossibility of separately studying people suffering double and triple experiences of discrimination (Collins 2000) based on an experience of oppression marked by gender, class and nationality (Oliveira 2010; Gomes and Granja 2015). The intersection of different forms of power and social vulnerabilities based on class, gender and nationality is fundamental for the comprehension of crime and the criminal justice system (Coster and Heimer 2006; Burgess-Proctor 2006; Potter 2015).

Data were collected during 2010 (from January to December) in two Portuguese female prisons. The individual files of all the foreign women prisoners from the nationalities under study were consulted. Interviewees were selected based on the crime for which they had been convicted (different crimes, if possible), the length of the sentence (different amounts of time but more than two years), recidivism (recidivist and non-recidivist) and age (different generations). Semi-structured interviews were conducted with 12 women; 5 were Africans from PALOP and 7 were Eastern Europeans.

Interviews were conducted under the Deontological Code of Sociologists and Anthropologists and the requirements of the applicable legislation, particularly regarding data protection, the guarantee of prisoners' privacy and voluntary participation. Therefore, they occurred only in situations where informed consent was obtained, and the use of the tape recorder was subject to prisoners' prior authorization. All interviews following the same procedure: (i) oral and written explanation of the study's objectives, and the researcher's commitment to maintain data confidentiality and provide all the information that requested by the participants and (ii) the participants' signature on an informed consent form.

Interviews were submitted to a thematic qualitative content analysis. We intended to look beyond the immediate meanings of the narratives, to make a more enriching or even more revealing contribution regarding what some messages intend to communicate, leading to rich, rigorous, objective and in-depth information and discussion about what was selected, produced and communicated by women prisoners' narratives. The steps followed for content analysis were those suggested by Bardin (1995)—pre-analysis, material exploration and treatment of results, inference and interpretation.

5 Interviewee Selection: Identifying the Prisoners

Within the group of foreign women prisoners, it was possible to select relatively diverse cases. The socio-demographic and legal–criminal characteristics of prisoners who narrated their trajectories to a trusted stranger—the researcher—are briefly presented here. A table and a tape recorder in a prison's empty room mediated the conversations. The women are identified by fictional names in order to maintain their anonymity.

The PALOP women prisoners interviewed were Noémia, Palmira and Marisa from Cape Verde, Neusa from Angola, and Mariama from Guinea-Bissau. Their ages ranged from 28 to 48 years old; school qualifications achieved out of prison varied from primary school to sixth grade; all were cleaning ladies or housekeepers before imprisonment; and the crime for which they were convicted was drug trafficking, combined with other crimes such as illegal weapon possession and the use of someone else's identification document. There is only one homicide case, and it was combined with a drug-trafficking crime case. Sentences ranged from three to nine years and six months of effective imprisonment.

The Eastern European women prisoners were Nicoleta, Ionela and Raluca from Romania, Ekaterina and Velislava from Bulgaria and Daryna and Laima from Ukraine and Lithuania, respectively. Although all had at least a high-school qualification or a university degree, their professional activities and occupations in most cases did not correspond to their qualifications: a seamstress, a cleaning lady, two waitresses, a prostitute and a student. Their ages varied between 20 and 49 years old. The crime that led to their imprisonment was mainly drug trafficking; and, in most cases, they were drug mules. There was only one woman convicted of pimping and criminal association; she received a sentence of 12 years. Those convicted of drug-trafficking offences had sentences ranging from four years and three months to six years of imprisonment.

Despite the specificities of these women's life experiences, the analysis of their life trajectories showed a set of common elements that allow us to understand how they ended up in prison. There are elements that are not disconnected from their social class, gender and nationality statuses, shaping not only the ways in which they expressed and narrated their lives, but also the ways in which they reflected on the long-lasting dispositions that have influenced the possible spectrum of options and chances. In the next sections we will discuss their life trajectories, expressed in the form of perception, thought and action (Bourdieu 1980, p. 91).

6 Pre-Prison Contexts: Objective Living Conditions Narrated

Observing these women's objective living conditions, despite the fact that the two groups of women experienced specific types of social inequality and exclusion, their trajectories before imprisonment show a set of common features that allow us to understand why they are in the same confined position, namely, their unequal and vulnerable positions as female, foreign and impoverished.

In the life trajectories that were narrated by PALOP women prisoners, there were three distinct types of trajectories: women who immigrated to Portugal during the last few decades—from the 1970s to the beginning of the new millennium—and, within this group, we have those who came to work and those who came when they were of school age; we also have the trajectories of those who were drug mules.

In the case of Eastern European women prisoners, it is possible to distinguish two trajectories: the immigrant trajectory linked to international networks—smuggling—and, in a larger number, the drug mules. Of the seven women interviewed, five were arrested for drug trafficking as mules and two were in Portugal because of international networks, one as part of the network and other as a victim of it.

6.1 Trajectories of Deprivation and Compliance of the PALOP Women

Women from PALOP who immigrated to find work are Marisa, in 2002 and Noémia, in the same year; and Palmira, in 2004. Family has a central role in the lives of these women and it shapes their entire storylines. Marisa, leaving her four-year-old son in Cape Verde with her grandmother, soon after separating from her boyfriend, immigrated to Portugal to work and earn enough money to be able to bring the child with her. In Portugal she lived initially with a cousin and then with a sister, who were already in the country and with whom she shared the household expenses. Noémia came to Portugal at the age of 20 with the expectation of being able to be with her son, who was with his father, but ended up getting a job as a domestic servant, which made it impossible for her to see the child frequently. Palmira left her nine-month-old son with his grandmother to travel on business and decided to stay in Portugal. There she got a job as a domestic servant and she ended up seeing her as her family. She does not ever intend to return to Cape Verde, because she met the person who became the father of her second child in Portugal. Therefore, the family, and especially children, are highlighted in their narratives as being the guiding thread of their lives. If, on the one hand, we understand that these women immigrated because the family was the centre of their concerns, on the other hand, we can see that work assumes a central role in their relationship with the country they emigrated to.

Their occupational paths are almost always related to domestic and cleaning work, even if they perform other jobs before and after. Marisa, for example, worked in a restaurant before working as a cleaning lady. She explained her difficulties in continuing to pay her taxes in order to maintain her visa when the employer would not assume these obligations:

> And since I arrived in Portugal…I entered legally, with a visa, I worked in a restaurant and after a while I worked in the house of my employer cleaning and such for two years and so. The visa was expiring, I wanted my employer to pay the taxes and… I found this job and she prepared everything for paying the taxes. But she was not the one paying the taxes, I was. I accepted anyway. And then she told me she could not give me vacations, holiday allowance, that it would be a little difficult to do so. I accepted anyway because I needed to have the visa.

The legal situation involving the "work permit" made her vulnerable to the employment possibilities and the conditions in which she ended up accepting the job. As is evident from her testimony, Marisa was involved in a number of duties that she was not responsible for, such as "taxes", and abdicated another set of rights in order to work legally in national territory. Throughout her experience in Portugal, she faced this type of situation several times, finding precarious work, depending on the conditions proposed to her. In 2003, she even describes accumulating three jobs, providing cleaning services to three employers at the same time.

Noémia and Palmira worked as domestic servants. They ensured that their salary was enough to send some money to relatives in Cape Verde and to those in Portugal. A regular week was divided into two parts: from Monday to Friday they were domestic servants in their employers' houses, where they would work and rest; and on the weekends they would stay at their relatives' homes. Noémia spent the weekends with her sister; Palmira, with her brother. As a consequence, these women did not know the city in which they lived. Palmira tells us the implications of this lack of familiarity:

...I came from Cape Verde and I do not know anything [in the city], I arrived at my brother's house that was there in Buraca, (...) later I started living at my work (...) I only know here [prison], Buraca and work. It's like this, if I go somewhere, I'm lost. I have to go with an address, or my employer would put me in a taxi with an address (...) If it was to get a bus, I would not go back home.

Next, we look at an interviewee who immigrated to Portugal at school age: Neusa, officially Angolan, arrived at the end of the 1970s, with her aunt, in order to study. She completed all her formal education in Portugal, finishing the sixth grade. During her school time, she recalls that her lack of documents made her go back to Angola, where she stayed for two years. This break prevented her from continuing her studies, and the urge to study no longer prevailed when she came back. She recounted that "colleagues either mocked about my clothes or...but it was not racism or anything like that, we were children". Although Neusa denies that it was racism, she ends up giving a testimony that contradicts this perception and assumes manifest racist experiences:

Once in school, (...) we were in an oral test, and my colleague from behind [my desk], the teacher asked the questions and she said to me "You will not make it, nigger! You will fail!" And I, with that, started to get disgusted even more.

Neusa admits that she did not like to study. She recounts, at different moments of the conversation, escaping from school to be with her boyfriends or to play outside. For that reason, she proposed to her mother that she would study and work simultaneously, a combination that was not possible due to her work conditions. Her dropping out had nothing to do with her mother's lack of commitment to her studies. On the contrary, according to Neusa, there was always family pressure to study, even if it was not on her own initiative. Eventually, she met her first husband, with whom she had three children and to whom she was married for 12 years. They lived together in social housing, but successive marital problems—which were almost all linked to the lack of money—eventually led to their separation. She had two other relationships and one more child. Her trajectory was marked by always having to manage different partners, since the first partner was always present in some way; but she maintained a strong bond with her children. In labour terms, her first jobs were as a cleaning lady or as a waitress, earning low wages. Her last professional experience was in an escort bar, which proved to be more remunerative than her previous jobs. Neusa explained that back then she would earn in one week the same amount she had earned in a whole month as a waitress. Thus, monetary reward was decisive for Neusa's entry into a world considered deviant.

Lastly, there are the women who were detained for having been drug mules. This is the case of Mariama, who came to Portugal at the age of 12 to work. She tells us about her family, the fact that she married early, having children and grandchildren, and reports that she lost her parents when she was three years old. The early days in Portugal for Mariama are narrated as positive, so good that she did not even have to work. Her marriage brought her some financial stability, to the point that her husband preferred that Mariama not work. However, the marriage did not last long, culminating in divorce. In the period immediately following, Mariama had two children as her entire responsibility and was forced to work in badly paid jobs to sustain them. Working was no problem for her; she states this while listing all the places where she worked and what she did. The problem was that the salaries were too low for her family's needs; until the moment of her confinement, she experienced monetary difficulties daily.

Through the narratives of these women with different life trajectories, we understand that they had objective living conditions marked by suffering economic deprivation, working at unskilled jobs, failing at school, having insufficient documentation and experiencing spatial segregation and episodes of racism. Nevertheless, their narratives demonstrate in general a conformity concerning their gender role as the person responsible for the family (see also Matos 2016). Further, this compliance narrative includes a certain acceptance of the social position they occupied, placing the family as the driving element of their trajectories, and not being critical of their disadvantaged social position in terms of social class or ethnicity, for instance. It does not mean they are not aware of it, because they are (Gomes 2014); but the whole narrative has a strong feeling of acceptance and resignation.

6.2 Trajectories of Deprivation and Violence Among the Eastern European Women

The woman who was smuggled into Portugal is called Daryna. She is Ukrainian and arrived ten years ago, when she decided to emigrate alone. Daryna tells us that she was working in her country, but the money she earned was not enough for daily expenses and for the university where she was studying for a psychology degree. So she decided to emigrate to work hard and to earn enough money to go back to university. However, the "one or two years" she planned lasted for an indeterminate time. Daryna was unaware that she was immigrating through a criminal network; and when she arrived, she was placed in a situation of legal defencelessness and forced to work in a brothel. Here, she became a drug addict, mainly due to the criminal network's pressure, which would threaten to hurt her family if she did not do what they were asking for, as well as her personal, emotional and legal fragility:

> I was working in the brothel and all the girls were using drugs. I…did not drink, did not smoke, and could not do it [have intercourse] the first times because I was always crying a lot and cutting my veins and all of that… they told me "Look, you have to work, otherwise something will happen with your family". I said I could not work anymore. And cried…but I could not talk to the police because I was afraid. (…) Because I entered illegally, I was illegal here. They took my passport. I arrived; I did not speak the language, I was afraid. (…) And then they said like this: "You will try something and you will see that it helps". Ok, I tried it. At the time I was just thinking about going home. After using one, two, four times…the fifth time I was already in pain, I felt… I was feeling ill. I need to consume [drugs] again.

In the early days, when she was completely dependent on the network, Daryna survived in Portugal like other women and men who were in the same situation: "We would go to the market (…), we stole food and so we ate. We had a house for more than 20 people". If, on the one hand, drug addiction imprisoned Daryna during the years she was out of prison, on the other hand, it was because of it that she was able to leave the

How Do Foreign Women End Up in Prison? An Intersectional... 91

brothel. A "blocked vein" led to a hospital admission; and, after that, she did not go back. When she left the hospital, she was alone, in the streets. That is when she met a Ukrainian man who welcomed her. As both were drug addicts, they engaged in drug trafficking in order to cope with their consumption needs.

In the case of the drug mules, we find two different patterns: women who regularly emigrated to Portugal or Spain and only subsequently became involved in drug trafficking, and women who drug trafficked within their home counties, without a previous immigration experience in Portuguese territory.

Ekaterina and Velislava, Bulgarian, and Laima, Lithuanian, are in the latter situation. Like the drug mules hitherto presented, they were in a fragile socio-economic situation before their criminal involvement. Ekaterina lived with her parents and a disabled cousin because she could not afford a house by herself. In addition to the poor living conditions— she was from a village where there were no roads, markets or shops— Ekaterina tells how her mother's illness, which forced her to be hospitalized for five years, and a dysfunctional health system obligated her to request credit to pay hospital expenses:

> In my country everything is paid for at the hospital, even the food. I send food to her. She has been there for 10 days and after 10 days she comes back because after 10 days you do not pay. You never stay in the hospital for more than 10 days because after that you don't need to pay more. (...) And then she goes back home and then she has to go back to the hospital because she is not well and she pays another 10 days and after that she comes back again. Always like this. (...) And all this for five years.

Laima, a single mother of two children and unemployed, was also living with her parents before she began drug trafficking. Velislava, a university student, did not live with her parents because she was studying abroad. The other two women had jobs, but their low salaries did not meet the basic needs of their families.

Raluca and Nicoleta, from Romania, immigrated to Portugal and Spain, respectively, before they began drug trafficking. Raluca travelled alone to reunite with her partner, who was already in Portugal. She had also two cousins with a successful immigrant trajectory in the country; they "were doing well". Therefore, as in traditional immigration, social networks influenced the choice of Portugal as a destination. In Romania, she "did not have money to eat or anything". After a while, she brought her daughter as well. Despite having higher educational credentials, she had always worked as a cleaning lady, as a waitress and in a factory. The Portuguese language was difficult in the beginning but, "since Romanian is also a Latin language" she ended up learning quickly. Nicoleta lived in Spain, and "worked and sent money to Romania every time she could". Her children lived with their grandmother, and she was living with her partner. Her conversation was not very long because Nicoleta did not express herself very well in Portuguese or in Spanish. Still, her talk was mostly related to poverty and difficulties in earning enough money for her and her partner, and sending money to the children back home.

The objective living conditions of Eastern European women show us contexts of deprivation and poverty, in and out of their national group. A female prisoner who came through criminal networks was being held by her own compatriots and blocked from attempting to enter a regular migratory trajectory. Prisoners who have been "drug mules" lived in their home countries or in other countries with economic difficulties. Therefore, we can affirm that there are processes of intragroup exclusion, either in the national territory or in foreign territory' and, at the same time, situations of intergroup exclusion, in which the national group segregates the immigrant.

Eastern European women also focus their narratives on the family, specifically on family care, either for mothers, fathers and/or children. In fact, family is described as being the driving force for their main life decisions (Cunha 2001). Substantiating this, women in this group report distance from family as one of the main difficulties in prison. What moves Laima the most during the interview is when she reports the process of separation from her children; the contact she has with them is sparse, only by telephone and limited by the money that is made available for phoning inside prison. The separation between women prisoners and their children is such a central issue that a number of researchers have studied it (see Ferraro and Moe 2003; Celinska and Siegel 2010; Granja et al. 2015); but it assumes specific configurations when we consider foreign women prisoners like those imprisoned for being drug mules who are serving a sentence in a country that is distant from their family's country. Family contact is only by phone or letter, and it depends on certain conditions (e.g., time, money). That is why foreign women, if they are able to work, are positively discriminated against inside Portuguese prisons in terms of having access to a paid occupation (Gomes 2014).

7 The Criminal Act: Reasons for Crime and Imprisonment

By combining reasons indicated by the prisoners for their criminal involvement or for their imprisonment with their previously described life trajectories, which are strongly influenced by disadvantaged objective living conditions, we promote an understanding of the factors and mechanisms that led these women to prison.

7.1 Economic Deprivation and Biased Justice in the Explanation of PALOP Women's Imprisonment

The life trajectories of all the PALOP women prisoners interviewed culminated in conviction for drug trafficking. One of them, Palmira, is also serving time for homicide, but it is related to a drug-trafficking case.

In the case of those women who immigrated to Portugal to work, drug trafficking appears to be a consequence of attempting to satisfy family needs. Seeing herself unemployed, Marisa, for example, had no way to keep up with the basic household expenses. Drug trafficking—transporting the product from one side of the river to the other side—was enough to be able to solve her situation promptly. It was a risk she consciously decided to take.

Other women maintain their innocence. Noémia, for example, claims that she was not involved in drug trafficking. During one of the weekends when she was visiting her son in the south of Portugal—he was living with his father—she got caught with him in a car with drugs, when he was taking her to the bus station to go back to Lisbon. The father of her son was already being tracked by police officers and they identified her as the black woman who usually accompanied him in the car when he was trafficking. She was convicted of being an accomplice, but she defends herself by stating she was working as a domestic servant in Lisbon; and, consequently, there was no way she could be the woman who police officers were identifying:

> And then I went to Algarve on a weekend to see my son and I was in the car with him [father of her son] and he had drugs in the car. And I did not know. (…) The police told him to pull over, and he did it. And then he told me that they [the police] were already following him because they already suspected of him (…) Except I had to go to Lisbon to work because I had to be at work on Monday morning, but I do not know what happened (…) they said that the girl who was usually with him in the car was me. But I only went that weekend to see my son. But the police did not believe me. And I ended up here. And here I am.

Although Palmira did not deny that she was trafficking in the neighbourhood where she was living, she refused to be associated with the particular drug-trafficking case for which she was judged and convicted. She accuses the police of trying to implicate her in order to find out the names of the traffickers. Palmira refused to do so for fear of suffering retaliation within the neighbourhood and was condemned.

> I sold [drugs]. Why did I sell them? I know why I am not going to sell anymore. I live in the hood. In Buraca. All the people there sell. I am not going to be the one saying that is Pedro or Manel. Police know that! Police know the people that sell, people that keep [drugs], people that buy; the police know everything! What can I do? I cannot do anything! I cannot say anything. Because if I say something, you think I am out of here alive? No, he orders to kill me! Are the police going to stop him from killing me? (…) The police will pick me, because I am fragile, and I don't have a family, don't have someone. If I were someone else, I would not be in prison!

Palmira outs the blame for her trafficking on the area where she lives, Buraca—a poor neighbourhood of Amadora, on the periphery of Lisbon. Like many others in the same area, she was involved in trafficking, and the police are perceived as knowing everything that is happening in the neighbourhood. In fact, these areas are extremely well monitored by the criminal justice agents. In areas where drug trafficking crosses several segments of the population, police intervention is, in most cases, limited to the detention of the lower layers of the trafficking networks (Cunha 2001). Therefore, urban space connected to social class and race/ethnicity play an extremely important role in understanding how the criminal justice system works, and on the perceived criminalization of these women, for being black—obviously in Noémia's case—and for being vulnerable.

Neusa, during her trajectory in Portugal, was involved in vulnerable situations and ended up entering an inescapable spiral linked to drug trafficking. She started working in an escort bar, where the police did not search women (due to their being women). Therefore, she, like others, transported and kept the drugs that were sold by male traffickers who frequented these places. Her first contact with drugs began like this and it was long-lasting—"for eight, nine years"—without her ever having been caught, detained or punished. During her "professional" activity, she got involved with one of the traffickers, and they started living together with the children she had from the first marriage. She was certain that he would treat her well, since he would not let her "put her hands on the drugs". Besides her partner's being a drug dealer, her eldest son also got involved in trafficking with him. Later both went to prison and Neusa was left helpless. Her family and her partners' family did not support her because they did not agree with the deviant and criminal lifestyle they led. So the solution she found to be able to provide immediately for the children at home and her partner and son in prison was to use her partner's contacts and also start trafficking. So Neusa ended up trafficking herself and did not leave this line of activity. It is a vicious cycle characterized by criminal activity, contact networks and the opportunity that is available to meet particular types of needs.

Women who got caught as drug mules mention economic factors to justify their criminal involvement. Mariama, for example, tells us that she did it voluntarily because she needed to pay for very delicate and expensive surgery for her granddaughter. Unemployed and knowing a person who needed to transport drugs, she did not think twice.

Hence, we can observe that economic factors are central in these women's narratives; family, professional and geographical factors also play an important role in these paths towards an illegal opportunity; but the lack of resources to provide for themselves and primarily for their families is a primary determinant in their criminal involvement. Moreover, we cannot ignore the situations in which women claimed to be innocent or wrongly convicted, revealing that race (being black), social class and socio-geographical background play a central role in their imprisonment (Gomes 2017).

7.2 Economic Factors and Drug Addiction Leading to Eastern European Women's Imprisonment

Eastern European prisoners who were convicted for being mules are assumed to have chosen the drug courier route because of economic reasons: paying debts for family health expenses, arranging money to pay school fees without parental help or because the family was so poor they needed the money to lighten their burden. They all point out that the whole process is very easy. The trafficker takes the initiative, approaching them and talking about the business. It is not the other way around. The trafficker explains to them that it is a good business and that "there is no way to go wrong"; thus, he encourages these women to start doing drug transportation.

Ekaterina and Laima are reported situations of greater poverty and economic vulnerability. Ekatarina describes the poverty in which she lived with her family and how the possibility of trafficking appeared as a viable opportunity to solve her family problems. Laima's story follows the same direction, revealing that she needed the money to get essential goods for herself and her children, which she could not otherwise afford in her own country. Ferraro and Moe (2003), when studying the relationship among motherhood, crime and imprisonment, points out that the responsibilities of childcare, combined with situations of economic marginality, led some women to choose drug trafficking as an alternative to hunger. Laima, a single mother, lived with her parents and her children. From the moment she became pregnant, she stopped working. The only person who worked at home was her father, but she claims that he had alcohol problems. Thus, in a poor and unstable family, money was not sufficient to meet the minimum needs, so Laima decided to carry drugs to obtain some money for her family.

On the contrary, Raluca was working at the time someone suggested drug courier work to her. However, the little money she earned was not enough to enable her daughter to take a degree at university, and she wanted her daughter to continue her studies. The possibility of earning 2,000 euros in one week was appealing. Raluca took the risk and ended up being arrested. Her goal was not fulfilled, and her daughter started working to sustain their family.

Doriana, even without experiencing the same economic difficulties as the other women interviewed, also decided to take a risk as a drug courier. She was a university student, studying abroad and working to be able to pay for university costs and her own living expenses. According to her testimony, her parents had no financial problems, but she wanted to be independent and to show that she could do things on her own without her family support. Hence at a certain point, instead of asking her parents for money to cover her expenses, she decided to carry drugs between countries. Now, while enduring the consequences of her illegal behaviour, the decision no longer seems so appealing and she describes it as "irresponsible". At one point in her speech she also compares herself with the other foreigners serving their sentence in the same prison and realizes that her situation was so much less serious than the others and how easily she could have had a different outcome.

In addition to these prisoners who were detained for being "drug couriers" and who are in the majority, a prisoner detained because of pimping and criminal association was interviewed: Ionela. She was engaged in this activity together with her husband; though not heading the network, she was one of the main people involved. Her husband was the key player and she did everything necessary to keep the network running smoothly. Her main tasks were to control women who were brought to Portugal for prostitution by watching them closely to prevent them from escaping or exposing the network as well as to collect the money resulting from their activity. Her response justifying her illegal act was that she "helping her husband"[4] to make money.

Daryna was on the opposite side of a similar situation when she arrived in Portugal through international networks: she was a victim. The motivation for drug consumption and, consequently, for drug trafficking, stems directly from the way in which she reached Portugal. During the sexual exploitation to which she was subjected, drugs were used as a way to keep her imprisoned and unable to escape or react. However, at some point, an overdose episode took her to hospital, where she was hospitalized, operated on and medicated. She then ran away from the illegal network but returned to drug consumption. Having no support when she left the hospital, without housing and without any knowledge of the country she was in, she was "rescued" by a fellow compatriot who, though working, also engaged in drug trafficking. She became involved in the drug industry with him and eventually got caught by the police. The road to prison is traced from the beginning to the end of her journey in Portugal.

As we can see, testimonies of women nationals from the Eastern European countries are diverse. However, there is one element that is central to all narratives: the economic deprivation or need they experienced before imprisonment. There are several situations that result in economic deprivation: unemployment, low wages and professional exploitation, among others. But, regardless of their marginalized and excluded positions, to these women crime appears as an "opportunity" to lessen their problems and as a way to change their social conditions positively. Additionally, we have one case where the crime was somewhere between a voluntary and involuntary action, when the offending individual was under the of drugs.

8 Final Considerations: Tying Loose Ends

In this study, foreign prisoners' life trajectories were categorized according to their relationship with migration and crime. Based on the trajectories narrated, and adding in the reasons for crime and/or imprisonment, it is possible to conclude that these women are not disconnected from the processes of exclusion and social inequalities, and from prejudice and racism. Thus, the economic factors and the factors deriving from the specificities of their social positions—social class, gender and nationality—systematically guided women's narratives, corroborating the studies which link crime and nationality as well as the those which advocate the relevance of introducing an intersectional slant to crime and criminal justice system studies.

These trajectories fall within the *single stories* of economic deprivation and criminal justice bias in the treatment of foreign and ethnic minority populations. These narratives cannot be changed, since the women are not middle class. They are specially monitored by criminal justice agents because they are poor, live in particular urban neighbourhoods and present a different phenotype; some of them are not even immigrants, and even the ones who are immigrants face so many deprivations that it would be difficult to imagine how they could survive without resorting to alternative ways of supporting themselves and their families. They all narrate a set of social and criminal constraints and opportunities that emerged along their trajectories, although with differentiated contours depending on the specific group to which they belong. When we consider the gender lens, and particularly the intersectional approach, we can confirm that women face multiple vulnerabilities and obstacles by virtue of their being women, foreign and poor, with different combinations of these positions throughout their trajectories until imprisonment. They presented conformity narratives regarding gender roles and a certain compliance because of their disadvantaged social position. However, it is interesting to note that they break out of their gender roles by immigrating—to change their own and their families' situations of social exclusion or inequality—or by involving themselves in criminal practices. But then, family is the core reason for their effort.

Finally, we can conclude that gender, class and nationality shaped their life trajectories on different levels: the way they understand and convey their life trajectories (subjective and interactional level); their long-lasting dispositions that influenced the possible spectrum of options and chances, by the action or reaction of the criminal system (organizational and institutional level); and the social constraints which determined the domains in which they could move (socio-structural level). Life trajectories analysed are therefore a tangle of relationships marked by the interdependence of diverse features at different levels. These foreign women's life trajectories are visibly constrained by social structures and their systems of oppression. Despite the fact that these women present through their narratives some relative degree of autonomy on key decisions, making their own stories, they do not do so in a way that is disconnected from their social position and objective living conditions.

Notes

1. It is entitled "Crime, Ethnicity and Inequalities: A comparative analysis between foreign groups from Eastern Europe and African Portuguese-Speaking countries and national Roma groups" and was based on my Ph.D. research (SFRH/BD/47010/2008).
2. Objective living conditions, a more comprehensive and elastic concept than class, encompasses other dimensions beyond class, such as gender, ethnicity and age, dimensions that are traditionally ignored or underestimated by the traditional Marxist perspective (Silva 2009a).
3. For a more extensive review of the literature on intersectional criminology, see Potter (2015).
4. The difficulties she had in expressing herself in Portuguese (or in a language we could both understand) were multiple, so it was not possible to explore further some questions that would be very interesting for richer analysis.

References

Aebi, M. F., Tiago, M. M., & Burkhardt, C. (2016). *SPACE I—Council of Europe annual penal statistics: Prison populations.* Survey 2015. Strasbourg: Council of Europe.

Agozino, B. (1997). Is chivalry colour-blind? Race-class-gender articulation in the criminal justice system. *International Journal of Discrimination and the Law, 2,* 199–216.

Albrecht, H. (1991). Ethnic minorities: Crime and criminal justice in Europe. In F. Heidensohn & M. Farrell (Eds.), *Crime in Europe* (pp. 84–100). London: Routledge.

Albrecht, H. (1997). Ethnic minorities, crime, and criminal justice in Germany. In M. Tonry (Ed.), *Ethnicity, crime, and immigration. Comparative and cross-national perspectives* (pp. 31–99). Chicago: The University of Chicago Press.

Alonso, C., Garoupa, N., Perera, M., & Vazquez, P. (2008). *Immigration and crime in Spain, 1999–2006*. Madrid: Fundaciòn de Estudios de Economia Aplicada.

Barak, G., Flavin, J., & Leighton, P. (2006). *Class, race, gender, and crime: Social realities of justice in America*. Lanham: Rowman & Littlefield.

Bardin, L. (1995). *Análise de Conteúdo*. Lisboa: Edições 70.

Bloom, B. (1996). *Triple Jeopardy: Race, class, and gender as factors in women's imprisonment*. PhD thesis, Riverside: University of California.

Bloom, B., & McDiarmid, A. (2000). Gender-responsive supervision and programming for women offenders in the community. In *Topics in community corrections annual issue 2000: Responding to women in the community* (pp. 11–18). Washington, DC: U.S. Department of Justice.

Bonelli, L. (2005, Dezembro). A revolta dos subúrbios: As razões da cólera. *Le Monde Diplomatique*, Edição Portuguesa.

Bourdieu, P. (1979). *La distinction. Critique sociale du jugement*. Paris: Les Éditions de Minuit.

Bourdieu, P. (1980). *Le sens pratique*. Paris: Les Éditions de Minuit.

Bourdieu, P. (1998). *La distinción: criterios y bases sociales del gusto*. Madrid: Taurus.

Bowling, B., & Phillips, C. (2002). *Racism, crime, and justice*. London: Longman.

Brown, G. (2010). *The intersectionality of race, gender, and reentry: Challenges for African-American women, Issue Brief, The American Constitution Society*. Washington, DC: American Constitution Society for Law and Policy.

Burgess-Proctor, A. (2006). Intersections of race, class, gender, and crime: Future directions for feminist criminology. *Feminist Criminology, 1*(1), 27–47.

Celinska, K., & Siegel, J. A. (2010). Mothers in trouble: Coping with actual or pending separation from children due to incarceration. *The Prison Journal, 90*(4), 447–474.

Collins, P. (2000). *Black feminist thought: Knowledge, consciousness, and the politics of empowerment*. New York: Routledge.

Coster, S., & Heimer, K. (2006). Crime at the intersections: Race, class, gender, and violent offending. In R. D. Peterson, L. J. Krivo, & J. Hagan (Eds.), *The many colors of crime: Inequalities of race, ethnicity, and crime in America* (pp. 138–156). New York: New York University Press.

Crenshaw, K. (1989). Demarginalizing the intersection of race and sex: A black feminist critique of antidiscrimination doctrine, feminist theory and antiracist politics. *University of Chicago Legal Forum, 8*, 139–167.

Crenshaw, K. (1991). Mapping the margins: Intersectionality, identity politics, and violence against women of color. *Stanford Law Review, 43*, 1241–1279.

Crenshaw, K. (2001). Intersectionality: The double bind of race and gender. *Perspectives*, Sheila Thomas interviewed Crenshaw.

Cunha, M. I. (2001). *Entre o Bairro e a Prisão: Tráfico e Trajectos*. Doctoral thesis, Braga: Universidade do Minho.

Cunha, M. I. (2005). Les Gitans, la prison et le quartier: une relation spÉcifique devenue le modèle ordinaire. *Études Tsiganes, 21*, 34–47.

Davis, K. (2008). Intersectionality as buzzword: A sociology of science perspective on what makes a feminist theory successful. *Feminist Theory, 9*(1), 67–85.

Diaz-Cotto, J. (2002). Race, ethnicity, and gender in studies of incarceration. In J. James (Ed.), *States of confinement: Policing, detention, and prisons*. New York: Palgrave.

Duarte, V., & Gomes, S. (2015). The (de)construction of a single story: Crossing crime, gender, social class, ethnicity, and nationality. *Psiquiatria, Psicologia & Justiça, 8*, 139–189.

Esteves, A., & Malheiros, J. (2001). Os Cidadãos Estrangeiros nas Prisões Portuguesas: Sobrerepresentação ou ilusão? In M. Pinheiro, L. Baptista, & M. J. Vaz (Eds.), *Cidade e Metrópole: Centralidades e Marginalidades* (pp. 95–114). Oeiras: Celta Editora.

Ferraro, K. J., & Moe, A. M. (2003). Mothering, crime, and incarceration. *Journal of Contemporary Ethnography, 32*(1), 9–40.

FitzGerald, M. (1997). Minorities, crime, and criminal justice in Britain. In I. H. Marshall (Ed.), *Minorities, migrants, and crime: Diversity and similarity across Europe and the United States* (pp. 36–61). London: Sage.

Girschick, L. (1997). The importance of using a gendered analysis to understand women in prison. *Journal of the Oklahoma Criminal Justice Research Consortium*, 4. Retrieved from http://www.doc.state.ok.us/offenders/ocjrc/97_98.htm

Gomes, S. (2014). *Caminhos para a Prisão—uma análise do fenómeno da criminalidade associada a grupos estrangeiros e étnicos em Portugal*. Famalicão: Editora Húmus.

Gomes, S. (2017, March 30). Access to law and justice perceived by foreign and Roma prisoners. *Race and Justice*. Article first published online. https://doi.org/10.1177/2153368717699972

Gomes, S., & Granja, R. (2015). *Mulheres e Crime—Perspectivas sobre intervenção, violência e reclusão*. Famalicão: Editora Húmus.

Granja, R., Cunha, M. I., & Machado, H. (2015). Mothering from prison and ideologies of intensive parenting: Enacting vulnerable resistance. *Journal of Family Issues, 36*(9), 1212–1232.

Guia, M. J. (2008). *Imigração e Criminalidade—Caleidoscópio de Imigrantes Reclusos*. Coimbra: Edições Almedina.

Heaven, O., & Hudson, B. (2005). Race, ethnicity and crime. In C. Hale, K. Hayward, A. Wahidin, & E. Wincup (Eds.), *Criminology*. Oxford: Oxford University Press.

Heitzeg, N. A. (1994). *Differentials in deviance: Race, class, gender and age*. Retrieved from http://minerva.stkate.edu/people.nsf/files/mina-82vm3a/$file/differnetialsindeviancel.pdf

Hood, R. (1992). *Race and sentencing—A study in the crown court*. Oxford: Claredon Press.

Junger-Tas, J. (1997). Ethnic minorities and criminal justice in the Netherlands. In M. Tonry (Ed.), *Ethnicity, crime, and immigration. Comparative and cross-national perspectives* (pp. 257–310). Chicago: The University of Chicago Press.

Kalunta-Crumpton, A. (2006). The importance of qualitative research in understanding the disproportionate black presence in crime figures in the United Kingdom. *African Journal of Criminology & Justice Studies, 2*, 1–32.

Marshall, I. H. (Ed.). (1997). *Minorities, migrants, and crime: Diversity and similarity across Europe and the United States*. London: Sage.

Matos, R. (2016). Trajectories and identities of foreign national women: Rethinking prison through the lens of gender and citizenship. *Criminology & Criminal Justice, 16*(3), 350–365.

McCall, L. (2005). The complexity of intersectionality. *Signs, 30*(3), 1771–1800.

Messerschmidt, J. (1997). *Crime as structured action: Gender, race, class and crime in the making*. Thousand Oaks: Sage.

Oliveira, J. M. (2010). Os feminismos habitam espaços hifenizados—A localização e interseccionalidade dos saberes feministas. *Ex aequo, 22*, 25–39.

Peterson, R. (2012). The central place of race in crime and justice—The American society of criminology's 2011 Sutherland address. *Criminology, 50*(2), 303–327.

Potter, H. (2015). *Intersectionality and criminology: Disrupting and revolutionizing studies of crime*. New York: Routledge.

Reasons, C. E., Conley, D. J., & Debro, J. (Eds.). (2002). *Race, class, gender, and justice in the United States*. Boston: Allyn & Bacon.

Rocha, J. (2001). *Reclusos Estrangeiros: Um estudo exploratório*. Coimbra: Edições Almedina.

Ruiz-García, M., & Castillo-Algarra, J. (2015). *Experiences of foreign-national female prisoners in Spain*. Retrieved from http://bordercriminologies.law.ox.ac.uk/foreign-national- female-prisoners-in-spain/

Schwartz, M., & Milovanovic, D. (Eds.). (1996). *Race, gender, and class in criminology: The intersection*. New York: Garland Publishing.

Seabra, H. M., & Santos, T. (2005). *A criminalidade de estrangeiros em Portugal: um inquÉrito científico*. Lisboa: Alto-Comissariado para a Imigração e Minorias Étnicas.

Silva, M. C. (2009a). *Classes Sociais: condição objetiva, identidade e acção colectiva*. Famalicão: Edições Húmus.

Silva, M. C. (2009b). Desigualdades e exclusão social: de breve revisitação a uma síntese proteórica. *Configurações, 5/6*, 11–40.

Sudbury, J. (Ed.). (2005). *Global lockdown: Race, gender, and the prison-industrial complex*. New York: Routledge.

Tonry, M. (Ed.). (1997). *Ethnicity, crime and immigration—Comparative and cross National perspectives*. Chicago: The University of Chicago Press.

Tournier, P. (1996). La dÉlinquance des Étrangers en France: analyse des statistiques pÉnales. In S. Palidda (Ed.), *DÉlit d'immigration/immigrant delinquency* (pp. 133–162). Brussels: European Commission.

Wacquant, L. (1999). 'Suitable enemies': Foreigners and immigrants in the prisons of Europe. *Punishment & Society, 1*(2), 215–222.

Wacquant, L. (2000). *As Prisões da MisÉria*. Oeiras: Celta Editora.

Wacquant, L. (2005). 'Enemies of the wholesome part of the Nation'. Postcolonial migrants in the prisons of Europe. *Sociologie, 1*, 31–51.

Webster, C. (2007). *Understanding race and crime*. New York: Open University Press.

Young, V., & Reviere, R. (2005). *Women behind bars: Gender and race in U.S. prisons*. Boulder: Lynne Rienner.

6

"To Kill or to Be Killed": Narratives of Female Victims of Intimate Partner Violence, Condemned for the Murder of Their Partners

Mafalda Ferreira, Sofia Neves, and Sílvia Gomes

1 Introduction

Intimate partner violence is an endemic problem in Portugal (Azambuja et al. 2013; Neves and Nogueira 2010), resulting in the death of an average of 40 women every year (UMAR 2017).

Although the country became a democratic regime in 1974, after about 50 years of dictatorship that culminated in the Carnation Revolution, gender asymmetries are still evident in different sectors of Portuguese society (Ferreira 2011). In fact, despite advances in Women's

---

M. Ferreira (✉)
Faculdade de Medicina da Universidade do Porto (FMUP), Oporto, Portugal

S. Neves
Instituto Universitário da Maia (ISMAI), Maia, Portugal

Centro Interdisciplinar de Estudos de Género (CIEG/ISCSP), Lisbon, Portugal

S. Gomes
CICS.NOVA Universidade do Minho, Braga, Portugal

Instituto Universitário da Maia (ISMAI), Maia, Portugal

© The Author(s) 2018
S. Gomes, V. Duarte (eds.), *Female Crime and Delinquency in Portugal*,
https://doi.org/10.1007/978-3-319-73534-4_6

Rights in the last decades, Portugal holds a Global Gender Gap Index of 0.737, occupying 31st place in a ranking of 144 countries (WEF 2016).

According to the European Union Agency for Fundamental Rights (FRA 2014), 19 per cent of Portuguese women have experienced physical and/or sexual violence from an intimate partner at some time in their lives. National data from the Annual Report of Internal Security (SSI 2017) confirms the severity of the phenomenon. Domestic violence[1] is the second-most-prevalent crime against persons in Portugal (28.1 per cent). In 2016, a total of 22,773 crimes were reported to police authorities; 79.9 per cent of all victims were female, and 84.3 per cent of all aggressors were male. Violence was committed by partners in 54.6 per cent of the cases and by former partners in 17.1 per cent of the cases. Psychological violence is the most significant (82 per cent), followed by physical violence (68 per cent), social violence (16 per cent), economic violence (9 per cent) and sexual violence (3 per cent). A total of 11.1 per cent of all victims were younger than 16 years old, 9.2 per cent were between 16 and 24 years old and 79.7 per cent were more than 25 years old. According to the Portuguese Observatory of Murdered Women (OMA), from January 2004 to December 2016, a total of 450 women were victims of femicide. In this chapter, the idea of femicide will be used as a broad concept which aims to characterize the end of a continuum of terror that includes psychological, physical and sexual acts against girls and women (Caputi and Russell 1992). In this sense, it addresses "the misogynous killing of women by men" and "the proportion of female deaths that occurred due to gender-based causes" (Radford 1992, p. 3). In 2016, a total of 22 Portuguese women died in femicide cases; 31 were victims of femicide attempts (UMAR 2017). Sixty-four per cent of these women were killed by a partner or a former partner. Ten victims were over 65 years old.

The prevalence of intimate partner violence must be borne in mind: research suggests that there is a huge discrepancy between the number of cases reported to police authorities and the number of convictions with effective prison sentences. Twenty-six murderers were condemned in 2015 for marital homicide (92.3 per cent were male) (DGPJ 2016), and 730 suspects were arrested in 2016 by police authorities (SSI 2017).

A recent study that aimed to evaluate judicial decisions in the field of marital homicide (2007–2012) concluded that this crime tends to be committed after years of intimate partner violence against the female partner, with violence occurring in the first year of the relationship (Agra et al. 2015). Ninety per cent of the murder victims were female, with the same percentage of male murderers. In about half of the situations (54.3 per cent) victims and aggressors were partners at the time of the murder. In about one-third of cases (36 per cent) violent relationships lasted more than 15 years. In only 18.3 per cent of the cases police authorities were notified of was there a previous history of violence. Previous convictions for domestic violence were verified in only 4.6 per cent of the situations.

Even though some national studies have tried to characterize the trajectories of women who are imprisoned for killing their partners (e.g., Pais 2010), little is known about the association between partner homicide perpetrated by women and previous exposure to domestic violence. In view of the lack of studies on this specific topic and considering that, as MacDonald pointed out (2013), there are probably many more women prisoners with a history of domestic abuse than is officially recognized, a qualitative study in the Portuguese context was developed, aiming to fill this gap and explore this issue in depth.

2 Hearing Women's Voices: A Qualitative Study

2.1 Women as Marital Murderers and Bias in the Criminal Justice System

Though mostly victims, women are also perpetrators of crime. Nevertheless, when we specifically refer to homicide, it almost always occurs in a family or conjugal context (Pais 1998). Exploring the association between partner homicide perpetrated by women and previous exposure to domestic violence is not possible without mentioning the concept advocated by Pais (1998) of homicide typology referred to as "battered homicide". This notion refers to a crime perpetrated exclusively by women on their companions who had mistreated them for long periods of time. In her study, the author refers particularly to situations in which women have lived solely in an intimate relationship in which violence has existed since its beginning and has continued over time, with the murder of their partners as the only means available to them to end their suffering.

Other studies, such as those of Pollock (1998), Siegel and Williams (2003) and McClellan et al. (1997), show that criminal women are more likely to have been victims of physical or sexual violence in their childhood and that this in turn often lead to an early entry into the world of delinquency and addiction to substances such as drugs and alcohol. Throughout history, women have more frequently been victims of marital homicide compared to men (Moracco et al. 2010, as cited in Almeida 2012). When the situation is reversed, that is, when women exercise violence or kill their partners, it is usually a situation of self-defence, a means to end the violence they have been experiencing (Almeida 2012; Mills 2001; Russell and Harmes 2001; Taylor and Jasinski 2011).

This perspective of self-defence is directly related to the literature focused on women who kill their partners after several years of victimization, when they feel that there is no escape or that their children are in danger (Websdale 1999; Wilson and Daly 1992).

Regarding the way in which the penal system addresses marital murder committed by women, Steffensmeier and Allan (1998) stated that the diversity of life experiences of men and women influences their criminal behaviour patterns. However, in the case of a penal system that should above all, be impartial, there is often a gender bias to the detriment of women, whether victims or offenders, in the interpretation and application of legislation (Matos and Machado 2007).

In general, feminist theories point to the influence that social constructs of gender stereotypes have on the justice system (Ballinger 2007; Machado 2007 cited in Gomes 2013), especially as this system judges according to a male model identified as the norm without considering women's different life experiences as a counterpoint to men's experiences (Carlen 2002; Fonseca 2008).

Despite the very different life experiences of men and women (Steffensmeier and Allan 1998), there are also criticisms of the tendency for women to receive the same punishments as men (Carlen 2002). This current of thought holds that this cannot occur, particularly in the case of "battered homicide" (Pais 1998), where the gender violence to which these women have been exposed throughout their lives should be considered (Carlen 2002) in order to lighten their sentences in some way.

Criminal law thus seems to judge women more by their appropriateness in terms of social gender roles than by the legal norms which we must all obey, thus punishing them for their social image more than their actual transgressions (Matos and Machado 2007). In fact, there are some studies that point to the application of more severe penalties for females than for males (Brown 1998), although according to the statistics there is not enough evidence that such segregation occurs (Carlen 2002).

2.2 Our Study and the Defence of the Victim as an Offender Within the Portuguese Justice System

This study emerged to address the social scourge that is domestic violence, through a distinct lens, which seeks to reflect simultaneously on women as victims and as marital murderers. Our research aimed to fill the existing gap in Portuguese academic literature, bringing a new perspective to the phenomenon by listening to women victims of intimate partner violence who have been condemned for the killing their partners, and by confronting them with the data contained in their judicial processes. The objective was to understand the possible relationship between prior exposure to intimate gender violence and the homicide of their partners or former partners.

The questions that we wanted to see answered by our study were the following: *How do women prisoners characterize their killing of partners or former partners? What is the relationship between prior exposure to intimate gender violence and the homicide? If there were a relationship between prior exposure to intimate gender violence and homicide, was it considered in the application of the judicial sentence?*

Regarding this last question, we sought to raise some hypothetical defences for these women which could minimize their sentences. To this end, we discuss the type of homicides these women committed, which is not identified in the Portuguese Penal Code, but remains a problem and should be judged differently: We are dealing with former victims, and we believe that they are being condemned within an inappropriate penal framework.

As previously mentioned, Pais advanced the concept of "battered homicide" to categorise the murders committed by female victims of domestic violence after long periods of abuse by their partners/offenders. Although many consider or commit suicide, the homicide of their partners appears as the most viable option to end their suffering, particularly in times of vulnerable emotional states, such as after episodes of verbal and/or physical violence (Pais 2010).

Furthermore, when we think of borderline cases such as the homicide of the abuser/companion of a domestic violence victim, we wonder about the victim's reasons for not abandoning this relationship. However, regardless of the victim's free choice, the Portuguese Law 112/2009 guarantees that their rights of defence and protection must always be assured. In this sense, we cannot ignore that the motivation of the victim's actions is to stop all the suffering (Feitor n.d.). In addition, studies have shown that one of the greatest risks for femicide is motivation for the rupture of the relationship and/or the separation itself (Brookman 2005; Dobash et al. 2004; Dutton and Kropp 2000).

Battered Woman's Defence is a concept that is directly related to the notion of Battered Woman's Syndrome (Beleza 1990). This strategy emerged with the purpose of protecting abused women in the face of the inefficiency of the police and the judicial system's minimal repression of the offender, leading us to consider a situation that attenuates the horror of a homicide that, although not justifiable for many theoreticians, becomes at least comprehensible (Rosen 1986).

Another justification used in the defence of these women would be the right of self-defence: that is, considering their situation as victims who became offenders as the only means of survival. However, this right is underpinned by several assumptions and circumstances, such as actual or imminent aggression that threatens a protected legal asset of another human (Palma 1990).

Still, given the nature of this research, it is essential to mention the existence of other doctrines that rely on other concepts, such as the "Legitimate Anticipated Self-Defence" (Carvalho 2004; Douglas 1995;

Garcia 2012), in which the subject is preparing to prevent eventual aggression by the creation of security measures such as traps, placement of glass on top of walls and purchase of weapons, among others (Garcia 2012). When we specifically think of situations that refer to cases such as "battered homicide", we understand that if the women suffering abuse had not anticipated their defence prior to the actual moment of the aggression, they would not be able to protect themselves properly because the delay in exercising their right to self-defence could make it dangerous or impossible to defend themselves (Carvalho 1998; Palma 1990).

Once the act of murder has been committed, we have to apply the 131st article of the Portuguese Penal Code: "Whoever kills another person is punished with imprisonment from eight to sixteen years", complemented by article 133, voluntary manslaughter, which diminishes the culpability of the subject, stating the following: "Whoever kills another person, dominated by understandable violent emotion, compassion, despair, or motive of significant social or moral value that appreciably diminishes his guilt, is punished with imprisonment from one to five years".

According to Bitencourt (2009), voluntary manslaughter is more lightly punished because of the reasons that led to the occurrence of the crime. The subject's emotional state during the criminal episode—despair, compassion, motives of high moral value or understandable violent emotion—all can considerably lessen the individual's guilt (Albuquerque 2010). Based on the scope of our investigation, it makes sense to look closely at two of the four influential elements relating to these emotional states: the understandable violent emotion and despair, which reduce the subject's psychological discernment and mental capacity, resulting in reduced criminal responsibility (Ferreira 1991; Palma 1983).

2.3   Description of the Study

This qualitative study was conducted between 2015 and 2016 in two Portuguese female prison facilities, and its main goal was to analyse the narratives of female prisoners condemned for the homicide of their partners or ex-partners, analysing the possible relationship between the practice of the crime and exposure to a previous history of intimate gender violence. Specifically, the study aimed to characterize, socio-demographically and criminally, female prisoners convicted of the murder of their partners or ex-partners, through documentary analysis of their individual files and content analysis of their narratives, collected through semi-structured interviews. These were focused on the subjects' socio-demographic origins and their views on gender relations in general and intimate gender violence in particular, on the (in)effectiveness of the justice system, on the effects of imprisonment on various dimensions of their lives, on the existence of previous (if any) victimization and on the influence of these stories of victimization (if any) on the homicide and the application of their judicial sentences.

We have combined documentary analysis of prisoners' individual files and content analysis of semi-structured interviews in order to provide more reliable conclusions (Igea et al. 1995).

Data was collected in two female Portuguese prisons (Special Prison of Santa Cruz do Bispo and Odemira Regional Prison). Before we entered the prison, an official letter to the General Directorate of Reintegration and Prison Services in Portugal (DGRSP) was sent, explaining the content of the study and requesting the authorization to conduct the study in all national female prisons. Our initial goal was to study the national complement of female prisoners condemned for the murder of their partners. The study was authorized to be held only in the two female prisons indicated, since according to the DGRSP, we would not have many women fulfilling the selection criteria in the other national prison (in total we have three female prisons).

In the Special Prison of Santa Cruz do Bispo, of the eleven women imprisoned for conjugal homicide, only four agreed to talk about this subject. Nonetheless, those who did gave extremely rich and extensive interviews. In the Odemira Regional Prison Establishment, two women were imprisoned at the time for marital homicide, and both agreed to be interviewed. This intentional sample had the following as inclusion criteria: female gender, victimization by domestic violence and imprisonment for marital homicide. All interviews were preceded by a brief explanation of the content of our study and the guarantee of total anonymity and confidentiality and followed by obtaining the interviewee's signature on an informed consent form ensuring confidentiality and anonymity as well as voluntary participation in the study. In both prisons, the semi-structured interviews were carried out in empty offices with a desk and two chairs, where we talked individually, on average for an hour and a half, with audio being recording for later transcription.

The treatment of our data was carried out through documentary analysis of the individual cases and through thematic-content analysis of the interviews. The documentary analysis consisted of identifying, verifying and evaluating the documents with a specific purpose; and in this case a parallel source of information was recommended to complement the data and allow the contextualization of the information contained in the documents (Souza et al. 2011); hence, we also used the semi-structured interview. Thematic-content analysis refers to a set of techniques that exploit content-rich communications using systematic and objective procedures (Bardin 1995). Thus, thematic-content analysis allows the deconstruction of the discourse in the interviews by identifying themes that facilitate a detailed analysis of the data (Guerra 2006). It is an elementary task of data analysis to categorize data into relevant units (Tesch 1990), that is, to select excerpts of text that allow simplification and, consequently, a better understanding of what we are studying, in order to obtain more insightful conclusions (Miles and Huberman 2003). The attainment of the categories results from an attentive reading of the texts, in this case from transcripts of the interviews, through ideas that determine their division sometimes still fragmented in other subcategories (Bardin 1995; Gómez 1995). In this concrete investigation, the categorization was performed after the complete transcription and reading of all the interviews.

2.4 Results

For this study six women were interviewed. Their ages ranged from 33 to 61 years (x = 49.6), with the age group 40–50 being the most prevalent, and their sentences varied from 11 (homicide) to 20 years (aggravated homicide). Regarding their school qualifications, two of them completed the fourth grade, three completed the ninth grade and only one finished high school. Their occupations prior to their confinement were diverse but equally menial: a caretaker in a nursing home, a street vendor, a psychic, a waiter, a monitor for drawing and painting. One of the subjects was unemployed. Only one of these women was married at the time of the crime, three were divorced and two cohabited with their partners. All had children, typically two.

This investigation allowed us to recognize gaps in the Portuguese criminal-legal system regarding the sentencing of women convicted of conjugal homicide, since the impact of the prior victimization to which all these women were subject was repeatedly verified as irrelevant in the determination of their judicial sentences. We cannot say that in all cases abuse was the fundamental motivation for the homicide; however, all the experiences of extreme violence that the women experienced from an early age in intimate relationships cannot be undervalued.

Regarding the moment when the homicide occurred, we found that half of these women were already divorced or separated, as we can see in this excerpt:

> Before what happened, I had been in my mother's house for three months. Only then he went there and convinced me, he promised that he would change and then I proposed that we moved from that house and he accepted. All this for my son's sake, because of my son. (Interview 2)

This fact is extremely significant because it allows us to affirm that, in fact, an initial period of separation of the couple constitutes an aggravated risk factor for both the occurrence of femicide (Dobash et al. 2004; Dutton and Kropp 2000; Moracco et al. 1998) and for the homicide of the victims' aggressors.

We also know that exposure to violence in family contexts (both aggressor and victim) or intimate relationships, alcohol abuse, death threats, low socio-economic status and access to firearms are highly predictive of the occurrence of femicide (Campbell 2004; Dobash et al. 2004; Gartner et al. 2001; Aldridge and Browne 2003). The following excerpts show the previous history of violence in the family context and in intimate relationships:

My mother also suffered from domestic violence. I grew up in the middle of domestic violence and my deceased partner too! (...) I had a lot of boyfriends and suffered a lot, I had many disappointments. (...) I do not know if this is genetic... it's not genetic, but it happens, it happened to me! I married at 22 [years old] and I was a victim of domestic violence. (Interview 2)

I would go to my mother's with my legs all black and she would say to me: "Oh daughter, what am I going to do for you? Just hang on, I also handle your father when he drinks a lot too". (Interview 4)

All these indicators can be recognized in each of our cases in some way, which shows that given the risk of femicide that these women faced, the judicial sentences for killing their aggressors could have been attenuated. In the words of one of the interviewees: "If I had not killed, I would be dead!" (Interview 1). This testimony clearly reflects the initial theoretical considerations of this study, that is, the need for a legal framework that allows the use of the concept of the "Legitimate Anticipated Self-Defence" or the insertion in the criminal frame of voluntary manslaughter motivated by understandable violent emotion or despair (Albuquerque 2010), and which gives voice to the Battered Woman's Defence (Rosen 1986; Beleza 1990).

While such consideration of mitigating circumstances would not be associated with a total remission of the women's guilt, it could result in a reduction of culpability leading to a reduced sentence. When we understand that this type of crime is committed by women in visibly altered emotional states, we also understand that the reason behind voluntary manslaughter are intrinsic to an attenuation of the offender's punishment, based on the emotional state of the offenders (Casal 2004), who kill under deep emotional stress that affects their capacity for judgement (Dias 1999) and corresponds therefore to reduced accountability for their actions (Pereira 1998).

Regarding premeditation, it was considered that in four cases there was some kind of premeditation, which, however, does not preclude the possibility of "Legitimate Anticipated Self-Defence".

We have also seen in the women's narratives that, over time, the cycle of domestic violence becomes shorter—that is, includes fewer phases—eliminating the honeymoon phase and alternating only between the phase of increased tension and the phase of the attack. The literature highlights this as a great predictor of the occurrence of femicide (Walker 2009).

> Well, to this day I wonder why he left the house laughing, and everything was fine, but then when he came back he looked like the devil! (…) He would spend 2/3 days out and then when he got back in that state, it seemed like I was the target to shoot down. It's the reality … and to this day I do not understand. (Interview 6)

Because of the violence the experience, some women tried to escape from their men without success and others experienced great difficulties in abandoning the abusive relationship due to social constraints concerning the female gender:

> I stayed because of my children. For their children, people do everything! If I did not have the children, I do not know what could have happened. (…) It was a shame at the time. I had to get beaten and shut up! Or it was a huge shame for the family. (Interview 4)

It was also possible to infer that these women felt extremely wronged by the defence they received from their lawyers, both private and state-appointed, but especially the latter. The women felt that state lawyers were not sufficiently dedicated to their cases, thus depriving them of the hope for a more favourable judicial sentence. In addition, the long prison sentences they received made them feel discredited and fearful about the life that awaits them after their imprisonment.

Furthermore, it is interesting and exasperating to notice in their cases judicial narratives highlighted the their abusers' roles as their life partners and the parents of their children as aggravating factors. This reveals how unaware criminal justice professionals are about the experiences and daily life of a victim of domestic violence, and is evidence of the perpetuation of stereotyped gender roles. In a society which perpetuates such stereotypes, homicidal women will all be considered as transgressors because they have deviated not only from criminal law, but also from the gender role they are expected to play socially (Lombroso and Ferrero as cited in Matos 2008).

3 Final Considerations

When we confront the results we obtained with our initial objectives, we realize that the primary objective of this study—to analyse the possible relationship between homicide and exposure to intimate gender violence—was effectively achieved, since although we cannot assert that their previous victimization was the motive for these women's crimes, we can state with certainty that their life paths were marked by multiple episodes of violence that affected who these women were and how they behaved in their daily lives.

Even though there is much public discussion about gender violence, in practice, not only do the victims themselves and their families (because they have also experienced it) tend to normalize the phenomenon, but also many members of the police and criminal and health institutions are not sufficiently sensitized to this social problem. Since domestic violence is a public crime in Portugal, authorities in several entities must be alert to these situations, denouncing them immediately as is their duty as professionals and as citizens.

It is also important to recognize the lack of attention given to women's prior victimization experiences, namely, their witnessing of inter-parental violence and exposure to physical, verbal and emotional violence by their partners. Agra et al. (2015) verified that penalties tend to be lower for women convicted of homicide, and the suspension of the prison sentence tends to be applied proportionally more with women than men. However, we realized that the sentences of these women go far beyond the period of suspension, with sentences ranging from 11 to 20 years of imprisonment, in the most serious case.

Therefore, we argue that alternatives such as "Legitimate Anticipated Self-Defence" or voluntary manslaughter for understandable violent emotion or despair should be considered to avoid the re-victimization of these women.

Moreover, data show that the exposure to intimate gender violence is not only a predictor of the occurrence of femicide, but also a predictor of the occurrence of the killing of the aggressor by the victim. Excluding or omitting the relevance of this information in the trials of women charged with homicide is also another form of gender violence that is reflected in a lack of confidence among women victims of intimate violence in the institutions that should protect them. This leads increasingly to under-reporting of this type of crime in society, making it nearly invisible and impossible to address. Domestic violence against women needs to be a target of public denunciation and awareness-raising campaigns, and become more than a mere article in the Portuguese Penal Code, as we are dealing with a public health problem, and a social, political and educational scourge.

Note

1. Intimate partner violence is seen as part of the crime of Domestic Violence – Article 152 of the Portuguese Penal Code: "Whoever, in a repetitive manner or not, imposes physical or mental abuses, including bodily punishments, deprivations of liberty, and sexual offences upon the spouse or ex-spouse; upon a person of another or of the same sex with whom the agent maintains or has maintained a relationship equal to a relationship of spouses, even if without cohabitation; upon the progenitor of common descendant in first degree; or upon a particularly defenceless person with regard to age, deficiency, disease, pregnancy or economic dependency, who cohabitates with him, is punished with a sentence of imprisonment from one to five years. If the agent commits the act against a minor, in the presence of a minor, in the common domicile or in the victim's domicile, he is punished with a sentence of imprisonment from two to five years. If these acts result in death, the agent is punished with a sentence of imprisonment from three to ten years and in cases resulting in grievous bodily injury, the agent is punished with a sentence of imprisonment from two to eight years".

References

Agra, C., Quintas, J., Sousa, P., & Leite, A. (2015). *Decisões conjugais em matéria de homicídios conjugais. Estudo de sentencing (sumário executivo)*. Lisbon: CIG.

Albuquerque, P. (2010). *Comentário do Código Penal à luz da Constituição da República e da Convenção Europeia dos Direitos do Homem*. Lisbon: Universidade Católica.

Aldridge, M., & Browne, K. (2003). Perpetrators of spousal homicide: A review. *Trauma, violence and abuse, 4*(3), 265–276.

Almeida, I. (2012). *Avaliação de Risco de Femicídio: Poder e Controlo nas Dinâmicas das Relações Íntimas*. PhD thesis in Psychology, Lisbon: ISCTE- IUL.

Azambuja, M., Nogueira, C., Neves, S., & Oliveira, J. (2013). Gender violence in Portugal: Discourses, knowledges and practices. *Indian Journal of Gender Studies, 20*, 31–50. https://doi.org/10.1177/0971521512465935.

Ballinger, A. (2007). Masculinity in the dock: Legal responses to male violence and female retaliation in England and Wales, 1900–1965. *Social and Legal Studies, 16*(4), 459–481.

Bardin, L. (1995). *Análise de Conteúdo*. Lisbon: Edições 70.

Beleza, T. (1990). *Mulheres, direito e crime ou a perplexidade de Cassandra*. Lisbon: Faculdade de Direito de Lisboa.

Bitencourt, C. (2009). *Tratado de Direito Penal* (9th ed.). Rio de Janeiro: Saraiva.

Brookman, F. (2005). *Understanding homicide*. London: Sage.

Brown, J. (1998). Aspects of discriminatory treatment of women police officers serving in forces in England and Wales. *The British Journal of Criminology, 38*, 265–282.

Campbell, J. (2004). Helping woman understand their risk in situations of intimate partner violence. *Journal of Interpersonal Violence, 19*(12), 1464–1477.

Caputi, J., & Russell, D. (1992). Sexist terrorism against women. In J. Radford & D. Russell (Eds.), *Femicide. The politics of women killing* (pp. 13–24). New York: Twayne.

Carlen, P. (2002). Introduction: Women and punishment. In P. Carlen (Ed.), *Women and punishment: The struggle for justice* (pp. 3–20). Devon: Willan Publishing.

Carvalho, A. (1998). A Legítima Defesa. PhD thesis in juridical sciences, Oporto: Faculdade de Direito da Universidade Católica Portuguesa.

Carvalho, A. (2004). Direito Penal – Parte Geral, Teoria Geral do Crime (Vol. II). Oporto: Universidade Católica Editora.

Casal, C. (2004). *Homicídio Privilegiado por Compaixão.* Coimbra: Coimbra Editora.

Dias, J. (1999). *Comentário Conimbricense ao Código Penal – Parte Especial.* Coimbra: Coimbra Editora.

Direção-Geral da Política de Justiça (DGPJ). (2016). Condenações por homicídio conjugal em processos-crime na fase de julgamento findos nos tribunais de 1ª instância (2007–2015). *Boletim de Informação Estatística, 45,* 1–4.

Dobash, R. E., Dobash, R. P., Cavanaugh, K., & Lewis, R. (2004). Not an ordinary killer – Just an ordinary guy: When men murder an intimate women partner. *Violence Against Women, 10*(6), 577–605.

Douglas, W. (1995). *Legítima Defesa Antecipada.* São Paulo: Revista dos Tribunais.

Dutton, D., & Kropp, P. (2000). A review of domestic violence risk instruments. *Trauma, Violence & Abuse, 1*(2), 171–181.

Feitor, S. (n.d.). *Battered Woman e Homicídio Conjugal: Legítima Defesa ou Estado de Necessidade Defensivo?* Lisbon: Universidade Nova de Lisboa.

Ferreira, A. (1991). *Homicídio Privilegiado.* Coimbra: Coimbra Editora.

Ferreira, V. (2011). Engendering Portugal: Social change, state politics and women's social mobilization. In A. C. Pinto (org.), *Contemporary Portugal – Politics, society and culture* (2nd ed., pp. 153–192). New York, Columbia University Press: Social Science Monographs, Boulder.

Fonseca, A. (2008). *Mulheres em Cumprimento de Pena: Um Estudo Exploratório no Sistema Prisional Português.* Master dissertation in Forensic Sciences. Oporto: Faculdade de Medicina da Universidade do Porto.

FRA. (2014). *Violence against women: An EU-wide survey.* Luxembourg: FRA – European Union Agency for Fundamental Rights.

Garcia, M. (2012). *O risco de comer uma sopa e outros casos de direito penal: Elementos da Parte Geral I.* Coimbra: Almedina.

Gartner, R., Dawson, M., & Crawford, M. (2001). Women killing: Intimate femicide in Ontario, 1974–1994. In D. Russell & R. Harmes (Eds.), *Femicide in global perspective.* New York: Teacher College Press.

Gomes, S. (2013). *Criminalidade, Etnicidade e Desigualdades Análise comparativa entre os grupos nacionais dos PALOP e Leste Europeu e o grupo étnico cigano.* PhD thesis in sociology. Braga: Universidade do Minho.

Gómez, A. (1995). O Pensamento Prático do Professor. In A. Nóvoa (Ed.), *Os Professores e a sua Formação.* Lisbon: Publicações D. Quixote.

Guerra, I. (2006). *Pesquisa qualitativa e análise de conteúdo – sentido e formas de abuso.* Estoril: Princípia Editora.

Igea, D., Agustin, J., Beltrán, A., & Martin, A. (1995). *Técnicas de Investigación en Ciencias Sociales*. Madrid: Dykinson.

MacDonald, M. (2013). Women prisoners, mental health, violence and abuse. *International Journal of Law and Psychiatry, 36*(3–4), 293–303.

Matos, R. (2008). *Vidas raras de mulheres comuns: Percursos de vida, significações do crime e construção da identidade em jovens reclusas*. Coimbra: Almedina.

Matos, R., & Machado, C. (2007). Reclusão e laços sociais: discursos no feminino. A prisão, o asilo e a rua. *Análise Social, XLII*(185), 1041–1054.

McClellan, D., Farabee, D., & Crouch, B. (1997). Early victimizaction, drug use, and criminality. A comparison of male and female prisoners. *Criminal Justice and Behavior, 24*(4), 455–476. California: American Association for Correctional and Forensic Psychology.

Miles, M., & Huberman, M. (2003). *Analyse des Données Qualitatives. Recueil de Nouvelles Méthodes*. Bruxelas: De Boeck Université.

Mills, S. (2001). Intimate femicide and abused women who kill: A feminist legal perspective. In D. Russell & R. Harmes (Eds.), *Femicide in global perspective* (pp. 71–87). New York: Teachers College Press.

Moracco, K., Runway, C., & Butts, J. (1998). Femicide in North Carolina, 1991–1993: A statewide study of patterns and precursors. *Homicide Studies, 2*, 422–446.

Moracco, K., Andersen, K., Buchanan, R., Espersen, C., Bowling, J., & Duffy, C. (2010). Who are the defendants in domestic violence protection order cases? *Violence Against Women, 16*(11), 1201–1223.

Neves, S., Gomes, S., & Martins, D. (2016). Narrativas mediáticas sobre o femicídio na intimidade: Análise de um jornal popular português. *Ex-Aequo: Revista da Associação Portuguesa de Estudos sobre as Mulheres, 34*, 77–92. https://doi.org/10.22355/exaequo.2016.34.06.

Pais, E. (1998, 2010). *Homicídio conjugal em Portugal: rupturas violentas da conjugalidade*. Lisbon: INCM.

Palma, M. (1983). *Direito Penal, parte especial. Crimes contra as pessoas*. Lisbon: AAFDL.

Palma, M. (1990). *A justificação por Legítima Defesa como Problema de Delimitação de Direitos*. Lisbon: AAFDL.

Pereira, M. (1998). *Direito Penal II: Os Homicídios: Apontamentos de aulas teóricas dadas ao 5º ano, 1996/1997*. Lisbon: AAFDL.

Pollock, J. (1998). *Counseling women in prison*. Thousand Oaks: Sage.

Radford, J. (1992). Introduction. In J. Radford & D. Russell (Eds.), *Femicide: The politics of woman killing* (pp. 3–12). New York: Twayne Publishers.

Rosen, C. (1986). The excuse of self-defense: Correcting a historical accident on behalf of battered woman who kill. *The American University Law Review*, *36*(1), 11–56. Retrieved from https://www.wcl.american.edu/journal/lawrev/36/rosen.pdf

Russell, D., & Harmes, R. (2001). *Femicide in global perspective*. New York: Teachers College Press.

Siegel, J., & Williams, M. (2003). The relationship between child sexual abuse and female delinquency and crime: A prospective study. *Journal of Research in Crime and Delinquency*, *40*(1), 71–94. London: Sage.

Sistema de Segurança Interna (SSI). (2017). *Relatório Anual de Segurança Interna*. Lisbon: SSI.

Souza, J., Kantorski, L., & Luis, M. (2011*)*. Análise Documental e Observação Participante na Pesquisa em Saúde Mental. *Salvador: Revista Baiana de Enfermagem*, *25*(2), 221–228. Retrieved from https://portalseer.ufba.br/index.php/enfermagem/article/view/5252/4469

Steffensmeier, D., & Allen, E. (1998). The nature of female offending. Patterns and explanation. In R. T. Zaplin (Ed.), *Female offenders: Critical perspectives and effective interventions*. Gaithersburg: Aspen Publishers.

Taylor, R., & Jasinski, J. (2011). Femicide and the feminist perspective. *Homicide Studies*, *15*(4), 341–362.

Tesch, R. (1990). *Qualitative research: Analysis types and software tools*. New York: The Falmer Press.

UMAR. (2017). *OMA – Observatory of murdered women. Data from 2016*. Lisboa: UMAR. Retrieved from http://www.umarfeminismos.org/images/stories/oma/2016/Relat%C3%B3rio_Final_OMA_2016.pdf

Walker, L. (2009). *The battered woman syndrome*. New York: Springer.

Websdale, N. (1999). *Understanding domestic homicide*. Boston: Northern University Press.

WEF (World Economic Forum). (2016). *The global gender gap report 2016*. Geneva: WEF.

Wilson, M., & Daly, M. (1992). Who kills whom in spouse killings? On the excepcional sex ratio of spousal homicides in the United States. *Criminology*, *30*, 189–215.

Part II

Female Juvenile Delinquency: Victimizations, Delinquencies and the Juvenile Justice System

7

Heterosexual Dating Violence and Social Gender Relations: Voices of Young Portuguese Girls

Sofia Neves and Joana Torres

1 Introduction

Intimate partner violence is a widespread problem in Portuguese society and is motivated by deep gender asymmetries (Azambuja et al. 2013; Neves and Nogueira 2010). Rooted in conservative values, a legacy of the Salazar regime that lasted for more than 40 years, the country remains trapped in a patriarchal ideology that reinforces the centrality of women's roles in families and highlights women's *natural* aptitude for child-rearing and domestic labour (Aboim 2010; Robinson 2015).

Data from the European Union Agency for Fundamental Rights (FRA 2014) revealed that almost every woman surveyed (93%) thinks that violence against women is either very common or common in her country

---

S. Neves (✉)
Instituto Universitário da Maia (ISMAI), Maia, Portugal

Centro Interdisciplinar de Estudos de Género (CIEG/ISCSP), Lisbon, Portugal

J. Torres
Universidade do Porto, Oporto, Portugal

© The Author(s) 2018
S. Gomes, V. Duarte (eds.), *Female Crime and Delinquency in Portugal*,
https://doi.org/10.1007/978-3-319-73534-4_7

and that 18% of Portuguese women have experienced physical violence, 3% sexual violence and 36% emotional or psychological abuse by a partner since the age of 15. In 2016, a total of 22,773 crimes of domestic violence were reported to the Portuguese police authorities, with women representing 79.9% of the victims. The offenders were male in 84.3% of the cases (Internal security system—SSI 2017).

In the last decades, national studies have been showing that young people are particularly affected by violent behaviour in their dating relationships (e.g., Machado et al. 2003, 2010, 2014; Magalhães et al. 2016; Matos et al. 2006; Neves et al. 2016a; Paiva and Figueiredo 2004; Perista et al. 2012; Saavedra 2011).

Dating violence is the concept usually adopted to describe the perpetration of (or at least the intention of perpetrating) physical, psychological and/or sexual abuse in youth intimate relationships (Teten et al. 2009). Evidence suggests that dating violence is one of the strongest predictors of intimate partner violence in adult relationships (White et al. 2001). Conceptualized as a human rights and a public health issue, the phenomenon has recently gained public attention in Portugal, becoming a public crime in 2013 (article 152.° of the Portuguese Penal Code), which means anyone, not only the victim, can and should report the occurrence.

It is estimated that one in every four Portuguese intimate relationships among young people is abusive (Caridade 2011). A recent study (Magalhães et al. 2016) conducted with 2500 teenagers showed that 7% admitted to having been victims of at least one form of violence in their intimate lives; psychological abuse was the most significant (8.5%), followed by physical violence (5%) and sexual violence (4.5%). This study also revealed that 22% of teenagers legitimize violence, with sexual violence being the most legitimized by young males (32.5%).

Although data from quantitative research indicates mutuality and reciprocity in dating violence, showing that girls and boys suffer from and perpetrate abusive behaviour, qualitative studies indicate gender asymmetries (Neves 2014; Molidor and Tolman 1998; Tjaden and Thoennes 2000). In fact, although in terms of prevalence girls seemed to be as aggressive as boys in intimate relationships, the former are still more susceptible to suffering from violence than the latter (WHO 2016) and are also more likely to experience greater injury, fear and psychological consequences (Dardis et al. 2014). Moreover, boys use strategies of intimidation or coercion to perform sexual acts much more than girls (Hickman et al. 2004). On the other hand, some data demonstrates that girls are more likely than boys to use physical aggression for self-defence purposes (Foshee 1996), rarely initiating violent acts (DeKeseredy and Schwartz 1998). While girls generally indicate self-defence as a motivating factor in committing violence against their partners, boys commonly mention the need to exert control over girls (O'Keefe 1997).

Considering the scarcity of qualitative studies aimed at understanding heterosexual dating violence in the light of a gender framework, and bearing in mind the need to capture the social meanings of violence perpetrated and suffered by girls, a critical approach will be developed in this chapter discussing how gender (re)constructs and (re)defines female practices and narratives.

2 Heterosexual Dating Violence: A Qualitative Study

Using focus groups, a method that uncovers aspects of understanding that often remain hidden in more conventional in-depth interviews (Liamputtong 2011), we questioned 107 young Portuguese girls, aged between 11 and 17 years old (M = 13.38) about youth social relations and dating violence.

In order to organize the focus groups, the following inclusion criteria were established: (a) being a girl, (b) being younger than 18 years, (c) not having serious psychological problems, (d) not having cognitive problems and (e) speaking and understanding Portuguese.

Thirteen focus groups, 12 composed of 8 members and one of 11 members, were conducted. Forty girls were attending 7th grade, 43 were attending 8th grade and 24 were attending 9th grade. Twenty-four participants were involved in intimate relationships at the time of the data collection and the average age of their male partners was 14.5 years old.

Two secondary schools in the Oporto district participated in the study and all the ethical procedures were assured, including informed consent. The focus groups took place in schools and were led by two junior researchers, one with an academic background in psychology and the other with an academic background in criminology. The focus groups had an average duration of one hour and the audio was recorded.

The interview script comprised five questions:

1. In general, how do you describe social relationships among young people?
2. How do you characterize intimate relationships among young people?
3. If dating violence is present, how would you describe it?
4. From your point of view, who perpetrates and who suffers most from dating violence at your age?
5. In your opinion, what motivates dating violence?

The interviews were fully transcribed and were then subject to a thematic analysis (Braun and Carkle 2006), a technique used with the aim of identifying themes and patterns, and their relationship with different epistemological and ontological positions. When conducted within a constructionist framework, which is the case here, thematic analysis "(…) seeks to theorise the socio-cultural contexts, and structural conditions that enable the individual accounts that are provided" (Braun and Carkle 2006, p. 14). In order to guarantee validity, codification was used by the two junior researchers who collected the data and by a senior researcher who supervised the study. Consensus among the researchers regarding the core themes was achieved. In the next section, the results will be presented and discussed.

2.1 Youth Social Relationships Reconfiguration: From Stability to Fugacity

Social relationships among young people have been characterized by Portuguese girls in descriptions of romantic or sexual interactions with the opposite sex, suggesting that they play a central role in teens' lives. Behaviour to initiate youth relationships is marked by the use of technology, with Facebook and/or Twitter being the most popular social network sites among the participants.

Not only do those relational strategies allow romantic or sexual interaction to begin, they facilitate the first approaches between potential partners, as they are mechanisms that are allegedly popular among young male and female audiences. As documented in previous research, there seems to be an association between the use of social networking sites and increased levels of young people's social capital (e.g., Ellison et al. 2014).

Portuguese children and young people are digital natives, using digital technologies from the age of 10 to achieve self-satisfaction and social interaction, to search for information and entertainment, incorporating media as spaces where autonomy is tested and intimate relationships are maintained (Almeida et al. 2013; Cardoso et al. 2009). A recent study conducted in Portugal revealed that among the children surveyed aged between three and eight years old, all watched television, half had played video games and 38% used the internet (Ponte et al. 2017).

When describing youth relationships, girls pointed out several gender differences. They see themselves as much more romantic than boys, bonding romantic interactions to emotional needs. In contrast, boys are described as seeking dating for sexual purposes, preferring not to establish long-term relationships.

From their point of view, youth partner relationships can be characterized in terms of two distinct categories: dating and sleeping together. The former—dating relationships—are described as being less frequent but more stable and durable. They are often preceded by a friendship that grows deeper over time. They are emotionally supported relationships, founded on trust and sharing. On the other hand, sleeping-together relationships represent non-affective interactions between partners, which are focused on satisfying sexual desire, although not necessarily through sexual intercourse. They are more common, fleeting and fortuitous and involve, in a large number of cases, constant changes in partners, especially by boys.

Although both boys and girls exhibit these kinds of interactions, girls consider them to be typical of boys. Still, their social connotations are different according to gender, and it is more acceptable for boys than girls to get involved in sleeping-together relationships. While boys who have multiple female partners are seen as popular and virile—the "players"—girls are labelled as promiscuous and easy, usually nicknamed "sheilas". So "players" are admired and valued, whereas "sheilas" are disparaged and devalued, suggesting that gender norms assign asymmetrical levels of acceptance regarding sexual conduct to girls and boys. Previous national studies have confirmed the tendency to stigmatize girls when they have sexual behaviour that does not conform with their traditional gender roles, elevating the hegemonic masculinity of the boys (Vieira 2012).

2.2 Practices and Social Meanings of Dating Violence: Reframing Gender Specificities

The Portuguese girls interviewed recognized the existence of intimate partner violence among young people. They understood dating violence as abusive and/or inappropriate behaviours that affect both sexes and cause harm in several areas of daily life, for example, at school.

In the girls' opinion, girls and boys suffer from and perpetrate all forms of violence, except sexual violence, which is almost exclusively perpetrated by males, as demonstrated in other national and international studies (e.g., Hines and Saudino 2003; Neves et al. 2016a). So, sexual harassment, sexting and exposure to pornography and violence during sexual intercourse are types of abuse perpetrated by boys, who frequently use digital strategies to threaten and intimidate victims. As demonstrated in a recent study by Zweig et al. (2015), just over a quarter of young people mention having been the victim of some form of cyber-dating abuse in a current or recent relationship, with females reporting more cyber-dating abuse than males, and particularly sexual cyber dating abuse.

Girls admit to using psychological violence more than boys, mainly justified by jealousy. When psychological violence is perpetrated by boys against girls, they usually use it to belittle their physical appearance. Insults like "you're fat" are common and are described as deeply affecting girls' self-esteem. In response to psychological abuse and to termination of relationships by partners, some girls mention self-harm, something which is reported in other studies (e.g., Motz 2008).

Physical violence is primarily characterized by slaps and pushes, and social violence by control, threats, restriction behaviours, prohibition and even invasion of privacy. Once again, digital social networks are often used to perpetrate social violence regardless of the perpetrator's gender.

Although girls are aware of the extent and complexity of dating violence, in some situations the same behaviours they interpret as abusive are considered inoffensive. In fact, occasionally, control is confused with proof of love and sexual violence with sexual stimulation, indicating that abuse is not always recognized as such. Some of them picture sexual intercourse as being naturally violent, naturalizing abusive behaviours and not realizing the risks they incur.

When asked about the causes of dating violence, girls pointed out a range of explanations that range from individual to cultural factors. Their own conduct emerged as one of the reasons boys are sexually violent towards girls, which means girls are guilty for being victims. They advocate that the way girls behave, expressed through clothes they wear or the attitudes they have, explains their propensity to victimization. Thus, boys are reactive to female sexual stimuli evoked by a certain provocative style (intentional or otherwise), which is an explanation that recovers the classical theories of victimology focused on blaming the victims (Neves and Fávero 2010).

Male *nature* is frequently mentioned to explain violence against girls, especially physical and sexual violence. Boys need to satisfy sexual impulses and prove their masculinity for biological and social reasons. To do so, they tend to be more aggressive than girls, seeking domination and power. As is widely documented in the literature, ideas and values related to gender influence how women and men view themselves as women and men and their social and intimate relationships (e.g., Jewkes et al. 2015).

Group influence is also seen as a cause of dating violence. Girls say that violent behaviours can be a strategy to achieve social prestige and recognition in peer groups. International findings attest that adolescents who typically have friends who use dating violence, and girls who are typically high in social status, run a higher risk of using dating violence throughout adolescence (Foshee et al. 2013).

To be exposed to family violence is a risk factor for being a dating abuser. Participants argued that boys who have been exposed to a history of abuse within their families, especially violence between their parents, are more likely to commit abuse against their partners. Previous studies show a link between witnessing inter-parental violence, attitudes about dating violence and teen-dating violence victimization (Karlsson et al. 2016). In fact, people with a history of exposure to interparental violence, particularly in early childhood, are significantly more likely to be both perpetrators and victims of dating violence in early adulthood (Narayan et al. 2013).

During the interviews, violence between parents was mentioned by some girls, which shows that this is a problem that affects adults as well as young people.

Concerning cultural explanations, the girls mentioned that Portuguese social organization is asymmetrical in terms of gender power distribution and that gender inequality is a reality. In intimate relationships, violence is an expression of a patriarchal society that reinforces male privileges.

As women have achieved formal and legal rights, including equality rights, girls who participated in this study believe they are legitimate in using violence to defend themselves from violence. So the use of violence against boys is considered both a right and a means of self-defence.

3   Problematizing Girls' Voices

Taking into consideration the girls' interviews, intimacy plays an important role in youth social relationships. Their discourse shows that a reconfiguration of intimate relationships is currently underway that involves a transition in relationship models from stability to instability, that is, a paradigm change regarding how romantic/sexual interactions are conceived and put into practice. The current study addresses the need to clarify the impact of this new romantic order on violent practices among teens, since dating violence constitutes a serious problem among young people.

According to participants—and evidenced by several studies (e.g., Caridade 2011; Magalhães et al. 2016; Straus 2008)—dating violence is mutual and reciprocal but gender specific. Not denying that they are abusers too, the girls point out specific reasons and dynamics that characterize violence they suffered and perpetrated, defending the use of physical violence as a way for girls to establish gender equality and ensure self-defence (e.g., Currie 1998; DeKeseredy and Schwartz 1998). The girls suggest that they are, generally speaking, less tolerant of the most serious physical violence perpetrated by boys, believing it to be their right—by equivalence—to use violence against them in similar circumstances. This shows that the young women appropriate a distorted idea of gender equality and, moreover, take an unsuitable and abusive view of the rights acquired through equality between the sexes. The right to use violence as a strategy for affirming equality suggests a perspective of false empowerment that ultimately places them not only at greater risk of becoming victims but also of perpetrating violence. So, the assessment of women's power, that is, their own power, by way of using the right to violence, calls into question one of the most emblematic principles of the peaceful feminist struggle, namely, a commitment to the democratic values of freedom and non-violence (Conover and Sapiro 1993). Naturalizing violence as a response to being a victim, that is, legitimating the right to be physically violent, may be an answer to the question of why the girls are aggressive in their intimate relationships today.

When invited to describe intimate relationships among young people, the girls distinguish between two different types with two distinctive focuses. A less common type usually known as dating and a more frequent type called sleeping together. Although both sexes tend to become involved in sleeping-together relationships, pursuing an eminently sexual goal, boys are more active than girls concerning sexual practices without emotional attachment. When girls have sleeping-together relationships, their conduct is labelled as promiscuous.

As Cristina Pereira Vieira pointed out (2012), it's not socially expected for girls to take a leadership position in intimate or sexual relationships. When they do so, their legitimacy and morality is questioned. Indeed, despite the sexual revolution, "(...) the possibility that girls might be interested in sexuality in their own right rather than as boys' objects of desire is met with resistance and discomfort" (Tolman 2005, p. 6). "Sheila" is the term used to emphasize the depraved condition of girls who do not meet the gender expectations of being "good girls". In the girls' opinion, "sheilas" are the type of girls every man wants to sleep with and no one wants to date, deserving the consequences their behaviour elicits, including violence.

Contrasting this sexual freedom apparently acquired by girls is the idea that girls are sexual victimized by boys due to their own conduct. Thus, the guilt associated with enjoying sexuality outside the context of a stable relationship seems to remain in the girls' thoughts. Moreover, male sexual conduct is valued, legitimized and associated with *natural* circumstances, making the perpetrators less responsible for their abusive acts. Boys seem to be allowed to experience sexuality without remorse and guilt.

This study therefore reveals the girls' self-blame connected to a very specific type of victimhood: sexual victimhood. While on the one hand, it can be seen that the girls are less tolerant towards suffered physical violence, with they themselves reacting with violence, when it is sexual violence that is suffered, they tend to take their own behaviour as the cause of their becoming victims. Their discourse therefore includes an attitude of self-blame alongside an attitude justifying their own violence and it alternates depending on the type of violence in question. The girls appear to feel legitimate in using physical violence but not sexual violence. Moreover, they seem to take responsibility for sexual violence away from the boys who perpetrate it, using the argument that they are unable to resist the impulses of nature. If we combine this justification with the reasoning that the crime is precipitated by the victim, we find a situation corresponding to the scientific perspective of blaming the victims (Neves and Fávero 2010), which is also spread by the media (e.g., Neves et al. 2016b).

Girls tend to attribute male-on-female dating violence to a mix of individual, situational and cultural factors, although with an emphasis on the first set of factors, while they attribute female-on-male dating violence almost exclusively to cultural factors, admitting to having learned to be violent in response to gender inequality. Indeed, previous findings on victims' explanations for their partners' intimate partner violence perpetration confirms a tendency towards individual explanations (e.g., Neal and Edwards 2015).

The occasional physical violence undergone by the girls is generally relativized and forgiven, while in some cases it is considered inoffensive (non-violence). There are other cases where physical violence, together with sexual violence, is considered *good violence*, in that, in their opinion, it stimulates the sexual relationship with their partner. Other studies indicate that the sexual violence disseminated by literature or the media (e.g., cinema, television) may have adverse effects in terms of normalizing the use of violence in intimate relationships, especially by younger people (Brown et al. 2006). The media impact arising from the publication of some books and the screening of some films in Portuguese cinemas may help explain such effects, since they propagate a discourse of *fetishization* of violence. One illustrative example is *Fifty Shades of Grey*, the plot of which develops around the idea of a supposedly transgressive sexuality as the traditional cornerstone of relationships (Enguix and Núñez 2015). Its impact was enormous in Portuguese society at the time when the data for this study was collected.

The negative implications of violence suffered that particularly affect health should also be noted in the young women's discourse. Self-harm arises frequently, which proves the marked suffering emerging from these types of abusive experiences. The impact of violence on young people's relationships in terms of mental health has been reported in several studies (e.g., Burton et al. 2013) and is another feature that justifies an investment in prevention and intervention.

4   Conclusions

This study provides important insights into Portuguese youth's social relationships and their social meanings. Furthermore, it enables a gender analysis focused on juvenile intimate interactions and, particularly, on dating violence practices and narratives.

Based on the girls' narratives, it was possible to conclude that juvenile intimate relationships are undergoing a reconfiguration process which invites us to rethink the theoretical concepts we have used to produce research in the field, such as the concept of intimacy and dating. In fact, relationships among young people are today less stable and long-lasting than in the past, and they contain a prominently sexualized component, without an affective bond, which opens the path to new possibilities and risks, especially for girls. These possibilities are not, however, free from restraints, because girls live with blame. The dilemma between adhering to the gender roles that are assigned to them socially and experiencing free sexuality often places them in the firing line for social disapproval. So girls who are involved in sleeping-together relationships are stigmatized and criticized, while the boys that do the same are instead valued and approved. The moral denigration of girls' sexual conduct is itself a risk factor, since it appears to pave the way for abusive sexual advances by boys (Esqueda and Harrison 2005). This evidence reflects the effects of socialization marked by the gender order (Connell and Pearse 2015), which is restrictive about which spaces boys and girls can occupy.

Social relationships, including those between partners, are also marked by the influence of digital networks. Initial approaches are often made over social networks, and they play an important role in how young people express their needs and interests.

It is clear in this study that, from the point of view of both the types of acts and the dynamics and motivations involved, there are differences according to sex regarding those who perpetrate and those who suffer from dating violence. While it is true that the participants recognize that violence in youth relationships is perpetrated by both sexes, it is less true that they agree with the idea of symmetry. Although physical, psychological and social violence is carried out by both boys and girls, the frequency, intensity and seriousness and contextual background of such forms of violence differs. According to the girls, they carry out more psychological violence than boys and, when they do perpetrate physical violence, it aims to respond to violence that has been previously experienced. Therefore, the physical violence perpetrated against boys is normally reactive and occasional and is understood as a self-defence strategy.

Sexual violence is mentioned as being an almost exclusively male conduct, arising from the boys' requirement to satisfy their biological needs and the unsuitability of female behaviour. This behaviour, when it is sexually promiscuous or provocative, is indicated as the principal reason for victimization. A legitimization of sexual violence can therefore be observed, which contrasts with the delegitimization of the physical violence perpetrated. Physical violence, when it is more serious, is even asserted with a justification for appropriation of women's right to use violence, which invites a reflection on what message is being transmitted and assimilated by younger generations regarding gender equality. Admitting that gender asymmetries persist, young women understand the use of physical violence against boys as being justifiable. The normalization of violence for different reasons not only makes it tolerable but also makes it acceptable, meaning that in certain situations it is hard to distinguish between what is and what is not violence.

The idea that sexual violence is normative in sexual relations, working as an enhancer of pleasure, is no less significant. In some situations, the media narratives on this connection may cover up cases of severe violence, so it is necessary to involve the media in their deconstruction.

It is therefore urgent to make early prevention of youth violence a goal, as is integrating it into the realm of public health. The consequences of violence appear to compromise young people's health in a very real way, so it is fundamental for the problem to be managed from a health standpoint, too. Examples of the negative effects of violence include self-harm by girls, which may, at an extreme level, cause them to die.

This study, while it cannot be generalized to the entire population of Portuguese young people, offers very important clues about putting in place an empirically validated action plan. As a result, we understand that more qualitative studies that also involve boys should be developed with the aim of achieving a more in-depth understanding of the representations and practices that young people display in terms of romantic relationships and violence in intimate relationships.

References

Aboim, S. (2010). Género, Família e Mudança em Portugal. In S. Aboim & K. Wall (Eds.), *A Vida Familiar no Masculino: Novos Papéis, Novas Identidades* (pp. 39–66). Lisbon: CITE.

Almeida, A. N., Alves, N. A., Delicado, A., & Carvalho, T. (2013). Crianças e internet: a ordem geracional revisitada. *Análise Social, XLVIII*(2), 340–365.

Azambuja, M., Nogueira, C., Neves, S., & Oliveira, J. (2013). Gender Violence in Portugal: discourses, knowledges and practices. *Indian Journal of Gender Studies, 20*, 31–50. https://doi.org/10.1177/0971521512465935

Braun, V., & Clarke, V. (2006). Using thematic analysis in psychology. *Qualitative Research in Psychology, 3*(2), 77–101.

Brown, J. D., L'Engle, K. L., Pardun, C. J., Guo, G., Kenneavy, K., & Jackson, C. (2006). Sexy media matter: Exposure to sexual content in music, movies, television, and magazines predicts black and white adolescents' sexual behavior. *Pediatrics, 117*(4), 1018–1027.

Burton, C. W., Halpern-Felsher, B., Rehm, R. S., Rankin, S., & Humphreys, J. C. (2013). "It was pretty scary": The theme of fear in young adult women's descriptions of a history of adolescent dating abuse. *Issues of Mental Health Nursing, 34*(11), 803–813.

Cardoso, A., Espanha, N., Lapa, A., & Araújo, T. (2009). *E-Generation 2008: Os Usos de Media pelas Crianças e Jovens em Portugal. Relatório Final de Apuramentos Estatísticos.* Lisbon: OBERCOM.

Caridade, S. (2011). *Vivências violentas. Uma abordagem científica.* Coimbra: Almedina.

Connell, R., & Pearse, R. (2015). *Gender: In world perspective* (3rd ed.). Cambridge: Polity Press.

Conover, P. J., & Sapiro, V. (1993). Gender, feminist consciousness, and war. *American Journal of Political Science, 37*(4), 1079–1099.

Currie, D. H. (1998). Violent men or violent women? Whose definition counts? In R. K. Bergen (Ed.), *Issues in intimate violence* (pp. 97–111). Thousand Oaks: Sage.

Dardis, C., Dixon, K., Edwards, K., & Turchik, J. (2014). An examination of the factors related to dating violence perpetration among young men and women and associated theoretical explanations: A review of the literature. *Trauma, Violence, & Abuse, 16,* 136–152.

DeKeseredy, W. S., & Schwartz, M. D. (1998). *Woman abuse on campus: Results from the Canadian National Survey.* Thousand Oaks: Sage.

Ellison, N. B., Vitak, J., Gray, R., & Lampe, C. (2014). Cultivating social resources on social network sites: Facebook relationship maintenance behaviors and their role in social capital processes. *Journal of Computer-Mediated Communication, 19,* 855–870.

Enguix, B., & Núñez, F. (2015). Género, sexualidad y posfeminismo en 50 sombras de Grey. *Revista de Antropología Iberoamericana, 10*(1), 49–74.

Esqueda, C. W., & Harrison, L. A. (2005). The influence of gender role stereotypes, the woman's race, and level of provocation and resistance on domestic violence culpability attributions. *Sex Roles, 53*(11–12), 821–834.

Foshee, V. (1996). Gender differences in adolescent dating abuse prevalence, types and injuries. *Health Education Research, 11,* 275–286.

Foshee, V. A., et al. (2013). The peer context and the development of the perpetration of adolescent dating violence. *Journal of Youth and Adolescence, 42*(4), 1–22.

FRA. (2014). *Violence against women: An EU-wide survey.* Vienna: FRA.

Hickman, L. J., Jaycox, L. H., & Aronoff, J. (2004). Dating violence among adolescents: Prevalence, gender distribution, and prevention program effectiveness. *Trauma, Violence, & Abuse, 5,* 123–142.

Hines, D. A., & Saudino, K. (2003). Gender differences in psychological, physical, and sexual aggression among college students using the revised conflict tactics scales. *Violence & Victims, 18,* 197–217.

Internal security system—SSI. (2017). *2016 annual internal security report.* Lisbon: SSI.

Jewkes, R. K., Flood, M. G., & Lang, J. (2015). From work with men and boys to changes of social norms and reduction of inequities in gender relations: A conceptual shift in prevention of violence against women and girls. *The Lancet, 385*(9977), 1580–1589.

Karlsson, M., Temple, J., Weston, R., & Le, V. (2016). Witnessing interparental violence and acceptance of dating violence as predictors for teen dating violence victimization. *Violence Against Women, 22*(5), 625–646.

Liamputtong, P. (2011). *Focus group methodology: Principle and practice.* Thousand Oaks: Sage.

Machado, C., Matos, M., & Moreira, A. I. (2003). Violência nas relações amorosas: Comportamentos e atitudes na população universitária. *Psychologica, 33,* 69–83.

Machado, C., Caridade, S., & Martins, C. (2010). Violence in juvenile dating relationships self-reported prevalence and attitudes in a Portuguese sample. *Journal of Family Violence, 25,* 43–52.

Machado, C., Martins, C., & Caridade, S. (2014). Violence in intimate relationships: A comparison between married and dating couples. *Journal of Criminology, 2014,* 1–9.

Magalhães, M. J. M., Pontedeira, C., Guerreiro, A., & Ribeiro, P. (2016). *Cenas. Igualdade. Programa de Prevenção da Violência e Delinquência Juvenil.* Lisbon: UMAR.

Matos, M., Machado, C., Caridade, S., & Silva, M. J. (2006). Prevenção da violência nas relações de namoro: Intervenção com jovens em contexto escolar. *Psicologia: Teoria e Prática, 8*(1), 55–75.

Molidor, C., & Tolman, R. (1998). Gender and contextual factors in adolescent dating violence. *Violence Against Women, 4*(2), 180–194.

Motz, A. (2008). *The Psychology of female violence: Crimes against the body* (2nd ed.). New York: Routledge.

Narayan, A., Englund, M., & Egeland, B. (2013). Developmental timing and continuity of exposure to interparental violence and externalizing behavior as prospective predictors of dating violence. *Development and Psychopathology, 25*(401), 973–990.

Neal, A., & Edwards, K. (2015). Perpetrators' and victims' attributions for IPV: A critical review of the literature. *Trauma, Violence, & Abuse, 18*(3), 239–267.

Neves, S. (2014). De vítimas a agressoras: A (aparente) dupla posição das raparigas na violência no namoro heterossexual. In V. Duarte & M. I. Cunha (Coord.), *Violências e Delinquências juvenis femininas: género e (in)visibilidades sociais* (pp. 63–76). Famalicão: Editora Húmus.

Neves, S., & Fávero, M. (2010). A Vitimologia e os seus percursos históricos, teóricos e epistemológicos. In S. Neves & M. Fávero (Coord.), *Vitimologia: Ciência e Activismo* (pp. 13–48). Coimbra: Almedina.

Neves, S., & Nogueira, C. (2010). Deconstructing gendered discourses of love, power and violence in intimate relationships. In D. C. Jack & A. Ali (Eds.), *Silencing the self across cultures depression and gender in the social world* (pp. 241–261). Oxford: Oxford University Press.

Neves, S., Cameira, M., Machado, M., Duarte, V., & Machado, F. (2016a). Beliefs on marital violence and self-reported dating violence: A comparative study of Cape Verdean and Portuguese adolescents. *Journal of Child and Adolescent Trauma.* Retrieved from https://link.springer.com/article/10.1007/s40653-016-0099-7

Neves, S., Gomes, S., & Martins, D. (2016b). Narrativas mediáticas sobre o femicídio na intimidade: Análise de um jornal popular português. *Ex-Aequo: Revista da Associação Portuguesa de Estudos sobre as Mulheres, 34*, 77–92. https://doi.org/10.22355/exaequo.2016.34.06

O'Keefe, M. (1997). Predictors of dating violence among high school students. *Journal of Interpersonal Violence, 12*, 546–568.

Paiva, C., & Figueiredo, B. (2004). Abuso no relacionamento íntimo: Estudo de prevalência em jovens adultos portugueses. *Psychologica, 36*, 75–107.

Pereira Vieira, C. (2012). *"Eu faço sexo amoroso". A sexualidade dos jovens pela voz dos próprios.* Lisbon: Editorial Bizâncio.

Perista, H., Cardoso, A., Silva, M., & Carrilho, P. (2012). *Delinquência e violência juvenil em Portugal. Traçando um retrato a diferentes vozes.* Lisbon: Centro de Estudos para a Intervenção Social. Retrieved from http://www.youprev.eu/pdf/YouPrev_NationalReport_PT.pdf

Ponte, C., Simões, J., Baptista, S., Jorge, A., & Castro, T. (2017). *Crescendo entre ecrãs: Usos de meios eletrónicos por crianças (3–8 Anos).* Lisbon: ERC.

Robinson, H. (2015). The changing role of women in Portugal. *Perspectives on Business and Economics, 33*(6), 49–60.

Saavedra, R. (2011). *Prevenir antes de remediar: prevenção da violência nos relacionamentos íntimos juvenis.* PhD thesis, Universidade do Minho, Braga.

SSI—Sistema de Segurança Interna. (2016). *Relatório Anual de Segurança Interna 2016*. Lisboa: Sistema de Segurança Interna. Retrieved from http://www.ansr.pt/InstrumentosDeGestao/Documents/Relat%C3%B3rio%20Anual%20de%20Seguran%C3%A7a%20Interna%20(RASI)/RASI%202016.pdf

Straus, M. A. (2008). Dominance and symmetry in partner violence by male and female university students in 32 nations. *Children and Youth Services Review, 30*, 252–275.

Teten, A., Ball, B., Valle, L., Noonan, R., & Rosenbluth, B. (2009). Considerations for the definition, measurement, consequences, and prevention of dating violence victimization among adolescent girls. *Journal of Women's Health, 18*(7), 923–927.

Tjaden, P., & Thoennes, N. (2000). Prevalence and consequences of male-to-femaleandfemale-to-maleintimatepartnerviolenceasmeasured by the National Violence Against Women Survey. *Violence Against Women, 6*, 142–161.

Tolman, D. (2005). *Dilemmas of desire: Teenage girls talk about sexuality*. Cambridge, MA: Harvard University Press.

White, J., Merrill, L., & Koss, M. (2001). Predictors of premilitary courtship violence in a navy recruit sample. *Journal of Interpersonal Violence, 16*(9), 910–927.

WHO. (2016). *Global plan of action to strengthen the role of the health system within a national multisectoral response to address interpersonal violence, in particular against women and girls, and against children*. Geneva: WHO.

Zweig, J., Dank, M., Yahner, J., & Lachman, P. (2015). The rate of cyber dating abuse among teens and how it relates to other forms of teen dating violence. *Journal of Youth and Adolescence, 42*(7), 1063–1077.

8

Constructing Meaning About the Delinquency of Young Girls in Public-Housing Neighbourhoods

Maria João Leote de Carvalho

1 Girls' Delinquency in Disadvantaged Neighbourhoods

Young girls' delinquency is a growing topic of public debate in contemporary societies, and its study is important in the analysis of social change in a given context and time. Early anti-social behaviour is one of the best predictors of future anti-social behaviour; children under 13 years of age who are involved in delinquency have an increased risk of recidivism, and are two to three times more likely to become violent and chronic offenders (Loeber and Farrington 2001; Loeber et al. 2008). Evidence shows that there tends to be a period of seven years of warning before a juvenile becomes a violent and serious offender, which means more special attention should be given to child offending (Augimeri et al. 2011).

Social concern about the relationship between gender and delinquency is neither new nor exclusive to the present. It has been proved that the prevalence of offending in Western societies tends to increase from late

---

M. J. Leote de Carvalho (✉)
CICS.NOVA FCSH Universidade Nova de Lisboa, Lisbon, Portugal

© The Author(s) 2018
S. Gomes, V. Duarte (eds.), *Female Crime and Delinquency in Portugal*,
https://doi.org/10.1007/978-3-319-73534-4_8

143

childhood, peak in the teenage years (15–19 years) and decline afterwards in the early 20s (Piquero et al. 2012; Blokland and Palmen 2012). Girls tend to peak earlier (Wong et al. 2010) and to desist being delinquent more quickly than boys. They are also less likely to victimize strangers, to become involved in physical aggression or to carry or use weapons (Steffensmeier and Haynie 2006). The age–crime curve is higher and wider for males (particularly minorities) growing up in disadvantaged neighbourhoods (Fabio et al. 2011).

The female juvenile offences highlighted by the media and the constant dramatization and politicization of delinquency in Western societies tend to suggest we are now living in a unique social setting, where girls have become more violent than ever. It is a fact that in many countries, such as Portugal, there is increased justice system involvement among girls, mainly those from disadvantaged neighbourhoods (Duarte and Carvalho 2017).

Girls' delinquency is seen in this context as an expression of a social problem associated with a range of factors and circumstances brought into play in a specific environment. This stems from the Chicago School's traditional combination of sociological views with the most recent perspectives on social ecology and childhood studies. The physical and social environment which influences, and simultaneously suffers the effects of the action and social control exercised by individuals (Elliot et al. 1996; Morenoff et al. 2001; Kingston et al. 2009), is that to which girls, as social actors, ascribe a particular meaning by appropriating, integrating, (re)constructing and (re)producing it in their lives (Corsaro 1997; Schneider 2016).

Sampson and Groves (1989) suggested that the structural factors of certain residential areas—low socioeconomic status, residential mobility, ethnic heterogeneity and family breakdown—tend to be the external sources of social disorganization that lead to the weakening and collapse of institutions and social networks. The residents' low level of agency, and the dilution of informal social controls in a neighbourhood could emerge and reinforce the lack of regulation, causing an increase in disorder, violence and crime. Thus, delinquency arises as a result of the social learning process (Akers 1998) associated with the existence of opportunities that facilitate the practice of delinquent acts. Among these opportunities, special attention should be given to the prevalence of certain patterns of social networks in certain areas (Cloward and Ohlin 1970; Kingston et al. 2009; Sampson 2012).

For decades, girls were absent from the focus of neighbourhood studies; only recently has the role of neighbourhood variables in determining gender differences in violence and delinquency become more visible, but the available research has pointed out mixed effects (Kling et al. 2005; Goodkind et al. 2009; Zahn and Browne 2009; Zimmerman and Messner 2010; Haynie et al. 2014; Lei et al. 2014; Duarte and Carvalho 2017). In spite of the methodological differences that could explain the discrepancy of results in this field (Fagan and Wrigth 2012), there is strong evidence demonstrating differences between girls who are exposed and those who are not exposed to structural disadvantage and violence where they live (Augimeri et al. 2011).

The neighbourhood effects have an impact on gender socialization and children's delinquency in complex ways (Kling et al. 2005; Lei et al. 2014). Socially disadvantaged children tend to display higher levels of mobility in public spaces and more autonomous activity with little or no parental supervision (Schneider 2016). Boys are more frequently associated with offending behaviour in disadvantaged neighbourhoods than girls. Nevertheless, strong gender similarities in the links between structural disadvantage and arrest rates were proved by authors in the United States and Canada, who suggested exposure to criminogenic neighbourhoods and witnessing or experiencing violence affect both male and female delinquency (Steffensmeier and Haynie 2000; Jacob 2006; Mrug and Windle 2009). In contrast, Fagan and Wright (2012) showed that neighbourhood variables, such as collective efficacy and disadvantage, may have more impact on girls' delinquency than on male offending.

Recent studies focusing on the gender gap found that differences between boys and girls who commit violence are less pronounced in gender-equal neighbourhoods compared to those characterized by gender inequality. Gender- equality levels in a specific context may explain why boys and girls are affected in different ways by neighbourhood effects (Zimmerman and Messner 2010; Lei et al. 2014).

Based on the perspective of traditional gender roles, girls are less exposed to street influences than boys because families place more restrictions and control on their actions (Giordano 1978; Chesney-Lind 1997; Fagan et al. 2007; Zahn 2009). Girls tend to spend more time at home, while boys are allowed more freedom outside; this results in boys' being more exposed to neighbourhood social and structural factors (Fagan and Wrigth 2012). However, when exposed to community violence or abuse and maltreatment at home, girls are more affected than boys (Augimeri et al. 2011). As a result, girls are mainly regarded as in need of more protection and supervision than boys, and their behaviour is more likely to be regulated by the family.

Gender differences are also expressed in peer influence on delinquency (Moffitt et al. 2001; Piquero et al. 2005), mainly on violent offending, as females are more likely to be influenced by peer involvement in such practices than males. Girls tend to select friends according to their behaviour, and to have more intimate friendship ties with other girls than boys have with their peers (Zimmerman and Messner 2010; Haynie et al. 2014).

2   The Research

This paper is based on a larger Ph.D. research project in sociology concerning childhood, violence and delinquency in Portugal (Carvalho 2010).[1] Rooted in social ecology approaches and in childhood studies that recognize children as social actors, this study aimed to achieve a better understanding of children's socialization processes in multi-problematic spaces, particularly concerning their involvement in delinquency. Between 2005 and 2009, a case study based on ethnographic research and child-centred methods (neighbourhood drawings, semi-structured interviews and community photography) was carried out in six public-housing neighbourhoods in the Lisbon metropolitan area; subjects were chosen because they experienced relatively high levels of social deprivation, violence and crime, although they are located in one of the richest counties in the country, the first to eradicate slums in 2003 by promoting public-housing policies. Five of the subjects form a homogeneous continuum in this county territory, and the sixth is less than a half a mile away from the other five.

Participants were 312 schoolchildren aged 6–13 (M = 8.38) attending two primary state schools (1st–4th grade), living in one of the neighbourhoods selected. Exactly half of the participants were girls (n = 156). Most were of African origin from the former Portuguese colonies (62.8 per cent), mainly The Cape Verde Islands, 9.2 per cent were Roma, and 28.0 per cent were Caucasian. Nearly all were from lower SES households, with 86.7 per cent getting financial support from social services at schools.

Given the extent of the study, this text presents only some of the most important results relating to girls' social practices in order to learn from the resident girls, aged 6–12 years old, and the reasoning and meanings assigned by them to their own actions in this context. Based on the analysis of the girls' drawings of these neighbourhoods, interviews (18 girls were interviewed, aged 7–11 years), and field notes, we discuss the features of girls' socialization in the field and examine their perspectives on offending behaviours.

All procedures performed in this study were in accordance with the ethical standards of the institutional national research legislation. According to Portuguese law, as the participants were under the age of 18, the researcher had to explain the project beforehand to the girls and to their parents or legal guardians who had to give permission. Letters of consent were sent to them in order to obtain permission for the girls' participation, and through informed consent they also expressed their willingness to take part in the research. Informed consent was obtained from all individual participants included in the study. For ethical reasons, to protect participants and guarantee their privacy and anonymity, the girls' names are replaced by alphanumeric codes in this paper. Though translated from Portuguese, the original language and expressions have been retained as far as possible.

As the exploratory qualitative research study focused on a specific context at a particular time, the findings presented in this text cannot be generalized to other urban settings.

3 The Gendered Social Learning of Delinquency

One of the first issues is to analyse and focus on the way in which the girls perceive the position of 'being a child' in the context under study, according to gender.

> I think… and I do not think that being a child in this neighbourhood is different from other places. I think it's good because now and then you get along with other people and learn good things. But other times I think it is not good being a child here because I see the boys smoking, doing crap and they try to steal and then they will stay like the others. I think the girls are less naughty [laughs], the boys like to go out at night and do other crap. Girls… only a few do the same, we are more timid. (…) But some girls are rude and also go in the same way of the boys … I'm not saying that the boys are naughty, not all, right? But some are bad, they are very bad. (Girl01, 9 years old) (Carvalho 2010, p. 312)

Within a gender typing culture, children's socialization results in different gender roles and behaviours sustained in gender-based beliefs, as expressed by this girl in what she considers to be acceptable for each gender. Traditional gender stereotypes are present at an early age among girls, determining their preferences, a trend also visible in their delinquent practices.

In this study, the interviewed girls were mostly involved in offences against property, primarily shoplifting in commercial spaces for the most part located near their neighbourhoods. This is a delinquency of acquisition, in which girls want to obtain consumer goods, mainly those associated with fashion and women's lifestyles.

> – No, I didn't choose, I only chose one thing. (…) I chose the coat, she [Gir27, 11 years-old] gave me some T-shirts and trousers, and we went to put them on in the changing rooms. (Girl36, 11 years old)
> – Then I took a sweater, just one sweater. I put on two sweaters and a pair of trousers. Girl [27] told us to put on some shoes, but if they didn't fit, I didn't put them on. (Girl37, 8 years old)

- Me neither, it was a red coat with a brand name, like this, short. And she [27] chose a [brand name] track suit (Girl35, 9 years-old)
- And your sister [8 years-old], did she get something too?
- Yes, socks (…) she didn't have them on her feet, but she put them in her bag, and she had two pairs of trousers, one pair [brand name] and another pair, three sweaters, a top, a sweater, and her own sweater (Girl36).
- And how were they caught?
- They said that she [27] took something out of the trousers to turn off the alarm and put it in the rubbish bin. The police let her go into the toilet to take them off. Then I saw [27] and [35] with a policewoman. After, the police told us to take the clothes off. We took them off and the police said we had to go to the police station. (Girl36). (Carvalho 2010, p. 394)

This gender-biased trend in stealing goods was pandemic with girls, often acting with peers of a similar age, in pairs or in small groups, stealing clothes, accessories (earrings, chains, bracelets, assorted decorative accessories and handbags) or school materials. The current status and organization of families, schools and of the media (particularly new social media) as sources of socialization promote new relationships through the growing development of horizontal socialization processes with peers, in a fragmented puzzle of social and educational references, social bonds and roles in constant flux that replace some of the traditional forms of vertical socialization (Corsaro 1997; Piquero et al. 2005; Zahn 2009).

The willingness to follow other girls is strongly present, and the gendered character of peer influence emerges as an important variable when examining their explanations and understanding of their offending behaviours (Giordano et al. 2002; Miller 2007, Haynie et al. 2014; Duarte and Carvalho 2017). Close interaction between young boys and girls involved in delinquency has not been observed or mentioned by the interviewed girls. It is not surprising in these age groups based on gender, and is a trait common to childhood experiences anywhere in the world. However, very little is known about the phenomenon of young girls' delinquency, as literature mainly focuses on delinquency among older girls. This study intends to contribute to our knowledge of the offending behaviour in younger age groups.

Fig. 8.1 My neighbourhood

Shopping centres and hypermarkets become places of pleasure, representing a kind of large and very attractive playground, which some girls use frequently, often removed from any family supervision. To some extent, this might occur because of the lack of playgrounds in the neighbourhoods, either because they have not been built or because the existing ones have been vandalized by adults and youngsters who have used them for other purposes (Fig. 8.1).

These are the buildings, the cars and the boys playing when there were slides and swings and seesaws. I used to go there to play but now there's nothing because they pulled it all down and I don't know why. (…) A playground is very much needed here so we can have a space where we can go play. We need space to play, we can go to the street and there we have space, but then the balls go into the road and sometimes the cars are driving so fast in street races that someone can be killed (Girl16, 7 years old).

Not having playgrounds was one of the girls' major complaints. Associated with a notion of territoriality, a playground was a collective aspiration in all these neighbourhoods, regarded as a social symbol perceived to be accessible to social groups living in other places. Without specially designed areas for recreational use in their neighbourhoods, children are mainly sent to the street. While giving them the opportunity to explore their physical and social environment fully, the street simultaneously exposes them to a range of other situations that are clearly more unfavourable and potentially generate different risks. Not surprisingly, the commercial areas outside their neighbourhoods should be understood as primary socialization spaces that fulfil some of the girls' most important social and educative needs, providing them with access to opportunities that they would otherwise not have.

Most girl offenders' actions tend to bring their potential for creativity and practical ability to solve problems to the surface, based on a logical plan developed to meet challenges and take greater risks (some real, some imagined). The ineffectiveness of social controls, both informal and formal, turns out to be decisive in how they perceive and anticipate the effects of delinquency. The girls' initial experience of success with their first delinquent act may assume increasing importance, and accumulated successful experiences encourage acceptance that delinquency should continue. Society's investment in them might be perceived as inadequate. This perception does not facilitate the internalization of conventional internal controls, as reflected in the distinction between what they considered a violation of legal norms according to the categories of morality constructed and internalized by these girls themselves.

- I never did it; I've never stole clothes!—[GirlF35, 9 years old,]
- Your mother said all the clothes you have are all stolen! [Girl F36, 11 years old]
- No, but my mother has already stolen … [F35]
- My mother never stole or steals but you and your mother stole clothes [F36]
- I had already 'taken' clothes from the [name of the shop], on Friday we went there too. [F35] (…) I only 'caught' socks. [F35]
- I also only 'brought' socks, she [F27, 11 years old] 'took' more things, she removed all the alarms … then you leave. [F36] (Carvalho 2010, p. 395)

For some girls, delinquency appears to be based on their distorted perception of its severity. The frequent use of terms such as 'catch', 'grab', 'bring' and 'take' was identified as common amongst them and many of the neighbourhoods' adults. This perception was associated with codes of conduct where the disapproval of illegal acts tended to be voiced only when the acts went above a certain level. The predominant view of a petty theft as a trivial experience is expressed by a significant number of the girls. However, this does not mean they do not demonstrate an understanding of good or evil, though this trend becomes more visible only when they also become victims of crime. Nevertheless, such victimization was no impediment or obstacle to continuing with delinquent practices. What is more significant is the dissolving of the clear boundaries between conformity and deviation. This leads to the notorious undervaluation of the importance and consequences of the violation of social norms and rules, a perspective that stems largely from the neighbourhoods' social disorganization.

The girls' passive role also emerges, even against their will or their family's wishes, when they are exposed to a high incidence of disorder and violence from which they cannot escape simply because it happens where they live. When comparing risks in different urban settings, it is clear that children living in socially disadvantaged neighbourhoods are not only more frequently referred to as aggressors, but also more likely to be victims of violence (Elliot et al. 1996; Morenoff et al. 2001) (Fig. 8.2).

This here is a man running over a little boy… On the other side is the youngster who killed the other near my house. He went home to pick up the gun and then came back and killed him… In the building there is a man shooting at his wife. He pushed her away and she fell out of the window. The neighbours called the firemen and there's nothing more… I don't like living here. There are too many sad things and it's very sad to live here. It's like this… (Girl02, 9 years old).

The area where children live clearly influences the choices and opportunities they have at their disposal in daily life (Kingston et al. 2009; Sampson 2012). Not surprisingly, there are girls in this context who use physical violence as a resource for their defence and social inclusion in the area where they live as a result of the 'normalization' of violence to which they are often subjected.

Constructing Meaning About the Delinquency of Young Girls... 153

Fig. 8.2 My neighbourhood

Yeah! All the people go fighting here, there is always someone against me and (…) Bang! There she goes! I give her a punch hard too! (Girl06, 8 years old) (Carvalho 2010, p. 396).

The girls interviewed do not reject conventional values, but violence can emerge as an attractive socialization strategy, varying from what is considered to be play to the need to obtain social recognition nor even to defend themselves from others.

- Teacher, are you missing Valentine's Day? [Girl21, 7 years old,]
- Do you have a boyfriend?—asked the teacher.
- Yes, I have it in T [other public housing neighbourhood] [21]
- How old is he?
- He's eight years old.
- So he's older than you! [Girl05, 7 years old]
- Yeah, but I have the strength to beat him up, I'm not afraid of him! (Carvalho 2010, p. 306)

While exploring the contexts in which the girls emerge as aggressors, the social dynamics which still make many of them victims become even more visible. Domestic violence affects a significant proportion of the neighbourhoods' households, regardless of their composition. Males tend to be identified more often as aggressors toward women and children, but several cases where women were the main aggressors, especially towards their own children, were also mentioned. In other cases, females seem to react more against males.

> My father hit my mother, and then my mother tried to kill my father. (Girl24, 8 years old) (Carvalho 2010, p. 317)

Gender assumes another expression, which is particularly visible in the case of assault. When examining the profile of the victims of delinquency committed by the young girls, is it common for victims to be from the same gender. This could be regarded as a sign that these girls perceived female victims to be more vulnerable and were thus able to incorporate this understanding into their own offending behaviour. Moreover, those who are aggressors can also become victims at the hands of older girls in what seems to be a social reproduction of gendered violence patterns among females.

> I like playing in my neighbourhood, but what I don't like are the older girls who come beating on us and steal. (Girl38, 10 years old). (Carvalho 2010, p. 396)

Zimmerman and Messner (2010) showed that neighbourhood disadvantage increases exposure to peer violence and has a significant impact on girls' violent offending, promoting the reduction in the gender gap at higher levels of disadvantage. Social disadvantage is manifested in a low level of confidence in relation to others, which reduces the residents' expectations about lessening social control, while also lowering their expectations of taking collective action for children's socialization (Sampson 2012). Wherever children live, discovering the existence of the *other* implies raising questions about identity, difference, otherness and power. Taking into account the complexity of social life it can be observed

Constructing Meaning About the Delinquency of Young Girls... 155

that the relationships between cultural and ethnic groups are often conflicting. This is something that girls become aware of and point out as one of the major problems in their neighbourhoods (Fig. 8.3).

It's my street and the buildings on the side of the 'Gypsies' and on the other it's me and my friends. What I like least in my neighbourhood are the 'Gypsies' and if I could, I would move them to another neighbourhood because they are noisy and rude and throw litter on the streets (Girl13, 9 years old).[2]

Many families have been relocated by local authorities to specific streets according to their ethnic origin. Of particular relevance in these neighbourhoods is the divisions and boundaries inside them, which are mainly associated with ethnic origin and hierarchies among different cultural groups. This trend simultaneously encourages and (re)constructs permanent social dissatisfaction by reinforcing the neighbourhood's stigmatization, and is at the origin of many disorders and violence in which young girls are heavily involved.

Fig. 8.3 My neighbourhood

4 Girl's Delinquency as a Female Business

It is worth mentioning the importance of family in the girls' involvement in delinquent practices, while recognizing that there is a reciprocal effect between the family and the environment (Augimeri et al. 2011). There are many possible relationships among families, informal social control and delinquency, but it is important to note that as families influence the development of their members through social control, they are also influenced by the context in which they live (Kingston et al. 2009).

Factors associated with families and the parental exercise of informal social control and supervision, as well as the educational learning processes parents and relatives build with girls—in particular, those involving adherence to social and legal values—are frequently addressed in research and strongly related to delinquency (Belknap and Holsinger 2006; Loeber et al. 2008; Zahn et al. 2010; Piquero et al. 2012; Kruttschnitt 2013).

> Do you know a group [of 4 young adult females] called the Gang of the [name of a famous Portuguese clothing brand]? They bring me clothes, but my mother [who is living abroad] tells me not to accept [them] because if I have a lack of clothing, it is because I damage it. She always brings a suitcase of clothes. (…) They are smart; they have a 'silver suitcase' [lined with aluminium foil and silver inside] to pass the alarms without being caught. One is my aunt and they do not give clothes to others in the neighbourhood, they only give it to me; to the other girls, they sell at the same price. (…) People here buy a lot. (Girl27, 11 years old) (Carvalho 2010, p. 430)

Female participation in delinquent groups is not a recent phenomenon—what seems to be new are some of the ways in which girls participate, how they build gender relationships and how they orchestrate various forms of femininity through their delinquent practices. These practices are seen as 'girl's things' and 'girl's business' by the girls interviewed. The social learning of delinquency tends to occur within the matriarchal family context under the direct influence of relatives of the same gender—mothers, aunts, girl cousins, grandmothers and sisters—and not necessarily from any male influence. The gender schemas that female relatives provide for girls significantly influence their delinquent practices.

> We talked to the mother of [Girl35, 9 years old] and she explained every-thing. She put on the clothes, picked up her clothes, put on the clothes in the [shop] and then she told us to do what she was doing. She told us to take something off (…) that (…) the alarm tag. Her mother taught us, do it like this with your teeth (…). We managed to get it off, one took it off and we put on the clothes (…). Her mother told us, and she told us to go because there are stolen clothes at home and some bought, but most were stolen and then the case went to the court once. (Girl27, 11 years old) (Carvalho 2010, p. 394)

The intergenerational transmission of crime has been extensively described in scientific research and affects both girls and boys. The most complex challenge emerges when the girl offenders' families are also involved in crime and delinquency; this is not a new problem, but an intergenerational one, passed from one generation to the next, within a process of social reproduction that is similar to that of other social problems (that is, poverty, social exclusion).

5 Final Remarks

Debating girls' delinquency necessarily implies talking about social dynamics and the multiplicity of challenges and risks that influence genderized social roles and the construction of identity during childhood in societies marked by changes in the role and position of women. At the origin of delinquency are gendered social processes and dynamics in which analysis in general, both scientific and social, is relevant, as it allows insights into the social construction of gender in broader terms.

For the 6–12 year-old girls involved in this research, the ties to deviant and criminal models present in the neighbourhoods were more obvious and significant than others related to social conformity. The girls' family and group relationships, especially with older female peers or relatives, are key-factors in their involvement in delinquency. Results suggest that the deviant influence of female adults on girls seems to be encouraged by the influence of the social environment, which easily turns into a particular knowledge that could be used amongst the younger ones for their own purposes. Moreover, talking about their participation in delinquency could give them personal recognition at the local level and increase their local social status. These girls do not reject conventional values, but in their offending practices there is more excitement, pleasure and adhesion to notions that are highly valued in these neighbourhoods, such as 'being smart' and 'having power and money', which are recurrently associated with a code of the street (Anderson 1999).

Delinquency has a functional and instrumental role, offering girls attractive and rewarding forms of socialization. So it seems that girls are more present in the same spaces as boys and subject to the same tensions and conflicts in these neighbourhoods. This could lead to an understanding of how girls are increasingly challenging the traditional gender behaviours of children in Portuguese society.

In this process, special attention should be paid to what happens in the public spaces that influence girls' social practices and gender roles. As in the case of boys, the street plays a central role in the socialization of many girls', and parental supervision does not always provide adequate protection; often, girls referred to how they were involved in social disorder, violence and delinquency with their own parents or relatives. This forces us to question the nature of the existing social networks and how the residents' lack of intervention in social control reflects insufficient collective action to improve children's socialization, which may endanger social cohesion (Morenoff et al. 2001; Sampson 2012). As a part of the context where they grow up, violence and crime seem 'normalized' to many girls. This 'normalization' strengthens the risk of the girls' under-valuing the seriousness and effects of these kinds of actions and some even start participating when very young. Ultimately, girls' social development through delinquency is already structuring how they interact with peers and adults now, and it will be reflected in their future roles in society.

As revealed by the high levels of autonomy and mobility of some girls outside their neighbourhoods, delinquency seems to be influenced by the spatial and social neighbourhood features. As a result, two aspects arise as fundamental: concentration and stigmatization. Located on the 'other side of the city' (Carvalho 2010), these neighbourhoods do not benefit from a closer relationship with socially differentiated residential areas where the expectations of the social control of children are higher. This was probably one of the most critical limitations in the urban planning of these neighbourhoods, resulting in areas that promote girls' delinquency in different ways.FundingThis work was supported by the Fundação para a Ciência e Tecnologia through individual research grant reference SFRH/BPD/116119/2016 under POCH funds, co-financed by the European Social Fund and Portuguese National Funds from MCTES, and by the CICS.NOVA—Interdisciplinary Centre of Social Sciences of the Universidade Nova de Lisboa, UID/SOC/04647/2013, with the financial support of FCT/MCTES through National funds.

Notes

1. Research supported by the Fundação para a Ciência e Tecnologia (SFRH/BD/43563/2008).
2. The term 'Gypsies' was kept instead of the use of 'Roma' because it was most common among the girls living in these neighbourhoods, including those who are Roma.

References

Akers, R. (1998). *Social learning and social structure: A general theory of crime and deviance*. Boston: Northeastern University Press.

Anderson, E. (1999). *Code of the street*. New York: Norton.

Augimeri, L. K., Walsh, M. M., Liddon, A. D., & Dassinger, C. R. (2011). From risk identification to risk management: A comprehensive strategy for young children engaged in antisocial behavior. In D. W. Springer & A. Roberts (Eds.), *Juvenile justice and delinquency* (pp. 117–140). Sudbury: Jones & Bartlett.

Belknap, J., & Holsinger, K. (2006). The gendered nature of risk factors for delinquency. *Feminist Criminology, 1*, 48–71.

Blokland, A. A. J., & Palmen, H. (2012). Criminal career patterns. In R. Loeber, M. Hoeve, N. W. Slot, & P. van der Laan (Eds.), *Persisters and desisters in crime from adolescence into adulthood: Explanation, prevention and punishment* (pp. 13–50). Aldershot: Ashgate.

Carvalho, M. J. L. (2010). *Do Outro Lado da Cidade. Crianças, Socialização e Delinquência em Bairros de Realojamento*. PhD thesis, Universidade Nova de Lisboa, Lisbon.

Chesney-Lind, M. (1997). *The female offender: Girls, women and crime*. Thousand Oaks: Sage.

Cloward, R., & Ohlin, L. (1970). Differential opportunity structure. In M. Wolfgang & E. Ferracutti (Eds.), *The sociology of crime and delinquency* (pp. 300–318). New York: Wiley.

Corsaro, W. (1997). *The sociology of childhood*. Thousand Oaks: Pine Forge Press.

Duarte, V., & Carvalho, M. J. L. (2017). Female delinquency in Portugal: What girls have to say about their offending behaviors. *Gender Issues, 34*, 258–274.

Elliott, D. S., Wilson, W. J., Huizinga, D., Sampson, R. J., Elliott, A., & Rankin, B. (1996). The effects of neighborhood disadvantage on adolescent development. *Journal of Research in Crime and Delinquency, 33*, 389–426.

Fabio, A., Tu, L. C., Loeber, R., & Cohen, J. (2011). Neighborhood socioeconomic disadvantage and the shape of the age-crime curve. *American Journal of Public Health, 101*(S1), 325–332.

Fagan, A. A., & Wright, E. M. (2012). The effects of neighborhood context on youth violence and delinquency: Does gender matter? *Youth Violence and Juvenile Justice, 10*(1), 64–82.

Fagan, A. A., Van Horn, M. L., Hawkins, J. D., & Arthur, M. (2007). Gender similarities and differences in the association between risk and protective factors and self-reported serious delinquency. *Prevention Science, 8*, 115–124.

Giordano, P. (1978). Girls, guys and gangs: The changing social context of female delinquency. *Journal of Criminal Law and Criminology, 69*, 26–132.

Giordano, P., Cernkovich, S., & Rudolph, J. (2002). Gender, crime and desistance: Toward a theory of cognitive transformation. *American Journal of Sociology, 107*(4), 990–1064.

Goodkind, S., Wallace, J. M., Shook, J. J., Bachman, J., & O'Malley, P. (2009). Are girls really becoming more delinquent? Testing the gender convergence hypothesis by race and ethnicity, 1976–2005. *Children and Youth Services Review, 31*(8), 885–895.

Haynie, D. L., Doogan, N. J., & Soller, B. (2014). Gender, friendship networks, and delinquency: A dynamic network approach. *Criminology, 52*(4), 688–722.

Jacob, J. C. (2006). Male and female youth crime in Canadian communities: Assessing the applicability of social disorganization theory. *Canadian Journal of Criminology and Criminal Justice, 48*, 31–60.

Kingston, B., Huizinga, D., & Elliot, D. S. (2009). A test of social disorganization in high-risk urban neighborhoods. *Youth and Society, 41*, 53–79.

Kling, J. R., Ludwig, J., & Katz, L. F. (2005). Neighborhood effects on crime for female and male youth: Evidence from a randomized housing voucher experiment. *The Quarterly Journal of Economics, 120*, 87–130.

Kruttschnitt, C. (2013). Gender and crime. *The Annual Review of Sociology, 39*, 291–308.

Lei, M. K., Simons, R. L., Simons, L. G., & Edmond, M. B. (2014). Gender equality and violent behavior: How neighborhood gender equality influences the gender gap in violence. *Violence and Victims, 29*(1), 89–108.

Loeber, R., & Farrington, D. P. (Eds.). (2001). *Child delinquents: Development, intervention and service needs*. Thousand Oaks: Sage.

Loeber, R., Slot, N. W., & Stouthamer-Loeber, M. (2008). A cumulative developmental model of risk and promotive factors. In R. Loeber, N. W. Slot, P. H. Laan, & M. Hoeve (Eds.), *Tomorrow's criminals. The development of child delinquency and effective interventions* (pp. 133–161). Farnham: Ashgate.

Miller, K. (2007). Traversing the spatial divide? Gender, place, and delinquency. *Feminist Criminology, 2*, 202–222.

Moffitt, T. E., Caspi, A., Rutter, M., & Silva, P. (2001). *Sex differences in antisocial behaviour: Conduct disorder, delinquency, and violence in the Dunedin longitudinal study*. Cambridge, UK: Cambridge University Press.

Morenoff, J. D., Sampson, R. J., & Raudenbush, S. W. (2001). Neighborhood inequality, collective efficacy, and the spatial dynamics of urban violence. *Criminology, 39*, 517–560.

Mrug, S., & Windle, M. (2009). Mediators of neighborhood influences on externalizing behavior in preadolescent children. *Journal of Abnormal Child Psychology, 37*, 265–280.

Piquero, N., Gover, A., MacDonald, J., & Piquero, A. (2005). The influence of delinquent peers on delinquency: Does gender matter? *Youth & Society, 36*(3), 251–275.

Piquero, A., Hawkins, J. D., & Kazemian, L. (2012). Criminal career patterns. In R. Loeber & D. P. Farrington (Eds.), *From juvenile delinquency to adult crime: Criminal careers, justice policy, and prevention* (pp. 14–46). New York: Oxford University Press.

Sampson, R. (2012). *Great American city: Chicago and the enduring neighborhood effect*. Chicago: University of Chicago Press.

Sampson, R. J., & Groves, W. B. (1989). Community structure and crime: Testing social-disorganization theory. *American Journal of Sociology, 94*, 774–802.

Schneider, B. (2016). *Childhood friendships and peer relations: Friends and enemies.* New York: Routledge.

Steffensmeier, D., & Haynie, D. L. (2006). Gender, structural disadvantage, and urban crime: Do macrosocial variables also explain female offending rates? *Criminology, 38,* 403–439.

Wong, T., Slotboom, A. M., & Bijleveld, C. (2010). Risk factors for delinquency in adolescent and young adult females: A European review. *European Journal of Criminology, 7*(4), 266–284.

Zahn, M. (2009). *The delinquent girl.* Philadelphia: Temple University Press.

Zahn, M. A., & Browne, A. (2009). Gender differences in neighborhood effects and delinquency. In M. A. Zahn (Ed.), *The delinquent girl* (pp. 164–181). Philadelphia: Temple University Press.

Zahn, M., et al. (2010). *Causes and correlates of Girl's delinquency.* OJJDP girls study group: Understanding and responding to girl's delinquency. Washington, DC: US Office of Justice Programs.

Zimmerman, G. M., & Messner, S. F. (2010). Neighborhood context and the gender gap in adolescent violent crime. *American Sociological Review, 75,* 958–980.

9

Gender and Crime in the Life Pathways of Young Women Offenders: Contrasting the Narratives of Girls and Professionals

Raquel Matos

1 Introduction

In this chapter, two empirical studies developed in Portugal are presented in order to contrast young women offenders' perspectives with those of professionals on women's involvement in crime and deviance. They are based on the feminist approaches that criticize, deconstruct and propose to reconstruct the way women offenders have long been conceptualized in criminological theories. As these approaches claim, in these empirical studies a fundamental status was conferred on gender and on variables such as class and ethnicity, and no specific pre-conceptions (e.g., *double deviance, irrationality*) were adopted about the way women are involved in criminal activity. We begin by discussing the impact that those theoretical perspectives had on several empirical studies on women and crime that have been developed since the 1990s, both globally and in the specific context of Portugal. We then present the most relevant findings of

R. Matos (✉)
Universidade Católica Portuguesa, CEDH, Oporto, Portugal

© The Author(s) 2018
S. Gomes, V. Duarte (eds.), *Female Crime and Delinquency in Portugal*,
https://doi.org/10.1007/978-3-319-73534-4_9

163

both studies to discuss gender and crime in the pathways of young women offenders. We end the article by contrasting the narratives of young women inmates with those of the professionals. We conclude that the latter are shaped by gender stereotypes and, as such, do not consider the diversity of paths and forms of involvement in crime that are evidenced by the young women themselves.

2 The Feminist Contributions to the Study of Women and Crime, Globally and in the Portuguese Context

The first theoretical approaches that aimed at understanding female criminal behaviour first appeared in the context of a highly positivist and androcentric late nineteenth-century criminology. Together with some of the psychological and sociological theories developed later on, also deterministic to female deviance (e.g., Pollak 1950), these bio-anthropological approaches prevailed as dominant models during the first half of the twentieth century. New perspectives on women as crime perpetrators were enabled by the incursion of the feminist movements into criminology after the 1960s (Matos and Machado 2012). However, it was only in the context of a more open and diverse late 1980s criminology (Gelsthorpe 1997) that several feminist approaches started to re-contextualize female criminality in the criminology discourse (Carlen 1987, 1988; Rafter and Heidensohn 1995; Smart 1990, 1996). Also in Portugal, following the international trend, some studies have been carried out since the 1990s to understand women offenders' trajectories and prison experiences from a feminist critical perspective.

To mention some of the most relevant literature, we can start with Cunha's (1994, 2002) ethnographic studies on women's experiences in Portuguese prisons. In a first approach, Cunha (1994) drew attention to identity and cultural aspects of women's experiences of imprisonment. Later on, she focused on women convicted for drug offences to analyse the intersections between the prison and the "neighbourhoods". Among other findings, Cunha (2002) showed that imprisonment may emerge as an expected life transition in the trajectories of many women who come from the same marginalized neighbourhoods. As she concluded, criminal activity based on the drug market is common in the lives of women who do not have many other options in the "normative job market" (Cunha 2002).

Later on, Matos (2008) interviewed nearly all the women under 21 years old detained in the Portuguese prison system. The 49 interviews revealed several different pathways directing young women to prison. While some were in prison for violent crimes against persons but had no evidence of previous deviant behaviour, drug use, or the involvement of relatives in crime, others were convicted for various crimes, presented a past as drug users and had previous records of delinquency; in addition, some of their relatives had already been in prison. Others were serving time for drug trafficking, which was linked to problematic and continued use of hard drugs. Finally, some young women presented themselves as working women, whose lives did not escape the socially determined standards, except in their daily work in the narcotics trade. This study made it possible to question the stereotyped discourses about female crime not only because of the diversity of trajectories found but also because it allowed us to look at women as entrepreneurs in crime, as was the case with the latter example (Matos 2008).

More recently, we can highlight the work of Granja (2016), who focused on the intersections between the experiences of incarceration and the prisoners' family relationships. By taking a critical stance towards the dominant discourse that links family and crime, Granja (2016) evidenced how prison sentences have an impact that goes far beyond the prison walls affecting family members who were not convicted. She also concluded that prison contributes to emphasizing gender asymmetries, which in turn reinforce the gender-related vulnerabilities in women's lives (Granja 2016).

The feminist perspectives that supported these national and many of the international studies on women, crime and imprisonment criticized three fundamental ideas in the way discourses on women who commit crimes tend to be constructed.

The first is that women offenders are considered twice as deviant, for transgressing both the law and the conventional gender roles. As Cunha (1994) points out, the double deviance attributed to women is due to the fact that "the transgression of legality that has led to imprisonment is in one way or another concomitant with the denial of the norms that define appropriate female conduct" (1994, p. 24). Underlying the dual construction of the deviant woman is a "dichotomous view of the feminine": on the one hand there is the "chaste, domestic and maternal" woman and on the other "the woman attending the public sphere, neglecting family and domestic responsibilities" (Cunha 1994, p. 24).

The second criticism concerns the narrow view of female criminality, focusing only on specific types of crime because of the dominant stereotypes. The stereotyped characterization of crimes committed by women thus contrasts with male crime, considered not only more frequent and violent, but also much more diverse (Matos and Machado 2012). This argument for the existence of "typical female crimes" is seen by the feminist authors (e.g., Carlen 1983, 1987) as having negative implications for women, including the way they are treated in the penal system. Studies that evidenced the heterogeneity of women's transgression (e.g., Matos 2008) as well as the involvement of women in deviant activities traditionally associated with men, such as terrorist acts (Cruise 2016) or gang violence (e.g., Campbell 1992; Laidler and Hunt 2001; Miller 2001), have contributed to the deconstruction of the argument of the specificity of female criminality. The feminist authors suggested that the differences between men and women offenders rested on the frequency and severity of the crimes rather than the type of crimes committed. In addition, they have argued that many differences in the statistics are particularly due to a differential structure of opportunities, to different forms of socialization and to gendered social control, rather than to "innate characteristics of the offender" (Matos and Machado 2012).

Finally, the feminist perspectives criticize the construction of a transgressive woman who does not rationally choose to commit crimes. According to them, women who commit crimes have been unduly represented and treated as "unstable and irrational" in the various traditional criminological approaches (Rafter and Heidensohn 1995). The argument of the hetero-determination of female criminal behaviour has also been central in conventional discourse about the offending woman, described as committing crimes not by her choice, but coerced by others. Given such discourse, feminist authors have sought to deconstruct it through the exploration of social factors, such as the social and economic marginalization of women, patriarchal power and the informal devices for controlling women's behaviour (Matos and Machado 2012).

The feminist conceptualization has been more difficult to find in studies that focus specifically on girls' delinquency. Indeed, when it comes to analysing youth and delinquent behaviour, many studies present a more positivistic and less critical epistemological framework. The approaches that explore socialization and gender roles, however, although sometimes remaining close to a deterministic and stereotyped reading of female delinquency, have the merit of going beyond biology and the supposedly innate characteristics of women to include sociological dimensions.

An example is the analysis of girls' transgression from the point of view of how social expectations of them (e.g., subordination to men, compliance with norms) may determine or constrain their own deviance (Matos 2008). Other authors discuss the influence of a normative feminine socialization on girls' delinquency based on the argument that delinquent acts are related to an ideal of masculinity and to the roles conventionally attributed to men. According to them, boys' socialization tends to legitimate deviant acts while girls' socialization occurs in terms of compliance to the norms. On the one hand, it is suggested that girls' socialization promotes higher compliance than boys' socialization, because when committing delinquent acts girls are violating gender expectations. Some studies show, for example, that girls feel more shame and guilt when they get into trouble with the law and they legitimate delinquent acts less than boys do (e.g., Morris 1965 cited in Shoemaker 2010). On the other hand, some authors argue that the delinquent acts committed by young women result from a socialization similar to men's, leading to participation in typically male roles, something that does not happen to non-delinquent girls (Shoemaker 2010). In a more critical perspective, other authors suggest that young women who transgress move away from normative expectations of femininity. According to this perspective, when subjected to a stricter gender control, especially in the family context, girls can choose to break with the expectations of corresponding to an ideal of femininity that relies on them (Matos 2008; Matos and Machado 2012).

In Portugal, among the studies on juvenile delinquency, we highlight the critical approach by Duarte (2012) on the trajectories of girls who comply with youth justice measures. Duarte systematizes four different trajectories for girls: those with a history of family victimization and violence, and significant paths in terms of deviant behaviour and regulation by the control authorities ("Emphasized transgression"); the trajectories of girls who don't have a history of family victimization nor previous institutionalization, and whose transgression seems to be associated with the "rebellion of being young and trying to experiment" ("Rebel-transgression"); the paths of girls whose positioning in relation to their deviant behaviour is hetero-determined, centred on factors which do not depend on themselves ("Transgression-influence"); and finally, the trajectories of girls whose deviant behaviour assumes an exceptional character (Duarte 2012). This study emphasizes the relevance of gender in girls' delinquent behaviour and highlights differentiated social control and various forms of gender discrimination that the girls themselves associate with their delinquent paths.

As previously mentioned, the feminist perspectives on criminology brought new conceptualizations of the woman offender and, consequently, a new focus and new methodologies for understanding female delinquency. Globally, several approaches have specifically targeted girls' criminal pathways (e.g., Carlen 1987; Daly 1994; Miller 2001). However, in the Portuguese context, with the exception of the aforementioned study by Duarte (2012), we can say that these critical feminist approaches to feminine youth delinquency are still scarce. The studies we are about to present may be seen as important contributions, as the first one focuses on the way young women offenders attribute meaning to their criminal experiences and the second analyses the perspectives of the professionals on girls' deviant pathways.

3 Girls' Narratives: Life Pathways, Meanings of Crime and Identity Construction in Young Women in Prison

This study is part of a research project about "life pathways, meanings of crime and identity construction in young women in prison".[1] In this project we intended to understand how circumstances such as inequality of opportunities or gender relationships were relevant constraints in the pathways of young female inmates (Matos 2008). We conducted in-depth interviews with twelve young female prisoners, 16–22 years old, selected after a preliminary study with 49 young women prisoners in Portugal. As such a study evidenced different deviant experiences concerning the type of crime, previous contact with the justice system, drug use and relatives' involvement in crime (Matos 2008), for this study we selected young women with contrasting paths in those dimensions (Table 9.1). The interviews were recorded, transcribed and later analysed according to the grounded analysis principles.

From the analysis of the young women's discourses, some findings may be highlighted. To begin with, the girls themselves identify gender constraints that were negative turning points in their life pathways. For example, they report instances of rejection by their family for not behaving according to the expected gender roles. They also report being abused by male partners, as was the case for Helga—

> With him I couldn't say no. I was afraid. [...] If I didn't do what he wanted, I'd go home and be beaten. I think I wasn't even addicted to drugs anymore... it was the fear ... I had to make money. I think the price I'm paying is too much because if I did it, it was out of fear, otherwise I wouldn't have done it. (Helga, 22)

Also worth mentioning is the diversity of life paths and deviant experiences of these young women. Their discourses reveal different narratives about their engagement in crime and deviance.

Some girls present very *normative* life courses, without any deviant occurrence up to the moment when the crime happened. Consequently, imprisonment is kind of a time-out in their lives and an obstacle to

Table 9.1 Participants, with a description of: crime, prison sentence, criminal record, drug use and relatives involved in crime

Alias (age)	Crime	Prison sentence	Previous crimes and sentences	Drug use	Family and crime
Helga (22)	Trafficking	4 years and 6 months	Assault (without conviction)	Cocaine	Partner, mother, father, brother, sister- in-law, cousin
Iris (21)	Trafficking	3 years and 4 months	–	Heroin Cocaine	Partner, father
Joana (22)	Trafficking	4 years	–	–	Mother, sister
Katia (19)	Trafficking	4 years	–	–	–
Dalia (19)	Crimes against property	4 years	Crimes against property (without conviction)	Heroin	–
Emma (21)	Crimes against property	3 years and 9 months	Crimes against property; (18 months on probation)	Heroin Cocaine	Partner
Flora (20)	Crimes against property	4 years	Crimes against property; (3 years on probation)	Heroin Cocaine	Partner; 2 brothers
Guida (21)	Crimes against property	7 years and 6 months	Crimes against property; (2 years in prison)	Heroin Cocaine	Partner, father, cousin
Alexandra (18)	Homicide	6 years	–	–	Mother
Bárbara (20)	Homicide	4 years	–	–	–
Carla (22)	Homicide	7 years and 9 months	–	–	Uncle
Lisa (19)	Crimes against property and homicide	8 years and 9 months	–	–	Brother

accomplish their main goal—to study and be successful. In this group, crimes are clearly gender-based. These girls' single criminal act could be the result of the experience of being sexually abused, being subject to strict control by the family related to being a girl, or the lack of means to deal with an unwanted pregnancy. In fact, this is the only group where gender and crime are associated in a relevant manner. On the one hand, these girls present normative paths characterized by the acceptance of gender norms. Paradoxically, gender norms are at the basis of the crimes they committed. Take the words of Barbara below:

> I've always been a good student. As a little girl, I always wanted to study… and I still do. I wanted to study so badly that I even skipped First Grade. I've always believed that "you can never learn too much" and I still do believe it now; As far as my path in prison is concerned, everything is running smoothly. I like to do stuff, to participate, to lead, I have had a few ideas and I have implemented a lot of projects in here […] I have joined reading sessions, the soccer team, I do gym ….I have already done a play… (Barbara, 22)

Other young women present themselves as victims—of abuse during childhood, or "of drugs" or of violent partners later in their lives. They adopt a "pathological" perspective of their own transgression, describing being out of control and excluding any agency and rationality from their involvement in crime. In the case of Dalia, as she describes, it was the drugs that took over her life:

> If I wanted to stop I couldn't do it. In order to use drugs I had to steal […] all I cared about was drugs, that was all I cared about […] I was a drug addict…My life was all about drugs. (Dalia, 19)

Some attribute meaning to crime describing a rational choice for the criminal activity and the idea that they would again take the same option, showing no regret. In terms of criminal experience, they dedicate themselves to drug trafficking, without using drugs. Their involvement in crime is not ruled by a criminal lifestyle; instead, it is governed by a style close to normative patterns. Drug trafficking is, however, the activity they choose to make money, not only for paying their bills, but also for a better life which, according to their statements, would be difficult to attain by simply performing other available activities. Take, for instance, the words of Katia about her involvement in trafficking:

> I wanted to have everything, just like everybody else had. I've always been like this; whenever I go past a clothes shop I want it all. (Katia, 19)

Finally, some girls' statements on their life trajectories, and particularly on delinquent behaviour, lead us to associate them with the construction of deviant identities. They already have a significant track record in terms of delinquency and contacts with the youth justice system and their delinquent activity is heterogeneous, with a particular incidence of crimes against property. These girls present themselves as users of the so-called "hard" drugs, although they refer that they have never lost control over their drug use. They constantly refer to this dimension of control, when using expressions such as being "proud" of surviving in the streets or "being capable of stopping their use of drugs". Deviance seems to be a way for these young women to gain control over their lives (Batchelor 2005a). We also found, implicit in their statements, a dimension of pleasure and excitement associated with crime, which leads us to the positive feelings taken from criminal action proposed by Katz (1988/1996) and found in other studies on young women offenders, like the work of Batchelor (2005b). This dimension of pleasure is revealed through a "street life" discourse, characterized by a marginal lifestyle, by the association with deviant peers with whom they use drugs and survive in the streets, by sleeping in uncertain places and by an intense nightlife. Take the words of Emma below:

> This was our lives for many years, we stole a lot of money and then we went, bought and smoked [...] we always had money, we always had drugs; life always felt good. You know what street life is like ... there's drugs and stuff and here and there ... it may take one, two, three years, four, five years or more, but there will be one day, if you keep living on the street, there will be one day when you will... touch it. [...] We lived in sort of abandoned houses, [...] we managed to set up the water [...] We even had a key because we installed a locker. [...] I had to take care of myself, I had to do all this stuff ... I have no complaints. After all I did well, am I right? (Emma, 21)

The diversity of these narratives allowed deconstructing the idea of a typically female criminality, so criticized by the feminist perspectives in criminology. In addition to the four pathways previously identified, Lisa's particular case shows the combination of extreme meanings of crime: related to a criminal lifestyle or as an exception in a "normative" pathway.

> I had a schedule, on Fridays and Saturdays…at night…because those were the days when I had my parents' permission to go out…was when I robbed, and during the rest of the week my days were perfectly normal. If I had to, I went with my school friends to a disco or a bar or something like that, and only when they went home I would go and meet the group […] It's that adrenaline feeling, the thought of getting caught. Danger gives me a real thrill… (Lisa, 19)

In this case, a single trajectory contains several ways of attributing meaning to crime, oscillating between normative and deviant identities. Analysing this case leads us to conclude that it is impossible to reduce female transgression to one given typology; despite the regularities identified in the discourses of the different women, each of their pathways is idiosyncratic (Matos 2008). Based on this study it is also possible to state that young women's transgression is quite further from the most traditional conceptions; hence it makes sense to refuse the gender-stereotyped approaches to this phenomenon. In fact, the emerging narratives evidenced that, most of the times, (juvenile) female criminality is not so distant from male deviant experiences (Batchelor 2005b). This finding shows that even the expression "female criminality" should not be used, in order to avoid reinforcing the traditional argument that there is women-related criminality.

4 Narratives of Professionals on the Involvement of Girls in Delinquent Groups

The second study was part of a research project about "youth delinquent groups" (Matos et al. 2014),[2] with the purpose of analysing how practitioners dealing with young offenders characterize the phenomenon of

174   R. Matos

Table 9.2 Number of participants, according to the type of institution where they work

Type of institution	Number of participants and roles
Justice system (n = 16)	Six police officers Four magistrates Six youth justice practitioners
Protection system (n = 8)	Four practitioners from child protection services Four practitioners from children emergency shelters
Community institutions (n = 14)	Five practitioners from schools Nine practitioners from community intervention projects
Universities (n = 4)	Four academic researchers
Other institutions (n = 1)	One clinical psychologist

youth delinquent groups in Portugal. Forty-three professionals (Table 9.2) working in the main Portuguese urban areas were interviewed. As in the previous study, the interviews were recorded, transcribed and analysed under the grounded analysis principles. In this chapter, we will focus only on the practitioners' narratives on the involvement of girls in delinquent groups.

Based on the analysis of the practitioners' narratives, emphasis will now be put on their conceptualization of the involvement of girls in delinquent behaviour.

To begin with, the participants tend to portray the youth gangs as a "boys" phenomenon and to depict girls as having other types of deviant behaviours, namely, "running away from home" or "early pregnancy". According to this perspective, illustrated by the words of a woman working in protection services, belonging to a gang is an essentially male phenomenon: "Boys. Boys. Girls have different deviant behaviours […] Gang members are boys. The boys". (Woman, 42, Protection Services). The idea conveyed here that there is a boys' delinquency and a girls' delinquency is also present in the discourse of other professionals. Take, for instance, the words of a woman working at a community institution:

Gender and Crime in the Life Pathways of Young Women... 175

...I think girls have a different way of...even female delinquency is a little different from male delinquency, isn't it? I think they are a little more subtle, I don't know... I think girls' delinquency at this age is more a matter of shoplifting, at least here, what we register is shoplifting perfumes, stealing from school, stealing from the other girls... (Woman, 41, Community Institutions)

These references reveal the same tendency found in the classical approaches to crime, which associate women with "typically female deviances". This trend is based on gender stereotypes and on the idea that there are male and female crimes (Matos and Machado 2012).

When they characterize the girls that join juvenile gangs, several professionals mention qualities that, in their opinion, are "typically feminine". On the one hand, they argue that there are characteristics that differentiate girls from boys, such as, for example, being more "manipulative", "strategist", "subtle" and "seductive". On the other hand, the professionals mention that the girls try to take advantage of their "female condition". This is well illustrated by the words of a 35-year-old woman working in the justice system: "They have a mind of their own, they know how to use their girlish attributes to rule... ahm.... and they do it with, how do we say it, with an iron fist, right?" (Woman, 35, Justice System).

There are also professionals that argue that girls who join gangs step away from the "female standard", becoming more masculine than expected. A woman working at a community institution says "it depends on the girls we are talking about because there are some manly girls, right? [...] There are girls who present themselves as actual boys and, in those cases, the difference is not that big" (Woman, 32, Community Institutions).

Considering the role girls play as gang members, some practitioners describe it as different from the role played by boys. As two participants report, girls do not take on leadership, but keep secondary roles:

"Quite often their role is secondary, we don't see them as leaders. I can't imagine that in a group composed of boys and girls, I can't imagine a girl being the leader. Ahm, I think in that case boys will stand out and will sort of keep that position. Probably do not lose, do not let the power of being a, in quotation marks, leader, slip from their hands." (Woman, 35, Protection System); "I honestly think they play a limited role because they end up being the wives, the girlfriends…" (Woman, 28, Community Institutions)

There is also the idea that girls are sometimes "strategically used by boys" for diverse purposes such as, for example, "to outwit the police". Take the words of two professionals below:

> If you see a vehicle late at night with four people inside it may be a bit suspicious. If you see two couples inside the vehicle, it no longer becomes suspicious (…) these days many women are used. (Man, 41, Justice System)
>
> A girl helps to disguise … We are less suspicious of girls. So, it may be useful to have girls in the group. (Woman, 47, Academia)

But the dominant trend is to present dichotomized perspectives on girls' delinquency, just like in the most traditional criminological discourse. On the one hand, many practitioners say that women offenders have "typical female attributes"—they are "strategists", "subtle", "experts in seduction"—and that they know how to take advantage of those attributes. On the other hand, many participants consider that young women offenders are "less feminine" and "similar to boys". They may even be "worse than boys", "more violent" and "fearless". Two women working in the justice system make clear statements about this:

> [...] In cases that I have worked, women end up acting in a much more primitive way, hit more, and hit each other more and have a very clear sense of burglary and theft; They can steal in a more shocking way compared to many boys. (Woman, 40, Justice System)

> I think we still have less violence because there aren't many girls (offending); when we start having more I think we'll have more violence [...] I think that girls are much more capable of acting violently and to encourage physical aggression [...]. (Woman, 35, Justice System)

Overall, from the analysis of the practitioners' narratives on the involvement of girls in delinquent groups, stereotyped ways of giving meaning to the girls' behaviours were evidenced. These stereotyped perspectives seem to worsen when it comes to deviant behaviour, which tends to be even more subject to bias. In addition, the findings revealed that the professionals tend to present perspectives shaped more by gender stereotypes when they work in the formal justice system, when compared to those who work more closely with the communities.

5 Contrasting the Narratives of Girls and Professionals

Though we discussed two distinct studies, with different aims and participants and with a time gap, we believe that contrasting them is relevant and may give us interesting insights about gendered perspectives on young women's transgression.

The first one is that there were some convergences in the perspectives of the young women offenders and of the professionals. Both groups adhere, to some extent, to the dominant discourses on women and crime. Even those girls with a "criminal lifestyle", distant from the image of a "good girl", tend to adhere to the dominant conceptions of femininity, like the central role of motherhood or of family life, when describing themselves. In addition, for both groups, hesitations were found between a perspective embodied in stereotypes and in the dominant discourse of femininity and a more critical perspective outside such discourse.

Still, divergences are worth mentioning. First of all, various understandings of crime emerged in the young women's narratives, supporting the rejection of the traditional concepts of female delinquency. These diverse understandings contradict the idea that there are specific "female crimes". And the diversity in their interpretations and positioning regarding delinquency also contradicts traditional views on women and crime. In turn, the dimension of rationality associated with crimes committed by some young women contradicts the argument of its *pathology or madness*.

Such findings contrast with the gender stereotypes and ambivalence that prevail in the professionals' perspectives on female delinquency. According to them, "female characteristics" may prevent the involvement of girls in delinquent behaviour or, on the contrary, make them "leaders" of deviant groups. Paradoxically, the professionals also suggest that there is a "lack of femininity" in girls who get involved in delinquency, particularly in delinquent groups.

Thus, gender stereotyping and ambivalence that have dominated, for quite some time, the discourse on female delinquency seem to persist among those who deal on a daily basis with young offenders. Also worth mentioning is the fact that among the professionals, the closer they are to the justice system, the more stereotyped their narratives are. That means that police officers and magistrates present more a penalizing discourse about women and crime than the practitioners working in communities or in the protection system.

To sum up, we highlight in the first place that the findings from both studies reinforce our questions about the traditional approaches to female criminality. The diversity in the life paths and in the deviant experiences of all the women included in our sample contradicts the idea that there are "typical female crimes", which is one of the most criticized traditional arguments on female transgression (Rafter and Heidensohn 1995). The heterogeneity of the meanings and stances women assume regarding their deviant behavior—specifically, concerning the dimension of pleasure that sometimes seems to underlie deviance—also contradicts the traditional view of women and crime. In turn, the dimension of rationality associated with the crimes perpetrated by certain young women goes against the argument of their pathology or irrationality.

Some of the positionings regarding delinquency that have been identified show that the criminality of young women seems to come closer to the criminality that is traditionally associated with boys, either due to the diversity of criminal experiences, or specifically due to the criminal lifestyle noticed in certain women. However, no changes regarding the women's own dominant conceptions of femininity are noticeable (e.g., motherhood central role, family life). Women who commit crimes are still considered double-transgressors, which is actually reflected in their narratives about crime in their life pathways.

On the other hand, the analysis of the professionals' narratives reveals a contrasting scenario as their conceptualization of female transgression is often in line with the most traditional discourses.

The analysis of the professionals' perspectives highlights a view of female delinquency largely framed by gender stereotypes. To begin with, it is framed by the belief that the "feminine woman" is not violent and, for that reason, female delinquency is perpetrated by women who deviate from the ideal of femininity. By doing so they are considered "worse than men", more violent, and more cruel. We are then faced with the classical dichotomized female representation: when a woman commits a crime, she goes quickly from "angel to demon" (Matos 2008). It seems paradoxical, but the gender stereotypes are present not only in the idea that there are "typically female" crimes, such as "shoplifting", which was defended in criminological theories from the first half of the twentieth century (e.g., Pollak 1950), but also in the argument that there are "typically male" delinquent activities, for instance gang membership. Such stereotypes also mark the discourse on the tendency for girls to join gangs because of their dating relationships and on how boys "use" them within the gang activities, exactly the way it happens in the gender relationships established in any given context.

Therefore, we find that both the gender stereotypes and the ambivalence that characterize the discourse on female delinquency remain present and have an impact on the specific perspective about the participation of girls in gangs. It is noticeable in "typically feminine" characteristics that may bring advantages for the gangs and in the "lack of femininity" of the girls who get involved in gangs. It is also noticeable in the "feminine characteristics" that prevent them from playing a leading gang role or, on the contrary, that turn them into leaders, organizers and strategists or even "worse than them", for having "less fear", "inciting to more violence", and for "being colder".

6   Conclusion

To conclude, our first remark converges with what we have said in some of our previous work on women, crime and imprisonment (e.g., Matos 2008; Matos and Machado 2012): we still need to look at girls' and women's transgression through a gender lens. The work with the young women in prison evidenced that those who conform more to traditional gender roles seem to be more vulnerable to crimes related to their female condition. It also showed that strict social control in the family context may lead the girls to forms of delinquency traditionally associated with boys. On the other hand, the study with the professionals has shown that their perspectives on girls' delinquency may be highly shaped by gender stereotypes. It was interesting to see the divergence between the narratives of girls with delinquent behaviours and those of the professionals who deal with them. In fact, the diversity of paths and meanings of crime presented by the girls seems to be constructed as a dichotomy by the professionals. As we have seen, just as in some early criminological perspectives, they tend to see delinquent girls as mere "objects in the hands of their male counterparts" or as "evil women" who are worse than males who commit crimes.

The final remark relates to the fact that the professionals' narratives are more stereotyped the further they are from the community. This evidence suggests the importance of bringing judges and prosecutors as well as other staff from the formal justice system closer to the neighbourhoods. Possibly, if the professionals are closer to these social spaces, the process of constructing narratives about delinquent behaviour and pathways will be more informed by those who are part of the community and who, at some point in their lives, may pass through the justice system.

Notes

1. Research project funded by the Fundação para a Ciência e a Tecnologia (Foundation for Science and Technology) and by the Comissão para a Cidadania e a Igualdade de Género (Commission for Citizenship and Gender Equality) (PIHM-VG-0036-2008).
2. Research project funded by the European Commission (JLS/2009–2010/DAP/AG/1370).

References

Batchelor, S. (2005a). 'Prove Me the Bam!' Victimisation and agency in the lives of young women who commit violent offences. *Probation Journal, 52*(4), 358–375.

Batchelor, S. (2005b, July). *'Fer the Buzz o' It?'. The excitement and emotionality of young women's violence*. Paper presented at annual conference of British Society of Criminology, Leeds.

Campbell, A. (1992). *Girls in the gangs*. Cambridge: Blackwell Publishers.

Carlen, P. (1983). *Women's imprisonment. A study in social control*. London: Routledge & Kegan Paul.

Carlen, P. (1987). Out of care, into custody: Dimensions and deconstructions of the state's regulation of twenty-two young working-class women. In P. Carlen & A. Worrall (Eds.), *Gender, crime and justice* (pp. 126–160). Buckingham: Open University Press.

Carlen, P. (1988). *Women, crime and poverty*. Milton Keynes: Open University Press.

Cruise, R. (2016). Enough with the stereotypes: Representations of women in terrorist organizations. *Social Science Quarterly, 97*(1), 33–43.

Cunha, M. I. (1994). *The fabric of confinement. Identity and sociality in a women's prison* (Vol. 1). Lisbon: CEJ.

Cunha, M. I. (2002). *The prison and the neighborhood. Traffincking and trajectories* (Vol. 1). Lisbon: Fim de Século.

Daly, K. (1994). *Gender, crime and punishment*. New Haven: Yale University Press.

Duarte, V. (2012). *Discursos e Percursos na Delinquência Juvenil Feminina*. Famalicão: Editora Húmus.

Gelsthorpe, L. (1997). Feminism and criminology. In M. Maguire, R. Morgan, & R. Reiner (Eds.), *The Oxford handbook of criminology* (pp. 511–534). Oxford: Clarendon Press.

Granja, R. (2016). Beyond prison walls. *Probation Journal, 63*(3), 273–292.

Katz, J. (1988/1996). Seductions and repulsions of crime. In J. Muncie, E. McLaughlin, & M. Langlan (Eds.), *Criminological perspectives. A reader* (pp. 145–159). London: Sage.

Laidler, J., & Hunt, G. (2001). Accomplishing femininity among the girls in the gang. *British Journal of Criminology, 41*(4), 656–678.

Matos, R. (2008). *Vidas Raras de Mulheres Comuns: Percursos de vida, Significações do crime e Construção da identidade em jovens reclusas*. Coimbra: Editora Almedina.

Matos, R., & Machado, C. (2012). Criminalidade feminina e Construção do género. Emergência e consolidação das perspectivas feministas na Criminologia. *Análise Psicológica, XXX*(1–2), 33–47.

Matos, R., Almeida, T., & Vieira, A. (2014). Questões de Género em Gangues juvenis em Portugal. Perspetivas de atores que intervêm no fenómeno. In V. Duarte & M. Cunha (Coords.), *Violências e Delinquências juvenis femininas: género e (in)visibilidades sociais* (pp. 115–140). Famalicão: Editora Húmus.

Miller, J. (2001). *One of the guys. Girls, gangs and gender.* New York: Oxford University Press.

Pollak, O. (1950). *The criminality of women.* Philadelphia: University of Pennsylvania Press.

Rafter, N., & Heidensohn, F. (1995). *International feminist perspectives in criminology. Engendering a discipline.* Buckingham: Open University Press.

Shoemaker, D. (2010). *Theories of delinquency.* New York: Oxford University Press.

Smart, C. (1990/1996). Feminist approaches to criminology or postmodern woman meets atavistic man. In J. Muncie, E. McLaughlin, & M. Langlan (Eds.), Criminological perspectives. A reader (pp. 453–465). London: Sage.

10

Girls and Transgressive Paths: A Case Study of Portuguese Girls in the Juvenile Justice System

Vera Duarte and Ana Margarida Guerreiro

1 Introduction

In 2011, Portuguese social media introduced a new element in the juvenile delinquency scenario in Portugal: "More hate scenes between girls—other cases of brutal violence between them."[1] This resulted in feelings of indignation and a "zero tolerance" attitude expressed in the statements that young people are more violent, and that family and school have not been supportive and have failed in the integration process. Previously, only boys appeared on the delinquency scene, but now girls also do. Episodes such as these provided belated visibility for a phenomenon that had rarely been depicted in Portugal, whether in terms of describing the phenomenon by statistical analysis or via conducting other kinds of studies. The studies carried out in this country since the 1990s

V. Duarte (✉)
CICS.NOVA Universidade do Minho, Braga, Portugal

Instituto Universitário da Maia (ISMAI), Maia, Portugal

A. M. Guerreiro
Instituto Universitário da Maia (ISMAI), Maia, Portugal

© The Author(s) 2018
S. Gomes, V. Duarte (eds.), *Female Crime and Delinquency in Portugal*,
https://doi.org/10.1007/978-3-319-73534-4_10

have been mostly descriptive (Gersão 1990; Duarte-Fonseca 2000; Carvalho 2003). More recently, researchers focused on delinquency among young women (Matos 2008) and girls (Carvalho 2010; Duarte 2012; Duarte and Cunha 2014; Pedroso et al. 2016; Duarte and Carvalho 2017) because of girls' becoming visible in the official data.[2]

In the context of a perceived increase in violence involving young people, much research has been concerned with "violent youth" (Burman 2004) or with the relationship between gender and delinquency. In these investigations there has been little empirical examination of the meaning and effects of violence and delinquency in girls' everyday life. This is because, on the one hand, their behavior is often explained in the shadow of male juvenile delinquency, based on male samples (Chesney-Lind and Shelden 1992; Steffensmeier and Allan 1996; Batchelor 2005; Wong et al. 2010); and, on the other, because research tends to focus more on women than on girls (Zahn 2009). Furthermore, when females appear as offenders they are mainly portrayed as victims, and their behavior tends to be reduced to problems of sexual morality, exceptionality, or an expression of masculinity, which is why they are easily demonized and/or pathologized (Chesney-Lind and Shelden 1992; Garcia and Lane 2013; Belknap and Holsinger 2006; Zahn 2009).

Researchers from different areas and countries[3] acknowledged that the lack of research on girls' delinquency and this invisibility had consequences for the conceptual and analytical fields of study, as well for the way that girls have been processed in the juvenile justice systems and have been treated in correctional institutions. However, research still has a long way to go. After all, according to Artz (Burman 2004, p. 81), "the ideas about girls' violence have tended to be constructed out of existing theories premised upon male experience, and we have a limited theoretical and analytical vocabulary of violence that is not grounded in male behavior".

This invisibility began to change, in most Western countries, starting in the 1980s, when an increasing number of media accounts and official statistics portrayed violence by girls as a new and growing phenomenon (Campbell 1981; Chesney-Lind and Shelden 1992; Burman et al. 2001; Alder and Worral 2004). At this time, there was an increase in studies with delinquent girls, trying to shed some light on the nature of girl offending. But, what became most visible, in the first place, were their subjugation and their victimization paths and, only then, their subjectivity and agency (Batchelor 2007). Although girls experience a wide range of different forms of victimization and are increasingly reputed to be engaging in more delinquency, the voices of girls are rarely heard (Burman et al. 2001; Burman 2004).

Responding to this need to give visibility to a phenomenon that has hitherto only been a footnote, and accepting the challenge of the most recent studies which describe the need for exploratory investigations that give voice to at-risk and delinquent girls, this chapter offers some results, produced in the scope of a Ph.D. research study,[4] focusing on girls' views, experiences and paths to delinquency. By giving a voice to the girls and dimensioning them as social subjects we are providing an opportunity for them to construct different spaces of agency, in contexts of social constriction and accumulated risks.

2 Girls and Delinquency

"Girls do not commit as many crimes as boys because they are *betas*[5] or because they are much more enclosed at home and parents do not allow them out. Outside they can get pregnant ... so parents keep daughters at home. I know that's it. It's like that in my building" (Duarte 2012, p. 163). The narrative of Elisabete, a 14-year-old girl under liberty-depriving measures in an Educational Center in Portugal, allows us to take a journey through the social construction of the (in)visibility of the female figure in the realm of delinquency, which has shaped the way girls are seen (or not) in the theoretical and empirical universe of transgression.

One of the more perplexing areas of juvenile delinquency is the so-called gender gap. Boys commit more crimes than girls, which is what statistics and decades of research on juvenile delinquency tell us (Schwartz and Steffensmeier 2007; Junger-Tas et al. 2004). Further, if we go through traditional criminological theories, two main images have prevailed: the female "submerged" in explanations of male delinquency, as presented in mainstream theories which assume that girls become involved in delinquent practices for the same reasons as boys (Hirschi 1969); and female delinquent actions reduced to social problems and issues concerning sexual morality (Cowie et al. 1968). In general, they are images that reflect the female figure as a passive victim of risk, without much choice, because of her role and female condition (Chesney-Lind 1997). As Adichi (2009) points out "if you want to dispossess a people, the simplest way to do it is to tell their story and to start with, "'secondly'". Over the past 30 years, these images have been well documented and also criticized by some feminist researchers,[6] who have questioned their reliability to explain girls' delinquency.

Feminist criminologists and theories have transformed the gendering of lives into a priority area for study, by putting gendered development and socialization at the core of discussion (Belknap and Holsinger 2006), exploring the gendered pathways to delinquency (Chesney-Lind and Shelden 1992; Zahn et al. 2008), and the sexist and paternalistic responses of the juvenile justice system (Holsinger 2000). This critical standpoint emphasized the socio-cultural and gendered nature of the phenomenon, influenced by a new girl order debate that approaches a crossroads where competitive discourse prevails: "girl power" vs. "girls at risk" (Nayak and Kehily 2008; Duits 2008). This debate reshapes normative femininities, linking active girlhood to a set of moral/social concerns about teenage pregnancy, drug use or involvement in crime.

An increased visibility of girls in delinquency propelled a more gender-sensitive literature that challenged outdated assumptions about girls and their involvement in delinquency (Holsinger 2000), and revealed important considerations concerning gender differences (Hubbard and Pratt 2002; Junger-Tas et al. 2004; Belknap and Holsinger 2006; Chesney-Lind and Jones 2010) and the *Girls Study Group* (Zahn et al. 2008, 2010). These authors show there is growing evidence that some predictors and risk factors—such as poor family relationships, low parental supervision, low self-control, delinquent peer influence, and economic disadvantage—are gender invariant, but that the reactions to these stressors may not be (Kruttschnitt 2013). According to Chesney-Lind (1997), boys and girls do not express themselves in the same way and do not make the same choices. Girls' development, needs and pathways to delinquency seem to differ in some significant ways from their male counterparts, mainly because of the gendered nature of their lives (Piquero et al. 2005; Arnull and Eagle 2009; Zahn et al. 2010; Duarte 2012).

It is relatively agreed upon among researchers (McCarthy et al. 1999; Hubbard and Pratt 2002; Belknap and Holsinger 2006; Chesney-Lind and Jones 2010; Zahn et al. 2008, 2010) that girls have idiosyncratic features linked to their social conditions. They have a history of sexual abuse in greater proportions than boys, and a tendency to cognitive distortions that tend to accentuate mental health problems. Initiated earlier in sexual life than non-delinquent girls, unplanned pregnancy and adolescent motherhood emerge as a visible and problematic reality. They have more socio-tropic cognitive behaviors that increase the need for social acceptance as expressed by the greater impact that family and school relationships, and male and female friends and boyfriends, have on their lives. However, as underlined by Kruttschnitt (2013), some of these factors may not be uniquely explained or important to female offenders, because the relationship between girls' victimization and crime remains unclear (Moffitt 1993; Wong 2012).

This discussion also extends to gender differences in the nature and gravity of transgression (Zahn et al. 2010). Regarding nature, arrest data and juvenile court statistics have demonstrated that overall, girls' involvement in crime is lower than boys for most crimes, and is particularly low when examining the most serious crimes. The only crimes for which girls are more likely to be arrested than boys are prostitution, "runaway" and "unruly" behaviors (Chesney- Lind and Shelden 1992; Alder and Worral 2004; Schwartz and Steffensmeier 2007; Chesney-Lind and Jones 2010; Dennis 2012; Duarte and Cunha 2014; Duarte and Carvalho 2017). It is important not to forget that, historically, girls were more likely to come to the attention of the juvenile justice system because of sexual double standards related to their behavior—offending girls were generally considered to be breaking not only the law, but also gender role expectations (Gelsthorp and Sharpe 2006).

In relation to gravity, the studies emphasize that boys resolve their conflicts by resorting to direct confrontation and physical aggression, while girls tend to use indirect forms of anger, such as isolating a partner, ignoring or avoiding someone, lying, starting rumors and socially ostracizing. They become verbally abusive, due to a breach of trust, envy and stance of *"say-I-didn't-say"* (Artz 1998; Burman et al. 2001; Batchelor 2007).

The media tends to promote the idea there has been a change in the nature of the acts recorded, and probably girls' offenses have become more serious (e.g., there are more girls involved in theft and violent crimes) (Luke 2008; Chesney-Lind and Jones 2010). Therefore, a better knowledge of the nature, causes and reasons associated with female delinquency is needed because very little is known about this subject (Gelsthorp and Sharp 2006; Duarte and Carvalho 2017). Violence perpetrated by girls may depend on the context of production of such violence (Chesney-Lind et al. 2008; Batchelor 2007, 2009; Schwartz and Steffensmeier 2007).

There have always been delinquent girls. Decade after decade, older generations recycle the same panic about girls—the runaway, the wayward and incorrigible girl, the sex-delinquent girl. So, what else is new? (Gelsthorp and Sharpe 2006; Chesney-Lind and Jones 2010). The answer to this question is that what seems to be new is the way in which girls participate in delinquency, and the way they are socially controlled (Gelsthorpe and Worral 2009). On the one hand, the emergence of the image that many of the delinquent girls are no longer collaborators and accessories to their male partners revives the debate on "girl-object" vs. "girl-subject" (Lucchini 1997; Miller 2001; Batchelor 2007). According to Duarte and Carvalho (2017), supported by other studies (Batchelor 2007; Chesney-Lind and Jones 2010), "girls speak about other forms of femininity –"tomboy forms of femininity"—because they want to be recognized for performing acts similar to those practiced by boys whose freedom they envy (…) or "rebel forms of femininity," expressed in terms of more reactive identities, such as those involved in activities and cultures of experimentation and provocation". On the other hand, moral scrutiny of girls continued. Waywardness combined with offending behavior made girls more "risky". For Gelsthorpe and Worral (2009, p. 213) "there was simply a change in language and girls previously described as having 'immoral antecedents' came to be seen as being 'beyond control'", involved in everyday violence and disorder in a routine way (Pearce 2004) and their delinquent behaviors seen as "worse" than boys. Girls' purported violence is seen as a threat to the social order. These perceptions have not been positive for girls, as a group, because the regulation of acceptable gender-role behavior is still evident in the rhetoric and practice of the youth justice system's response to girls' offending (Gelsthorpe and Sharpe 2006). They continue to be seen as more vulnerable than boys and to the need for a lot of care, and these prevailing beliefs have been fueled by the way girls' offending has been described—girls are less criminally inclined, more emotionally unstable, more vulnerable and at-risk, more psychiatrically disturbed—contributing, according to Worrall (1990), to the increase in more punitive responses.

3   Methodology

The main objective of the research carried out was to analyze and discuss the experiences and meanings of transgression in the life paths of girls under educational court orders in Portugal. A strategy of qualitative research was developed. The focus was on concepts and methods emerging from theoretical approaches sensitive to the understanding of how people transform objective influences into subjective initiative. In this context, reading and discussion of the data were carried out in the interface of the symbolic interactions between the theories of structured action and feminist perspectives. Although these theories are on different analytical levels, they allow the exploration of different expressions of everyday life. In doing so, the theories place the debate in the realm of the subject (feminine), but would not lose sight of the fact that subjectivities are permeated by social conditions that shape the performance of transgression and gender.

The research was conducted with girls placed under liberty-depriving measures in custodial institutions (called Educational Centers), and with others subject to educational community measures, both supervised by the Directorate General for Social Reintegration (DGRS) (currently named the Directorate-General for Reintegration and Prison Services), which is the auxiliary body of the judiciary administration responsible for the enforcement of juvenile justice measures. In total, 27 individual files were examined and 19 interviews[7] were carried out.[8] By combining these two techniques, sociological portraits (Lahire 2002) of study subjects were constructed.

The data processing was carried out in two steps. In the first stage, content analysis (categorical and thematic) was favoured; and in the second stage we advanced with discourse analysis. From the analysis of the young girls' narratives we had access to their voice, which allowed us to explore the dominant discourse regarding transgression and profiling of transgressive paths.

The young girls with punitive educational measures included in this study sample (27 girls) are aged 16 and 17, predominantly Portuguese (20/27[9])—even though it is relevant to consider the number of girls of African origin (12/27) in the sample—and live in socio-economically deprived areas—council-housing neighborhoods, identified as problematic. They are serving educational tutelary sentences, mainly due to crimes against property, especially burglary (17/27), and against physical integrity (11/27). Young girls in Educational Centers tend to show more risk factors and greater vulnerability due to age, ethnicity and social class. Also, percentagewise, they are younger than girls with non-institutional measures (42% are in the range of 14–15 years old, against 6.7%). The majority of girls are African, either in terms of nationality or ethnicity. They are more prevalent in council-housing neighborhoods, identified as problematic.

4 Narratives and Transgressive Paths

From the narratives of the young girls, we came to realize that the reasons for transgression are diverse and how the girls (re)position themselves in relation to these reasons. It is through these narratives that they give sense to their actions and determine the various possibilities of the discursive constructions.

Some show how the transgression comes from the management of negative feelings, unresolved anguishes and periods of mourning, originating from stories of abuse, abandonment and institutionalization. For others, it was the search for the "risk–adventure" (Spink 2001), for the experience and the adrenaline of the transgressive act. *Enjoy life, live life as if every day is the last one,* or *life without risk is nothing,* are expressions used by young girls to highlight the importance of risk in the build-up of feelings of self-effectiveness and control in their lives, allowing them to grant some "normalcy" to their actions. Narratives of hetero-self-determination refer to the ambiguity of the position of young girls towards the transgression. Narratives of hetero-determination (it was the drugs' fault, boyfriend/companion, feelings of anger and rebellion, time spent in the institution…), are frequently combined with speeches of "I went because I wanted to or I went of my own free will". For others even, transgression comes as an exception.

As demonstrated by Duarte and Carvalho (2017) the debate on this issue should not be polarized as it runs the risk of failing to understand that pathways are built on choices and actions taken within a limited field of possibilities and a set of social, family, school, and cultural circumstances.

From the dialogue between the narratives and some expressive categories of the contexts of life of the young girls' experiences and accounts (e.g., family victimization, time spent in institutions, transgressive paths, motivations, meanings and moral conviction of the transgression), four profiles of transgressive pathways were constructed, namely: "emphasized transgression" (*by anger or in a spiral*), "rebellious transgression", "influence-transgression" and "circumstantial transgression", which should be understood from a dynamic and open perspective, capable of determining boundary situations and opening the possibility for trajectory changes.

"Emphasized transgression" is a path that gathers almost half of the young girls interviewed (9/19[10]) and almost all of the young girls who were admitted to an Educational Center (7/10). It focuses on paths of higher family victimization, heterogeneous stories of transgression and delinquency and successive institutionalizations related to negligence and family abuse, disciplinary and behavioral problems in school and running away from home. Passage through and time spent in protective institutions is marked by the constant episodes of running away and by the exacerbation of transgressive behaviors.

This is a divided path. Young girls whose transgression is emphasized *by anger,* show how the offence arose from an attempt to manage negative feelings, such as anxiety, as well as coping mechanisms to deal with history of abuse, physical and emotional mistreatment, abandonment and institutionalization:

> I have to explode, I have to explode (…). What gave me a rush was to see people on the ground crying… as crazy as that sounds. What came to my mind was: they did that to me, I have to do it to others, because if I don't do it, no one will feel what I felt. But today I understand that no one will ever feel what I felt, because it wasn't their parents beating them… [Elisabete, 14 years old, Educational Center]

For other girls, the transgression is emphasized *in a spiral*. There is the perception that the transgressive behavior has aggravated and reinforced itself along the paths of life. The motivation for the transgression is not only in the management of negative feelings (as happens in "emphasized transgression *by anger*"), but also in the experience and in the pleasure derived from it. This motivation appears to be related to the experiences lived on the street with friends from the neighborhood and to surviving on the street, after running away (from home and from institutions).

> I went to the neighborhood, went to meet with them [friends] and it was then that we would do silly things. Waiting for people from other schools to rob them, breaking windows and doors, steal cars. We always had something to do. [Isabel, 17 years old, Educational Center]

Hetero-determination in criminalinvolvement is combined with narratives of initiative, control and pleasure associated with the transgressive practice, which they do not condemn, only expressing some regret after the application of the corrective measure.

For other girls, seeking the "risk–adventure" of experimentation and adrenaline may also be what drives them into delinquency. Here we identified another path—"rebellious transgression". The group of young girls included in this path (3/19) do not show a history of significant family victimization, or records of residing in protection institutions. Motivations for the transgression are found in friends, in the rebellion of being young and in the desire to test limits.

Girls and Transgressive Paths: A Case Study of Portuguese Girls... 193

My objective is to enjoy life, live each day as if it was the last. (…) All in this life has a risk …see where you can get, what's your limit! I'm like this. I like to know what my limit is. In this life, either you die, are arrested or run! There is a quiet life… but life without risk isn't anything, a quiet life, only quiet, no… it doesn't make sense… it has no sense. [Inês, 17 years old, educational community measures]

The narratives reveal a certain self-determination in the transgressive involvement, not only in terms of the normality attributed to it, associated with being young, but also in terms of a certain control and dominance over their behaviors. According to Batchelor (2007), violence can be "fun" and, in this sense, the demand for it in its many facets can also be seen through the prism of risk-desire, and fascination with adrenaline and pleasure. This path intercepts with the other paths, not because rebellion and adventure are the triggers for action, but because they are instrumental in maintaining these behaviors, as was seen in the "transgression emphasized *in a spiral*", and as will be seen in "influence-transgression".

If the previous path is marked by borderline cases, the path of "influence-transgression" is, possibly, the one that gathers more diverse life stories (4/19). The central characteristic of this path is the hetero-determination in the transgressive involvement and the idea that it results from the influence of external factors (e.g. drugs, boyfriends and friends). The centrality of the influence factor in this trajectory tends to relegate to second place the weight of other variables. Without a history of significant family victimization, family—related problems are aggravated due to these factors of external influence.

All I did, I did it because I was completely drugged [Verónica, 16 years old, Educational Center]

I started doing silly things, (…) mistreating my parents all because of him (boyfriend) (…) I started running away from home to be with him. [Sónia, 18 years old, educational community measures]

Despite having spent time in promotion and protection institutions or changing schools, the great difference regarding the other young girls is that these processes were triggered by the parents, as an attempt to control their daughters' behavior. Having been institutionalized seems to have accelerated the transgressive behaviors, mainly due to constantly running away from home.

Young girls who personify the path of "circumstantial transgression" (3/19), all subject to educational community measures, organize their narratives around the ideas of exception and the casualness of the transgressive behavior, separating it from any deviant identity. It is seen as an exceptional path because the illegality is described as occasional and accidental and because their lives do not revolve around the transgressive practice. Narratives about the family context have predominantly positive meanings, though marked by the intergenerational conflicts of adolescence. As with all other young girls, it is with friends that they structure their daily lives, mainly marked by leisure activities that are common among young people: "we exchange messages on the Internet, we always go out clubbing; dating; have coffee every day and on Fridays and Saturdays we go out at night." (Anabela, 17 years old, educational community measures). The boundaries they tend to establish between themselves, friends and deviant "friends" is clear. In all the narratives they tend to separate themselves from a path of transgression.

When the interviewed young girls talk about their transgressive practices, they make it clear that there are various paths and that these are not chosen for only one reason. Giving space to the contexts in which girls appear as perpetrators of violence does not at all intend to deny the various social dynamics in which they continue to be victims. What stands out is that after knowing a little about these young girls' lives, it would be naive to think that they are mere spectators regarding what society imposes on them.

5 Final Considerations and Open Discussions

Female participation in delinquent and criminal groups is not a recent phenomenon. What seems to be new is some of the ways in which girls participate, how they build gender relationships and how they orchestrate various forms of femininity through their delinquent practices. So, describing the different speeches and transgressive paths built by young girls under educational court orders in Portugal provides an opportunity to overcome the traditional dichotomy: victimization vs. agency. The literature about this phenomenon is polarized, making it impossible to perceive how girls position themselves in terms of the demand and/or management of risky behavior (Batchelor 2007; Duarte and Carvalho 2017), and what boundaries exist in terms of the influence of peers, boyfriends, and family (Junger-Tas et al. 2004; Duits 2008).

The girls portrayed in this research are indeed victims—when we cross reference the number of social contexts in which they have negative connections—but are also protagonists—when we analyze how they construct, (re) create and negotiate the spaces of their agency. While they remain active and seek to conquer the space opened up for them, in their performance of femininities, they do not forsake their traditional gender conditions and tend to reproduce social constraints.

The dearth of studies on this theme, particularly in Portugal, turns this discussion, which is not new in other countries, into an opportunity to—

– Acknowledge the need to deepen and rethink the categories of femininities and feminine violence and delinquency, which continue to be defined in terms of male delinquency, maintaining conceptual voids that are an expression of this absence of discourse reflected in the policies and practices of the justice system. In Portugal, studies on female juvenile cultures are still sparse and ignore the different ways in which young girls live and experience life. Duarte-Fonseca (2000) argues that the moralizing view that characterizes countries of southern Europe, has a common denominator: to keep the girl circumscribed to the private space and give boys more freedom. This common denominator seems to be reflected in the life trajectories of girls and boys. As Fonseca demonstrates (2009),[11] the idiosyncrasies of female juvenile cultures are related to the specific ways in which they build their relationships and negotiate spaces of autonomy with their family, with housework, paid work, peers and management of free time and with street and neighborhood experiences. Despite restrictions and constraints, Laura Fonseca (2009) shows how "girls do not seem passive or victimized." Girls find strategies and activities of recreation, of pleasure, in particular, being with friends, the pleasure of being a confidant and confiding in (…) and in some respects, surpassing notions of what is believed to be adequate for girls (p. 203). Constraints of gender and the space that girls occupy in society have a close relationship with their behavior, whether they are normative, as in Fonseca's study (2009), or whether they are delinquents, as in Duarte's study (2012).

- Start developing a research-and-intervention agenda regarding this group and this issue. In Portugal, studies that allow us to delve further into the different contexts of transgressive and delinquent behavior committed by girls, and which question the judicial processes, "treatment" and intervention for girls under the juvenile justice system, are few and far between (Duarte 2012; Duarte and Vieites-Rodrigues 2015; Pedroso et al. 2016). Although international literature already provides consistent information on the risks, needs and trajectories of girls in the juvenile justice system (Holsinger 2000; Bloom and Covington 2001; Hubbard and Matthews 2008; Chesney-Lind et al. 2008; Zahn 2009), information on how to transfer this knowledge into practice continues to be lacking (Garcia and Lane 2013). Girls' delinquency represents a small minority in juvenile justice systems worldwide. As such, when one refers to evidence-based practice, the evidence tends to be based on the research findings from the male majority (Salisbury et al. 2009), not always questioning how gender inequalities can shape participation and intervention response (Goodkind 2005). Furthermore, gender-informed approaches are new and the research is limited by methodological challenges such as small sample sizes and low base rates of reoffending for girls, making it difficult to detect the effects of treatment. The question "*What works for who and why?*", is asked by Day et al. (2015). How does one answer it without fostering stereotypical ideas about gender roles and female behavior (Goodkind 2005), and/or without criminalizing their needs (Gelsthorpe and Worral 2009)? This highlights the need for cross-continental studies that gather evidence concerning the differences and similarities which girl-offenders exhibit. Almost all reviews and meta-analyses were based on US studies, and it is

unlikely that risk factors found for US females can be generalized to European females or to those in other geographies without special attention being paid to their specific contexts (Junger-Tas et al. 2004; Wong 2012; Duarte 2012; Duarte and Cunha 2014).
– Assume the heterogeneity of the phenomenon and the need for intersectional readings (Chesney-Lind et al. 2008). Having this perspective reminds us that *being, becoming* and *doing* feminine are very different things for girls/women of different race, gender, and social class, and that these dimensions inform their actions and the various institutional and interpersonal responses to their actions.

This is a discussion that must be had. Only then can legislators, politicians and practitioners be able to provide adequate services and ensure a debate based on scientific arguments and professional knowledge rather than on popular stereotypes and beliefs. This is a complex and demanding task that involves change at all levels, beginning with a critical examination of our own assumptions and stereotypes about girls in the juvenile justice system.

Notes

1. *Sábado Magazine,* number 370, June 2nd–8th, 2011.
2. Regarding juvenile delinquency and its distribution by gender, statistical dissemination by the Directorate-General for Reintegration and Prison Services (DGRSP) is the most rigorous observation instrument; however, it refers only to the evolution and nature of the requests made by DGRSP. It does not provide either the extent of crimes reported to the police or the number of the crimes judged in court. Moreover, these statistics are not always systematic and are often disclosed very late to the public, which does not allow a global view of the phenomenon. DGRSP data states young people between 12 and 16 years old who commit a criminal offence can only be subject to educational measures (in the community or under liberty-depriving measures in custodial institutions, called Educational Centers), as defined by the Educational Guardianship Law (LTE). The age of criminal majority has been maintained at 16 years although the age of civil majority is 18 years. According

to DGRSP statistics, the number of girls under liberty-depriving measures in Educational Centers has been growing since 2005 [December 2005: 5.6%; December 2008: 9.4%; December 2010: 10.2%; October 2012: 11.3%; December 2013: 8.7%; December 2014: 12.8%; December 2015: 12.6%].

3. E.g. Shaw and Dubois (1995), Artz (1998), Leschied et al. (2000) in Canada; Campbell (1981), Chesney-Lind (1997), Hoyt and Scherer (1998), Holsinger (2000), Miller (2001), Steffensmeier and Allan (1996), Zahn et al. (2008, 2010) in the USA; Burman et al. (2001) in Scotland; Gelsthorpe and Worral (2009), Arnull and Eagle (2009) in England; Assis and Constantino (2001), Abramovay (2010) in Brazil; Matos (2008), Duarte (2012) in Portugal.

4. Funding: The study was funded by the FCT—Fundação para a Ciência e Tecnologia, Portugal (Grant number SFRH/BD/35752/2007).

5. Who is overly well behaved.

6. For example, Naffine (1987), Carlen (1988), Campbell (1981, 1984), Worrall (1990), Chesney-Lind (1997), Hoyt and Scherer (1998), Belknap (2000), Holsinger (2000), Burman et al. (2001), Miller (2001), Giordano et al. (2002), Alder and Worral (2004), Messerschmidt (2004), Gelsthorp and Sharpe (2006), Matos (2008), Arnull and Eagle (2009), Zahn et al. (2010).

7. The fieldwork took place continuously between September and November of 2008, with occasional visits to the field during the year of 2009.

8. Ethical approval: All procedures performed in the study involving human subjects were in accordance with the ethical standards of the institutional and/or national research committee and with the 1964 Helsinki declaration and its later amendments or comparable ethical standards. Informed consent: Informed consent was obtained from all individual subjects included in the study. Conflict of Interest: The authors declare that they had no conflict of interest.

9. Should read: 20 young girls of a total of 27.

10. Should read: 9 young girls of 19 who were interviewed.

11. Qualitative research study, developed among female juvenile cultures and through the processes of preparation for and transition from school to paid work and family responsibilities, conducted with seven girls, between the ages of 15 and 21 years, born and raised in the historic center of Oporto—Sé Neighborhood.

References

Abramovay, M. (2010). *Gangues, género e juventudes: donas de rocha e sujeitos cabulosos.* Brasília: Secretaria de Direitos Humanos.

Adichie, C. (2009). *The danger of a single story.* New York/Vancouver: TEDGlobal. Retrieved from https://www.ted.com/talks/chimamanda_adichie_the_danger_of_a_single_story/transcript

Alder, C., & Worral, A. (Eds.). (2004). *Girl's violence: Myths and realities.* New York: State University of New York Press.

Arnull, E., & Eagle, S. (2009). *Girls and offending—Patterns, perceptions and interventions.* London: YJB.

Artz, S. (1998). *Sex, power and the violent school girl.* Toronto: Trifolium Books.

Assis, S., & Constantino, P. (2001). *Filhas do Mundo: infracção juvenil feminina no Rio de Janeiro.* Rio de Janeiro: Editora FioCruz.

Batchelor, S. (2005). Prove me the bam!' Victimization and agency in the lives of young women who commit violent offences. *Probation Journal, 52*(4), 289–294.

Batchelor, S. (2007). 'Getting mad wi' it': Risk-seeking by young women. In K. Hannah-Moffat & P. O'Malley (Eds.), *Gendered risks* (pp. 205–228). New York: Routledge.

Batchelor, S. (2009). Girls, gangs and violence: Assessing the evidence. *Probation Journal, 56*(4), 399–414.

Belknap, J. (2000). *The invisible woman: Gender, crime and justice.* Belmont: Wadsworth.

Belknap, J., & Holsinger, K. (2006). The gendered nature of risk factors for delinquency. *Feminist Criminology, 1,* 48–71.

Bloom, B., & Covington, S. (2001). *Effective gender responsive interventions in Juvenile justice: Addressing the lives of delinquent girls.* Retrieved from http://www.centerforgenderandjustice.org/pdf/7.pdf

Burman, M. (2004). Turbulent talk: Girls' making sense of violence. In C. Alder & A. Worral (Eds.), *Girl's violence: Myths and realities* (pp. 81–103). New York: State University of New York Press.

Burman, M., Batchelor, S., & Brown, J. (2001). Researching girls and violence. *The British Journal of Criminology, 41,* 443–459.

Campbell, A. (1981). *Delinquent girl.* New York: St. Martin's Press, Inc.

Campbell, A. (1984). *The girls in the gangs.* Oxford: Basil Blackwell.

Carlen, P. (1988). *Women, crime and poverty.* Milton Keynes: Open University Press.

Carvalho, M. J. L. (2003). *Entre as malhas do desvio*. Oeiras: Celta Editora.
Carvalho, M. J. L. (2010). *Do Outro Lado da Cidade. Crianças, Socialização e Delinquência em Bairros de Realojamento*. PhD thesis, Universidade Nova de Lisboa, Lisbon.
Chesney-Lind, M. (1997). *The female offender*. Thousand Oaks: Sage.
Chesney-Lind, M., & Jones, N. (Eds.). (2010). *Fighting for girls, new perspectives on gender and violence*. Albany: State University of New York Press.
Chesney-Lind, M., & Shelden, R. G. (1992). *Girls delinquency and juvenile justice*. Pacific Grove: Brooks/Cole Publishing Company.
Chesney-Lind, M., Morash, M., & Stevens, T. (2008). Girls' troubles, girls' delinquency and gender responsive programming: A review. *The Australian and New Zealand Journal of Criminology, 41*(1), 162–189.
Cowie, J., Cowie, V., & Slater, E. (1968). *Delinquency in girl*. London: Heinemann.
Day, J., Zahn, M., & Tichavski, L. (2015). What works for whom? The effects of gender responsive programming on girls and boys in secure detention. *Journal of Research in Crime and Delinquency, 52*(1), 93–129.
Dennis, J. (2012). Girls will be girls: Childhood gender polarization and delinquency. *Feminist Criminology, 7*(3), 220–233.
Duarte, V. (2012). *Discursos e percursos na delinquência juvenil feminina*. Famalicão: Húmus.
Duarte, V., & Carvalho, M. J. L. (2017). Female delinquency in Portugal: What girls have to say about their involvement in delinquency. *Gender Issues*. https://doi.org/10.1007/s12147-017-9187-8. Springer.
Duarte, V., & Cunha, M. (Org.). (2014). Violências e Delinquências Juvenis femininas: género e (in)visibilidades sociais. Famalicão: Editora Húmus.
Duarte, V., & Vieites-Rodrigues, L. (2015). Intervenção com raparigas delinquentes: contributos para uma discussão focada no género. In S. Gomes & R. Granja (Eds.), *Mulheres e Crime—perspetivas sobre intervenção, violência e reclusão* (pp. 15–30). Famalicão: Editora Húmus.
Duarte-Fonseca, A. (2000). *Condutas desviantes de raparigas nos anos 90*. Coimbra: Coimbra Editora.
Duits, L. (2008). *Multi-girl-culture: An Ethnography of doing identity*. Amsterdam: Amsterdam University Press.
Fonseca, L. (2009). *Justiça Social e Educação. Vozes, silêncio e ruídos na escolarização das raparigas ciganas e payas*. Porto: Edições Afrontamento.

Garcia, C., & Lane, J. (2013). What a girl wants, what a girl needs: Findings from a gender-specific focus group study. *Crime & Delinquency, 59*(4), 536–561.

Gelsthorp, L., & Sharpe, G. (2006). Gender, youth and justice. In B. Goldson & J. Muncie (Eds.), *Youth crime and justice* (pp. 47–61). London: Sage.

Gelsthorpe, L., & Worral, A. (2009). Looking for trouble: A recent history of girls, young women and youth justice. *Youth Justice, 9*(3), 209–223.

Gersão, E. (1990). Raparigas em internato de reeducação—porquê? Para quê? *Infância e Juventude, 4*, 47–51.

Giordano, P., Cernkovich, S., & Rudolph, J. (2002). Gender, crime and desistance: Toward a theory of cognitive transformation. *American Journal of Sociology, 107*(4), 990–1064.

Goodkind, S. (2005). Gender-specific service in the justice system. A critical examination. *Affilia, 20*(52), 52–70.

Hirschi, T. (1969). *Causes of delinquency.* New Brunswick: Transaction Publishers.

Holsinger, K. (2000). Feminist perspectives on female offending: Examine real girls' lives. *Women & Criminal Justice, 12*(1), 23–51.

Hoyt, S., & Scherer, D. (1998). Female juvenile delinquency: Misunderstood by the juvenile justice system, neglected by social sciences. *Law and Human Behavior, 22*(1), 81–107.

Hubbard, D., & Matthews, B. (2008). Reconciling the differences between the "gender responsive" and the "what-works" literatures to improve services for girls. *Crime & Delinquency, 54*(2), 225–258.

Hubbard, D., & Pratt, T. (2002). A meta-analysis of the predictors of delinquency among girls. *Journal of Offender Rehabilitation, 34*(3), 1–13.

Junger-Tas, J., Ribeaud, D., & Cruyff, M. (2004). Juvenile delinquency and gender. *European Journal of Criminology, 1*, 333–375.

Kruttschnitt, C. (2013). Gender and crime. *The Annual Review of Sociology, 39*, 291–308.

Lahire, B. (2002). *Portraits sociologiques: Dispositions et variations individuelles.* Paris: Armand Colin.

Leschied, A., et al. (2000). *Female adolescent aggression: A review of the literature and the correlates of aggression.* Ottawa: Solicitor General Canada.

Lucchini, R. (1997). A mulher e a desviância ou o debate sobre a especificidade da delinquência feminine. *Infância e Juventude, 2*, 71–126.

Luke, K. (2008). Are girls really becoming more violent? A critical analysis. *Affilia. Journal of Women and Social Work, 23*(1), 23–38.

Matos, R. (2008). *Vidas raras de mulheres comuns: percursos de vida, significações do crime e construção da identidade em jovens reclusas*. Coimbra: Almedina.

McCarthy, B., Hagan, J., & Woodward, T. (1999). In the company of women: Structure and agency in a revised power-control theory of gender and delinquency. *Criminology, 37*, 761–788.

Messerschmidt, J. (2004). *Flesh and blood: Adolescent gender diversity and violence*. Oxford: Rowman & Littlefield.

Miller, J. (2001). *One of the guys: Girls, gangs and gender*. New York: Oxford University Press.

Moffitt, T. (1993). Adolescence-limited and life course-persistente antissocial behavior: A development taxonomy. *Psychological Review, 100*, 674–670.

Naffine, N. (1987). *Female crime: The construction of women in criminology*. Sydney: Allen and Unwin.

Nayak, A., & Kehily, M. (2008). *Gender, youth and culture: Young masculinities and femininities*. New York: Palgrave Macmillan.

Pearce, J. (2004). Coming out to play? Young women and violence on the streets. In C. Alder & A. Worrall (Eds.), *Girl's violence: Myths and realities* (pp. 131–150). New York: State University of New York Press.

Pedroso, J., Casaleiro, P., & Branco, P. (Eds.). (2016). *Justiça Juvenil: a lei, os tribunais e a (in)visibilidade do crime no feminine*. Porto: Vida Económica.

Piquero, N., Gover, A., MacDonald, J., & Piquero, A. (2005). The influence of delinquent peers on delinquency: Does gender matter? *Youth & Society, 36*(3), 251–275.

Salisbury, E., Van Voorhis, P., & Spiripoulos, G. (2009). The predictive validity of a gender-responsive needs assessment: An exploratory study. *Crime Delinquency, 55*(4), 550–585.

Schwartz, J., & Steffensmeier, D. (2007). The nature of female offending: Patterns and explanations. In *Female offenders: Critical perspectives and effective interventions* (pp. 43–75). Boston: Jones and Bartlett. Retrieved from http://www.jblearning.com/samples/0763741159/Ch2_Female_Offenders_2e.pdf

Shaw, M., & Dubois, S. (1995). *Understanding violence by women: A review of the literature*. Retrieved from http://www.csc-scc.gc.ca/text/prgrm/fsw/fsw23/toce-eng.shtml

Spink, M. (2001). Tropics of risk discourse: Risk-adventure as a metaphor in late modernity. *Cadernos de Saúde Pública, 17*(6), 1277–1311.

Steffensmeier, D., & Allan, E. (1996). Gender and crime: Toward a gendered theory of female offending. *Annual Review Sociology, 22*, 459–487.

Wong, T. (2012). *Girls delinquency. A study on sex differences in (risk factors for) delinquency*. Oisterwijik: Uitgeverij Box Press.

Wong, T., Slotboom, A. M., & Bijleveld, C. (2010). Risk factors for delinquency in adolescent and young adult females: A European review. *European Journal of Criminology, 7*(4), 266–284.

Worrall, A. (1990). *Offending women. Female lawbreakers and the criminal justice system*. Londres: Routledge.

Zahn, M. (Ed.). (2009). *The delinquent girl*. Philadelphia: Temple University Press.

Zahn, M. et al. (2008). *Violence by teenage girls: Trends and context, OJJDP girls study group: Understanding and responding to girl's delinquency*. Washington, DC: US Office of Justice Programs. Retrieved from http://www.ncjrs.gov/pdffiles1/ojjdp/218905.pdf

Zahn, M. et al. (2010). *Causes and correlates of girl's delinquency. OJJDP girls study group: Understanding and responding to Girl's delinquency*. Washington, DC: US Office of Justice Programs. Retrieved from https://www.ncjrs.gov/pdffiles1/ojjdp/226358.pdf

Index[1]

A

Agency, 14, 26, 34, 36, 37, 67, 144, 171, 185, 195
Aggravated homicide, 113
Aggressors, 32, 106, 107, 114, 115, 118, 152, 154
Altered emotional state, 115
Annual Report of Internal Security, 106
Anti-social behavior, 143
Asymmetrical, 132
At-risk girls, 185, 186, 189
Attenuation of the offender's punishment, 115

B

Banalization, 45, 47, 50
Bardin, L., 84, 113
Batchelor, S., 172, 173, 184, 185, 188, 193, 195
Battered homicide, 107, 109–111
Battered woman, 110, 115
Battered Woman Syndrome, 110
Beleza, T. P., 6, 7, 110, 115
Black feminism, 6
Bourdieu, P., 83, 85
Burman, M., 9, 10, 184, 188, 198n3, 198n6

---

[1] Note: Page numbers followed by 'n' refer to notes.

© The Author(s) 2018
S. Gomes, V. Duarte (eds.), *Female Crime and Delinquency in Portugal*,
https://Doi.org/10.1007/978-3-319-73534-4

206 Index

C

Caridade, S., 126, 132
Carlen, P., 5, 7, 8, 36, 58, 62, 71n7, 108, 109, 164, 166, 168, 198n6
Carvalho, M. J. L., 4, 9, 13, 144–146, 148, 149, 151, 153, 154, 156–158, 184, 187, 188, 191, 195
Causes of crime, 13, 76, 82
Chesney-Lind, M., 5–7, 9, 10, 146, 184, 186–188, 196, 197, 198n3, 198n6
Childhood, 108, 132, 144, 146, 149, 157, 171
Children, 4, 13, 28–31, 33–36, 63–67, 69n1, 75, 78, 86, 88, 89, 91, 92, 95–97, 108, 114, 116, 129, 143, 145, 146, 148, 151, 152, 154, 158, 159
City, 70n5, 77, 87, 158
Collective efficacy, 145
Community, 14, 26–28, 30, 31, 34, 37, 67, 81, 146, 174, 175, 177, 178, 189, 193, 194, 197n2
Conformity narrative, 99
Crenshaw, K., 6, 79, 80, 83
Crime, 1–15, 25–37, 43, 49, 51, 59–61, 70n3, 76–85, 93–100, 106, 107, 111, 112, 114, 115, 117, 118, 118n1, 126, 134, 144, 146, 152, 157, 158, 163–180, 185–188, 190, 197n2
Crime studies, 5, 6, 79
Criminal, 25–37, 75, 77–84, 86–97, 99, 100
Criminal control institutions, 13, 82
Criminal involvement, 13, 91, 93, 96, 192

Criminalization, 13, 77
Criminal justice system, 2, 3, 5–11, 13–15, 77–81, 83, 95, 99, 107, 108
Criminal label, 76
Criminal models, 157
Criminals, 2, 4–7, 10, 13, 14, 43, 49, 108, 109, 111, 115–117, 163–165, 167, 168, 170–173, 177, 178, 194, 197n2
Critical perspective, 51, 164, 167, 177
Cunha, M. I., 6, 9, 11, 12, 59–67, 69, 70n3, 70n4, 71n9, 81, 92, 95, 164–166, 184, 187, 197
Custodial institutions, 189, 197n2
Cycle of domestic violence, 116

D

Danger, 27, 45, 51, 108, 173
Deep emotional stress, 115
Delinquency studies, 2, 5, 10
Delinquent peer influence, 186
Deontological Code of Sociologists, 83
Deviance studies, 80
Directorate-General for Reintegration and Prison Services (DGRSP), 112, 189, 197–198n2
Disadvantaged social position, 89, 99
Discourses, 9, 35, 44, 45, 79, 113, 132, 134, 135, 164, 165, 167, 169, 172–174, 176–179, 186, 190, 195
Discrimination, 5, 26, 43, 75, 78, 83, 168

Divorce, 49, 89, 114
Dobash, 59, 110, 114
Documentary analysis, 112, 113
Domesticity, 8, 58, 62, 65, 68
Domestic roles, 5
Domestic violence, 29, 32, 36, 37,
   38n2, 41, 42, 106, 107, 109,
   110, 112, 115–118, 126, 154
Double transgressors, 179
Drug courier, 61, 96, 97
Drug mules, 85, 86, 89, 91, 93, 96
Drug trafficking, 25, 26, 29, 36,
   60–61, 70n6, 85, 86, 91,
   93–95, 97, 98, 165, 171
Duarte, V., 4–7, 9, 11, 14, 78, 144,
   145, 149, 168, 184, 185,
   187, 188, 191, 195–197,
   198n3

E

Eastern European, 76, 83, 85, 86,
   90, 96–98
Economic deprivation, 28, 89,
   93–96, 98, 99
Economic factors, 96–99
Economic violence, 106
Educational Center, 185, 189–193,
   197–198n2
Educational Guardianship Law
   (LTE), 4, 197n2
Ethnicity, 6, 8, 11, 12, 57, 67, 68,
   79, 81, 82, 89, 95, 100n2,
   163, 190
Ethnic minority populations, 99
European Union Agency for
   Fundamental Rights (FRA),
   42, 46, 106, 125

F

Family, 8, 10, 14, 30–35, 37, 61, 66,
   67, 70n6, 78, 81, 86, 88–97,
   99, 107, 114, 116, 117, 125,
   131, 144, 146, 149, 150, 152,
   155–157, 165, 166, 168,
   169, 171, 177, 179, 180,
   183, 186, 187, 191–195,
   198n11
Fear, 27, 28, 31, 37, 43, 94, 126,
   169, 179
Female
   crime, 1–15, 25–37, 165, 166,
      175, 177–179
   delinquency, 2, 5, 15, 145, 167,
      168, 175, 177–179, 188
   idiosyncrasies, 10, 173, 187, 195
   inmates, 12, 64, 65, 164, 169
   prison, 4, 8, 9, 12, 60, 69, 83,
      111, 112
   stalking, 45, 49
   victimization, 42
Femicide, 106, 110, 114–116, 118
Femininity, 7, 8, 44, 58, 156, 168,
   177–179, 186, 188,
   194, 195
Feminism, 6
Feminist approaches,
   6, 163, 164, 168
Feminist criminology, 3, 6, 8
Foreign prisoners, 75, 76, 98
Foreign women prisoners, 76, 83,
   84, 93
Foshee, V. A., 127, 131
FRA, see European Union Agency for
   Fundamental Rights (FRA)
Freedom, 28, 33, 133, 134, 146,
   188, 195

208 Index

G
Gelsthorpe, L., 7–9, 164, 188, 189, 196, 198n3
Gender
asymmetry, 105, 125, 126, 129, 132, 136, 165
differences, 5–11, 44, 129, 145, 146, 166, 186, 187
equality, 13, 69n1, 132, 133, 136
gap, 145, 154, 185
identity, 58, 65, 67, 68
ideologies, 62, 64
inequalities, 2, 7, 9, 12, 44, 68, 134, 145, 196
neutral, 57, 67, 69n1
role expectations, 187
roles, 34, 51, 58, 66, 81, 89, 99, 109, 117, 130, 135, 146, 148, 158, 166, 167, 169, 180, 189, 196
sensitive literature, 5, 10, 186
studies, 79
victimization, 12, 112
violence, 12, 13, 41–51, 109, 112, 117, 118
Gendercentric, 12, 59
Gendercentrism, 67
Gendered pains of imprisonment, 58, 65
Gendered pathways, 11, 186
General Directorate of Reintegration and Prison Services, *see* Directorate-General for Reintegration and Prison Services (DGRSP)
Girlhood, 186
Girl power, 186

Girls' delinquency, 7, 143–146, 149, 157, 159, 167, 174–176, 180, 184, 186, 196
Gomes, S., 4, 6, 9, 11, 13, 34, 76–78, 83, 93, 96, 108

H
Harassment, 41, 42, 45, 130
Hetero-determination, 167, 191–193
Hidden crime figures, 7
Holsinger, K., 7–11, 156, 184, 186, 187, 196, 198n3, 198n6
Homicide, 26, 32, 36, 38n2, 85, 93, 106–114, 117, 118
Human security, 12, 26–28, 37

I
Identities, 12, 36, 57, 59, 60, 65–69, 79–81, 154, 157, 164, 169–173, 188, 194
Imprisonment, 6, 8, 13, 25, 26, 58, 60, 61, 66, 69, 76, 77, 84, 85, 93–100, 111, 112, 116, 117, 118n1, 164–166, 169, 180
Incarceration, 25, 33, 60, 61, 76, 80, 81, 165
Individual prison sentences, 25
Informal social control, 156
Informed consent, 84, 113, 127, 147, 198n8
Initial period of separation, 114
Inmates, 169
Insecurity, 26–32, 34
Institutional level, 99
Interactional level, 99
Inter-parental violence, 117, 131

Intersectional approach, 6, 75,
77–84, 86–97, 99, 100
Intervention, 2, 4, 6, 9, 10, 26, 33,
34, 37, 71n7, 95, 135,
158, 196
Interviews, 12, 70n4, 83, 84, 92,
112–116, 127, 128, 132, 146,
147, 165, 169, 174, 190
Intimacy, 48, 49, 132, 135
Intimate partner violence, 105–107,
109, 110, 112–118, 125, 126,
130, 134
Istanbul Convention, 42, 43

J

Judicial system, 71n10, 77, 110
Juvenile delinquency, 1, 4, 6, 11, 13,
14, 168, 183–185, 197n2
Juvenile justice system, 2, 9, 10, 183

L

Legitimate Anticipated Self-Defense,
110, 115, 118
Liberal feminism, 6
Life trajectories, 76, 77, 81–86, 89,
93, 98, 99, 172, 195

M

Machado, C., 108, 109, 126, 164,
166–168, 175, 180
Machado, H., 5–7, 71n10
Magistrates, 32, 36, 38n2, 178
Male behavior, 184
Male stalking, 44–46, 49, 51

Marital homicide, 106, 108, 112
Marxist feminism, 6
Matos, M., 41, 42, 44–47, 51,
61, 126
Matos, R., 4, 6–9, 11, 14, 61, 81,
89, 108, 109, 117, 164–169,
173, 175, 179, 180, 184,
198n3, 198n6
Moral concerns, 186
Moral entrepreneurs, 76

N

Narratives, 14, 26, 31, 65, 66, 77,
81, 84, 86, 89, 92, 96,
98–100, 105–107, 109, 110,
112–118, 127, 135, 137, 163,
185, 190–194
Nationality, 11, 13, 77–79, 81–83,
85, 99, 190
Neighbourhood, 2, 67, 69, 81, 94,
95, 99, 143–159, 164,
165, 180
Nexus
security–criminality, 12, 25–37
Nogueira, C., 105, 125
Normalization, 45, 137, 152, 158
Normative femininity,
58, 186

O

Objective living conditions,
76, 77, 82, 83, 85, 86, 93,
100, 100n2
Odemira Regional Prison, 112
Official statistics, 78, 184

210 Index

P

Pais, E., 107, 109, 110
PALOP, 76, 83, 84, 86–89
Parental supervision, 145, 158, 186
Passive, 152, 186, 195
Paternalistic, 9, 10, 186
Pathways, 14, 75, 77–84, 86–97, 99, 100, 163, 186, 191
Pathways to prison, 169
Patriarchy, 6, 10
Peer influence, 146, 149, 186
People of colour, 75
Physical violence, 106, 110, 126, 130, 132–134, 136, 152
Police, 27, 31, 32, 77, 90, 94, 95, 98, 106, 107, 117, 126, 149, 178, 197n2
Portugal, 1–15, 25, 35, 43, 60–62, 64, 76, 81, 86–91, 93, 95, 97, 98, 105, 106, 117, 126, 129, 144, 146, 163, 164, 168, 169, 174, 183, 185, 189, 195, 196, 198n3, 198n4
Postmodern feminism, 6
Poverty, 33, 36, 65, 81, 92, 96, 157
Practitioners, 2, 10, 173–178, 197
Prejudice, 26, 77, 80, 99
Prison
cultures, 58, 59
life, 12, 62, 67
regimes, 58, 60, 63, 68
studies, 1, 8, 12, 38n1, 57, 59, 68
Prisoners, 4, 8, 12, 13, 34, 58–60, 62–68, 69n1, 70n4, 70n6, 71n9, 75–77, 81–86, 92, 93, 96–98, 107, 109, 112, 165, 169
Private lawyers, 116
Psychological violence, 25, 106, 130, 136

Psychopathology, 45, 48, 50, 51
Public health problem, 118, 126
Public space, 145, 158

Q

Qualitative interviews, 84
Qualitative methodology, 127, 189
Qualitative study, 107–116, 126–132, 137

R

Race, 6, 8, 12, 57, 67, 68, 79–82, 95, 96, 150, 197
Racism, 77, 80, 88, 89, 99
Relatedness, 66, 68
Relative deprivation, 78
Risk-adventure, 190, 192
Risk assessment, 50
Risk factors, 10, 114, 131, 136, 186, 190, 197
Risk of violence, 49
Risky behaviours, 7, 195
Romantic discourse, 44, 45
Rosen, C., 110, 115

S

Sentences, 8, 12, 14, 25, 32, 61, 70n6, 81, 83, 85, 93, 97, 106, 109, 112–117, 118n1, 165, 170, 190
Sexist, 9, 10, 186
Sexual double standards, 187
Sexual morality, 184, 186
Sexual violence, 42, 106, 108, 126, 130, 131, 134, 136, 137
Single story, 2, 8, 10, 78, 99
Social actors, 82, 144, 146

Index   211

Social awareness, 43
Social class, 8, 11, 13, 78, 80, 82, 85, 89, 95, 96, 99, 190, 197
Social cohesion, 158
Social constraints, 99, 116, 195
Social control institutions, 13, 82
Social disorganization, 144, 152
Social ecology, 144, 146
Social exclusion, 36, 81, 82, 99, 157
Social housing neighbourhoods, 143–152, 154, 155, 157–159
Social inclusion, 152
Social inequalities, 13, 77, 82, 85, 99
Social invisibility, 118
Socialist feminism, 6
Socialization, 7, 13, 14, 136, 145–149, 151, 153, 154, 158, 166, 167, 186
Social learning process, 144
Social mechanisms, 43
Social norms, 7, 80, 152
Social risks, 185
Social roles, 7, 45, 59, 157
Social violence, 106, 130, 136
Social vulnerabilities, 77, 81–83
Socio-economic inequalities, 78
Sociological portraits, 190
Socio-structural level, 83, 100
SPACE I, 4
Special Prison of Santa Cruz do Bispo, 112
Stalking
 by men, 12, 45, 46, 48–50
 by women, 12, 41–51
 perpetration, 12, 44–49
 victimization, 47
Stereotypes, 36, 108, 117, 148, 164–167, 175, 177–180, 197
Stigmatization, 65, 68, 80, 130, 136, 155, 158

Strategy, 10, 26, 29, 61, 62, 110, 126, 128, 130, 131, 133, 136, 153, 189, 196
Straus, M. A., 132
Street influences, 146
Subjectivities, 35, 65, 185, 189
Surveillance apparatus, 27

T
Territory, 87, 91, 92, 146
Thematic content analysis, 113
Thematic qualitative content analysis, 84
Traditional criminology, 6, 8, 166
Trajectories, 6, 8, 25, 26, 29, 31, 34, 35, 59, 81, 84–90, 95, 98, 99, 107, 164, 165, 168, 173, 191, 193, 196
Transgressive girls, 2, 11, 166
Transgressive paths, 14, 183–197

U
UMAR, 38n2, 105, 106
Urban violence, 152

V
Victim, 5, 7, 11, 26, 27, 29, 31, 32, 41–44, 46–50, 58, 86, 98, 105–107, 109–118, 126, 130–134, 152, 154, 171, 184, 186, 194, 195
Victimization, 2, 6, 12–14, 36, 42, 45–47, 108, 112, 114, 117, 131, 132, 136, 152, 168, 187, 191–193, 195
Victimization paths, 81, 185

212   Index

Violence, 6, 12–14, 29, 32, 34, 36, 37, 38n2, 41–51, 65, 90, 105–107, 109, 110, 112–118, 118n1, 125–137, 144–146, 152–155, 158, 166, 176, 183, 184, 188, 189, 193–195

Violence against women, 41–43, 45, 118, 125

Voice(s), 107–116, 125–137, 152, 185, 190

Voluntary Manslaughter, 111, 115, 118

Vulnerabilities, 12, 27, 32, 36, 77, 81–83, 96, 99, 165, 190

W

Wacquant, L., 7, 75

Western countries, 9, 184

White, J., 126

WHO, 126

Women offenders, 10, 11, 14, 15, 48, 163, 168

Women's rights, 105–106, 136

Women's crime, 5, 7, 117

Worrall, A., 10, 58, 189, 198n6

Y

Young offenders, 14, 173, 178

Young women, 14, 61, 133, 135, 136, 163, 184

Youth justice system, 172, 189

Z

Zahn, M., 9–11, 145, 156, 184, 186, 187, 196, 198n3, 198n6